Family Reunion Planning For Dummies®

Reunion-Planning Timeline

Planning a successful family reunion requires a lot of advanced planning. Here's a quick reference for you to glance at when in doubt about what to do and when to do it.

One year ahead

- Compile a list of names and addresses for the guest list.
- Locate missing family members.
- Start your reunion files.
- Send a postcard surveying family members about possible reunion dates.
- Start your genealogical research.
- Scout out prospective reunion sites and reserve your favorite spot.
- Set a date for your reunion.

Six months ahead

- Set a budget and collect fees.
- Scout out prospective lodgings for out-of-towners.
- Form your committees and assign duties to committees and individual helpers.
- Send family members reunion postcard reminder.
- Select a reunion theme.
- Interview prospective entertainers and book your favorite.
- Plan activities and prepare entertainment and activity schedule.

Three months ahead

- Mail invitations and log RSVPs.
- Count the RSVPs as they arrive and make lodging arrangements for out-of-towners.
- Plan the menu if you're doing the cooking or hiring a caterer.
- Assemble family-history information to bring to reunion, including family group sheets and pedigree charts.

One month ahead

- Assign potluck items.
- Gather family memorabilia to display at the reunion.
- Send a reunion reminder postcard.

Two weeks ahead

- Decide what you need to buy, borrow, or rent for the reunion.
- Purchase decorations, paper/plastic products, and drinkware.
- Reserve rental items.

For Dummies: Bestselling Book Series for Beginners

Family Reunion Planning Kit For Dummies®

Three days ahead

- Purchase grocery items and make any do-ahead food items.
- Make certain that you have extra film and batteries.
- Prepare name tags and welcome packets.

The day before

- Prepare last-minute foods.
- Pick up rented/borrowed items and prepare the reunion site.

The day of

- Decorate reunion site and place direction signs near site.
- Delegate duties and responsibilities to volunteers.
- Roll out the welcome wagon.

After the reunion

- Clean up site and remove direction signs.
- Check for belongings left behind.
- Remove trash and recycling.
- Relax and pat yourself on the back.

Estimating Seating for a Crowd

- A 36" round table seats 4
- A 48" round table seats 6–8
- A 60" round table seats 8–10
- A 72" round table seats 10–12
- A 34x34" square table (card/bridge) seats 4
- A 4'x30" rectangular table seats 6
- A 6'x30" rectangular table seats 6–8
- An 8'x30" rectangular table seats 8–10

Estimating Beverages

One case of wine (12 bottles)	60 glasses
One keg of beer	140 12-ounce glasses
One liter of soda	10 8-ounce servings
One gallon of punch	30 5-ounce servings
One gallon of coffee	25 6-ounce servings

Hungry Minds™

For Dummies: Bestselling Book Series for Beginners

Family Reunion Planning Kit

FOR DUMMIES®

Family Reunion Planning Kit FOR DUMMIES®

by Cheryl Fall

Hungry Minds™

Best-Selling Books • Digital Downloads • e-Books • Answer Networks • e-Newsletters • Branded Web Sites • e-Learning

New York, NY ◆ Cleveland, OH ◆ Indianapolis, IN

Family Reunion Planning Kit For Dummies®

Published by:
Hungry Minds, Inc.
909 Third Avenue
New York, NY 10022
www.hungryminds.com
www.dummies.com

Library of Congress Control Number: 2001093373

ISBN: 0-7645-5399-2

Printed in the United States of America

10 9 8 7 6 5 4 3 2 1

1B/RR/RS/QR/IN

Distributed in the United States by Hungry Minds, Inc.

Distributed by CDG Books Canada Inc. for Canada; by Transworld Publishers Limited in the United Kingdom; by IDG Norge Books for Norway; by IDG Sweden Books for Sweden; by IDG Books Australia Publishing Corporation Pty. Ltd. for Australia and New Zealand; by TransQuest Publishers Pte Ltd. for Singapore, Malaysia, Thailand, Indonesia, and Hong Kong; by Gotop Information Inc. for Taiwan; by ICG Muse, Inc. for Japan; by Intersoft for South Africa; by Eyrolles for France; by International Thomson Publishing for Germany, Austria and Switzerland; by Distribuidora Cuspide for Argentina; by LR International for Brazil; by Galileo Libros for Chile; by Ediciones ZETA S.C.R. Ltda. for Peru; by WS Computer Publishing Corporation, Inc., for the Philippines; by Contemporanea de Ediciones for Venezuela; by Express Computer Distributors for the Caribbean and West Indies; by Micronesia Media Distributor, Inc. for Micronesia; by Chips Computadoras S.A. de C.V. for Mexico; by Editorial Norma de Panama S.A. for Panama; by American Bookshops for Finland.

For general information on Hungry Minds' products and services please contact our Customer Care department; within the U.S. at 800-762-2974, outside the U.S. at 317-572-3993 or fax 317-572-4002.

For sales inquiries and resellers information, including discounts, premium and bulk quantity sales, and foreign language translations please contact our Customer Care department at 800-434-3422, fax 317-572-4002 or write to Hungry Minds, Inc., Attn: Customer Care department, 10475 Crosspoint Boulevard, Indianapolis, IN 46256.

For information on licensing foreign or domestic rights, please contact our Sub-Rights Customer Care department at 212-884-5000.

For information on using Hungry Minds' products and services in the classroom or for ordering examination copies, please contact our Educational Sales department at 800-434-2086 or fax 317-572-4005.

Please contact our Public Relations department at 212-884-5163 for press review copies or 212-884-5000 for author interviews and other publicity information or fax 212-884-5400.

For authorization to photocopy items for corporate, personal, or educational use, please contact Copyright Clearance Center, 222 Rosewood Drive, Danvers, MA 01923, or fax 978-750-4470.

Hungry Minds is a trademark of Hungry Minds, Inc.

About the Author

Cheryl Fall is the author of nine books and more than 1,500 magazine articles for publication. These include publications such as *Woman's Day*, *Family Circle*, *Country Living*, *Traditional Quilter*, *Quilt World*, *Sew Perfect*, and *Woman's World*, to name just a few. She is also the author of *Quilting For Dummies* and *Needlecrafts For Dummies*. Adept in Adobe Illustrator, Cheryl creates the electronic illustrations for her books and Web site. She enjoys illustrating and designing using colored pencil, oils, soft pastels and acrylics. Cheryl also enjoys gardening, crafts, needlework, and home decor, and has been seen by the locals slinking around antique shops on a regular basis.

She lives with her husband Tony, daughters Rebecca and Ashley, and Buster, their nutty cocker spaniel, in the southwest area of Washington state (Vancouver, Washington/Portland, Oregon area).

Dedication

This book is dedicated to my husband, children, parents, grandparents, aunts, uncles, and cousins. Without these wonderful people, a book like this would be impossible to write.

Author's Acknowledgments

This book would not have been possible without the help of some very special people — members of my family, both here and passed. Without them, I would not have been inspired to write this book. To my husband and children, thanks for all the terrific grilled cheese sandwiches that you brought me when I pulled an all-nighter. The caffeinated beverages were helpful, too. My sincerest thanks to all of you.

I also want to thank the following folks at Hungry Minds, Inc. — Acquisitions Editor Tracy Boggier for the opportunity to work on such a fun title. Allyson Grove, Project Editor extraordinaire! Where would I have been without your wonderful advice and assistance? Copy Editor Mary Fales for her invaluable assistance. And Assistant Editor Natasha Graf for helping to keep things running smoothly.

Also, I give special thanks to Brad Peru of Farmers Insurance, Vancouver, Washington, for all the great advice regarding insurance and liability issues for family-reunion planners. And last but not least, to Betty Crocker for providing the wonderful crowd-sized recipes featured in this book.

Publisher's Acknowledgments

We're proud of this book; please send us your comments through our Online Registration Form located at www.hungryminds.com.

Some of the people who helped bring this book to market include the following:

Acquisitions, Editorial, and Media Development

Project Editor: Allyson Grove

Acquisitions Editor: Tracy Boggier

Copy Editor: Mary Fales

Technical Editor: Joell Smith-Borne

Senior Permissions Editor: Carmen Krikorian

Media Development Specialist: Marisa E. Pearman

Editorial Manager: Jennifer Ehrlich

Cover Photos: © Scott Barrow/ International Stock

Production

Project Coordinator: Nancee Reeves

Layout and Graphics: Jackie Nicholas, Janet Seib, Jeremey Unger

Proofreaders: Susan Moritz, Linda Quigley, Marianne Santy, Charles Spencer, TECHBOOKS Production Services

Indexer: TECHBOOKS Production Services

Hungry Minds Consumer Reference Group

Business: Kathleen Nebenhaus, Vice President and Publisher; Kevin Thornton, Acquisitions Manager

Cooking/Gardening: Jennifer Feldman, Associate Vice President and Publisher; Anne Ficklen, Executive Editor; Kristi Hart, Managing Editor

Education/Reference: Diane Graves Steele, Vice President and Publisher

Lifestyles: Kathleen Nebenhaus, Vice President and Publisher; Tracy Boggier, Managing Editor

Pets: Kathleen Nebenhaus, Vice President and Publisher; Tracy Boggier, Managing Editor

Travel: Michael Spring, Vice President and Publisher; Brice Gosnell, Publishing Director; Suzanne Jannetta, Editorial Director

Hungry Minds Consumer Editorial Services: Kathleen Nebenhaus, Vice President and Publisher; Kristin A. Cocks, Editorial Director; Cindy Kitchel, Editorial Director

Hungry Minds Consumer Production: Debbie Stailey, Production Director

Contents at a Glance

Cartoons at a Glance

By Rich Tennant

page 215

page 7

page 241

page 39

page 101

page 167

page 139

Cartoon Information:
Fax: 978-546-7747
E-Mail: richtennant@the5thwave.com
World Wide Web: www.the5thwave.com

Table of Contents

Introduction

· ·

"Of all the nostalgias that haunt the human heart, the greatest of them all is an everlasting longing to bring what is youngest home to what is oldest."

—Laurens van der Post

When I was a kid (good heavens, it's hard to believe that I was ever a kid!), the biyearly family reunion gave me the perfect opportunity to reconnect with my cousins. As a group, we played games and wreaked a little havoc — for example, we hid toads in people's shoes and painted the side of the house with a mixture of mud and water. (You can be sure that Grandpa wasn't too thrilled about the last one.)

Now that I'm all grown up (and have decided to use paint instead of mud), I plan the reunions so my family members can reconnect with cousins and older relatives, meet the newest additions to the family tree, and watch the children grow and wreak their own brand of havoc. In addition, my relatives get to review the family history. With families spread out across the miles, hosting a reunion is often the only way to gather the generations in one place.

With these benefits, however, comes work. Planning a successful family reunion takes time and effort. Give yourself at least one full year to plan everything, and get ready to work hard — you'll be justly rewarded in the end.

About This Kit

If a family reunion is tugging at your heartstrings, this book is your new best friend and resource. Use it as a guide to help you plan all things reunion related, from creating the guest list and selecting a theme to cleaning up after the party and processing post-reunion surveys.

In this book and on the accompanying CD, you can find valuable information and resources to help you manage your party effectively. I give you various checklists, address and RSVP lists, ideas for games and family-oriented activities, cleanup tips, and lots of other helpful advice. I also provide menu-planning ideas and crowd-sized recipes from Betty Crocker. With these resources at your disposal, you may be able to pull off your reunion without a hitch — or at least with fewer hitches. (Hey, I'm talking *family* here — I don't know any clan that's hitch-free!)

Foolish Assumptions

I assume that the reason you're looking at this book is that you have a longing for your family. However, if you're looking for an "easy way" to plan your reunion, fugetaboudit!

I'm also assuming that you enjoy a good challenge. A reunion, whether large or small, requires planning and hard work on your part. This book doesn't do the work for you, but it guides you through the planning process and beyond.

And lastly, I assume that you own a good pair of tennis shoes or some comfortable walking shoes — you're going to need them for all the footwork required of a reunion planner.

How This Book Is Organized

Planning a family reunion isn't rocket science, but you definitely need a method of attack. I set up this book in a way that I think makes the most sense for reunion planning — starting with the thought processes that go into planning to setting up committees (delegate, delegate, delegate . . .) on through to making the guest list, budgeting, menu and activities planning, and cleaning up. Here's a closer look at how the book breaks down.

Part 1: Gathering the In-laws and the Outlaws

Tracking down the clan can be a challenge, especially if your kinfolk are spread out across the miles. In this part, I give you advice on locating your family members — including the "long-lost" relatives — through networking, the Internet, and some creative sleuthing.

I also show you how to get your reunion information organized, and I recommend ideas for setting up committees that can help make your planning go smoothly. I include helpful lists to keep your committees focused and on task, and I provide tips on keeping committee members happy throughout the planning process.

Part II: Getting into the Nitty-Gritty of Reunion Planning

In this part, you find out how to transform your reunion vision into a plan. I give you information about sending out invitations, selecting locations, creating themes, working out a budget, and locating supplies.

I also give you advice on finding accommodations for out-of-towners so you don't have wall-to-wall sleeping bags spread out on your living-room floor.

Part III: Keeping Everyone Busy

The last thing that a reunion planner needs is a bunch of relatives branching off into little groups to be with the folks they know best at the reunion. To get everyone talking and interacting with one another, you need to provide lots of icebreakers and activities — and I give you plenty of starter ideas in Part III.

Many of the activities in this book are *multigenerational*, meaning that both young and old folks can comfortably participate. You may have lots of older folks at your reunion, so you don't want to leave them out of the activities!

Part IV: After the Reunion

Eventually, all good things must come to an end, including the reunion. In this part, you find helpful advice on cleaning up the mess, recycling trash, and getting the reunion site back to normal.

You can also find information on evaluating what worked and what didn't during your gathering. You may even decide to make the reunion a regular event. Assessing your reunion helps immensely if you want to plan the next one.

Oh, and one more thing: Part IV features tips for using your family-reunion planning skills to plan other group events. After all, practice makes perfect!

Part V: From Branches to Roots: Researching the Family Tree

If you're thinking of planning a family reunion, you may also be interested in researching your family history and sharing your findings with everyone. The family reunion is the perfect time for younger generations to find out about the family history.

This part of the book guides you through the basics of genealogy, including finding data, compiling family group sheets, and keeping all your material organized. I also give suggestions about Web sites and computer programs that are helpful for family historians. Imagine how wonderful it will be to pass your family history along to future generations so they can bring it along to future family reunions.

Part VI: The Part of Tens

This is my favorite part of the book. Basically, it consists of groups of ten pieces of information most helpful to reunion planners. You can find tips for dealing with family dynamics at the reunion, some recommended reading for general entertaining and genealogy, ideas on preserving family memorabilia, and various inspirations for reunion themes.

Appendixes

The appendixes contain more useful information for family reunion planners including resources such as helpful reunion sites and information on your state's Department of Tourism. You can also find the CD appendix here, which will guide you through the contents of the CD-ROM supplied with this book.

The CD-ROM

The CD-ROM contains useful tools to keep you organized, including printable copies of the forms used throughout the book, links to the recommended Web sites, and other nifty items. In the back of the book, you can find an appendix that explains the CD and its contents.

Icons Used in This Book

Sprinkled throughout this book are cute little pictures called icons that highlight important information. Here's the key to what they mean.

The Tip icon points out lots of important information that you can really use when planning your reunion. It points out nifty ideas, time savers, or even little things to inspire you.

When planning a family reunion, you need to keep lots of little details straight in your mind. This icon marks information that bears repeating and remembering during the process.

 This icon signals important information that can keep you out of planning trouble. I'm not saying that blunders aren't going to happen, but heeding these warnings can help minimize them.

 This icon points out the goodies included on the CD-ROM.

 This icon denotes multigenerational activities that both young and old folks can participate in and enjoy.

Where to Go from Here

You may not need my advice on every aspect of reunion planning. In this case, feel free to jump to the chapters that interest you and go from there. You don't have to read this book from cover to cover to understand. In fact, you can always go through the material again if you miss something. To make surfing this book easier, check out the table of contents to find the sections that you need.

Part I

Gathering the In-laws and the Outlaws

In this part . . .

1 start this book off by giving you some basics about planning reunions. I include tips for creating your guest list and locating elusive family members. I also discuss your role as the reunion planner and the importance of getting the clan involved in the planning process. To make sure that you don't feel overwhelmed, I give you lots of tips for organizing your information so you'll know exactly what-goes-where and who-does-what.

Chapter 1

It's All Relative

*T*hinking of organizing a family reunion? Congratulations! You've taken the first step in bringing the generations together for food, fun, and frolic.

You may have many motivating reasons for wanting to plan a family reunion, but I'm betting that you've watched your children and grandchildren grow, and suddenly you realize that everyone else's kids are all grown, too! Where has the time gone? What became of the old homestead? When was the last time that you saw your nieces and nephews? Now is the time to renew family bonds and connect with your relatives.

Family reunions come in all shapes and sizes, from small groups of immediate family to large groups pulled together from all corners of the globe. Family reunions can be as simple as a handful of kinfolk getting together for a back-yard barbecue or a lakeside picnic, or something as elaborate as a catered affair for hundreds of family members in a convention center or hotel ballroom.

The type of reunion that you plan depends on the number of people attending and the activities involved. For example, activities like a friendly game of croquet or kick-the-can call for a casual atmosphere, whereas a ballroom-dancing competition calls for more of a *shooshefafa* (a silly pet term for a gala affair) atmosphere complete with black ties and evening gowns and some cute little finger sandwiches that barely fill a hole in your tooth.

In this chapter, I share some basic reunion planning ideas and tips to get you started on the right foot — or the left foot if you prefer. Either way, I guide you into jumping in with both feet.

Deciding Why to Hold a Reunion

Having a family reunion is a simple way for kinfolk to reestablish family ties. But most families have a "big why" — a main reason — to hold a reunion. Some families have a big why because it makes the amount of time and money spent on the reunion easier to justify.

You can choose from many big whys to have your reunion. Perhaps Granny is celebrating her 100th birthday, Beth is graduating from medical school, Pops is retiring, or Aunt Suzie and Uncle Joe are celebrating 50 years of marriage. These examples are terrific reasons to hold a family reunion. The nice folks at Reunion Research estimate that about 200,000 family reunions are held each year in the United States. That's a lot of people getting together for a lot of different reasons!

In addition to or instead of having a guest of honor, consider having a theme for your reunion. Simply getting a bunch of people together for a meal or a barbecue can be boring. Having a theme livens things up. Perhaps your great-grandparents came from the "old country," or maybe your relatives are chicken-eaters and like to get together for grandma's famous fried cluck. Use these common bonds to your advantage. I give you more information on reunion themes in Chapters 5 and 20 — in this chapter, I simply want to plant a seed in your noggin.

Although thoughts of themes and reasons to have a family reunion are probably foremost in your mind, I want to offer a bit of advice: Think of your reunion as a gift that you give to yourself and your family. After all, where would you be without your family?

Understanding the Importance of Proper Planning

Whatever the reason or theme that you choose for your get-together, remember this basic idea: With proper planning, hosting a family reunion can be one of the most rewarding experiences of your life; without it, one of the worst. Planning is the single most important aspect when coordinating a successful family reunion. Without proper planning, a seemingly harmless, oversized party can turn into a "relative nightmare."

To avoid that, you first need to decide who to invite and when and where to hold the big event. The following sections touch briefly on these areas, but I cover them in more detail in Chapters 3 and 4.

Figuring out who to invite

Inviting every member of your extended family to a reunion simply isn't feasible — unless you have a very tiny family. If you consider the number of people in your family (including yourself, your parents, and your spouse), the guest list can be overwhelming. So you may need to do some paring.

Here's a simple trick for formulating a guest list for a reunion: Compile the guest list based on a common or unifying factor. Having a common factor makes the reunion more enjoyable because everyone shares something special.

Within an extended family, no two families are the same, but they all share something special that you can tap for the guest list. For instance, you can gather all the children, grandchildren, and great-grandchildren of a couple celebrating their milestone wedding anniversary. This kind of gathering lets far-flung relatives reunite while it helps the parents and/or grandparents celebrate a very special day.

Another nifty guest-list idea is to gather all the descendents of a specific ancestor or of the first relative that arrived in the new country — whether that's the United States or elsewhere. This idea is great for families who are curious about their origins, and this interest is passed on to the younger generations during the reunion. In Chapters 13 through 16, I discuss some enjoyable ways to get everyone involved in the family research. This research includes such activities as sharing family stories, photos, the family tree, and other special memorabilia.

Try to keep friends and neighbors off the family-reunion guest list, unless they are very close to most of your guests. If you're planning a true family reunion, they really don't belong there!

Locating everyone

Sometimes finding the clan can make the reunion planner (you) feel like a gumshoe in a detective movie. Folks move or disappear from the family holiday card list without a trace.

In Chapter 2, I tell you how you can find your kinfolk, and I give you some great advice on where to look. Put on your overcoat, grab a pencil, and enjoy the hunt.

Pondering the time and location

The size of your guest list determines when and where you hold your reunion. *Note:* The larger the group, the more planning the reunion requires. I discuss the nitty-gritty of reunion planning in Chapter 4.

When to plan the reunion can be tough. Most family reunions take place during the summer, which makes it easier for families with kids and *usually* means that the weather will cooperate. However, if you live in the Pacific Northwest like I do, the weather is hit-or-miss even during the summer months. (But what's a little rain when you're with the family?)

But if you're planning to hold the reunion to celebrate a special event, such as a 50th wedding anniversary, dates can problematic. You may not be able to have the reunion on the exact date of the anniversary; in fact, it rarely works. When setting the date, keep families with school-age children in mind, or those families won't be able to attend. Pulling children out of school to go on a family trip isn't a simple matter. You can also try to plan this type of reunion on a three-day holiday weekend or during spring break. The families attending will thank you for it.

After you have ideas for a date and a guest list, start thinking about the location. You can choose from a wide range of reunion-location options, from hotel ballrooms or grange halls to campgrounds or the good old backyard. Wherever you decide to hold the reunion, be sure that the place can accommodate the guest list. I give you more location ideas in Chapter 4, along with a location checklist that you can use to evaluate the potential sites.

Organizing the big event

Family reunions are big events — usually too large for one person to manage efficiently. You may need some help.

You can find that help in the form of *reunion committees,* which are groups of fellow kin that you put together to help you hash out all the reunion details. You also need a method of keeping your reunion information organized and handy. In Chapter 3, I go over all the pertinent details.

Likewise, in Chapters 4 though 6, I give you lots of tips and advice on budgeting the reunion, renting equipment, and figuring out where everyone is going to sleep. I also go over some insurance issues that every reunion planner should keep in mind.

Keeping everyone busy

I pity the uninformed reunion planner who selects the site and date and sends out the invitations without thinking about ways to keep everyone occupied after they arrive. Imagine how dull the reunion can be if everyone just sits in a chair and stares at one another. Activities keep everyone mingling and visiting, and they give the generations an opportunity to work together, instead of having the kids do one thing and the grown-ups do another.

A successful reunion needs activities. These activities can be as simple as storytelling and scavenger hunts or as energetic as carnival-sized games and the family Olympics. In Chapters 7 and 8, I give you lots of ideas for icebreakers to get everyone talking, as well as games to keep every generation busy.

Feeding the tribe

Everyone loves to eat — myself included. Your family reunion is a great time for everyone to show off their cooking skills by participating in a potluck meal. If you're not into potlucks (or cooking), you can hire a catering service to provide the eats.

For potluck planners, I include a who-brings-what Potluck Tracking Sheet in Chapter 5. This list can help you organize the menu and avoid the common problem of having too few salads and too many desserts (if you consider this a *problem*). If you prefer to hire a professional, Chapter 5 is also full of tips for working with vendors or caterers.

Cleaning up the mess

Reunions are messy affairs, so prepare yourself for some hefty cleanup! To make this task run smoothly, I include a special section in Chapter 10 specifically aimed at the cleanup process, and I give you a checklist to help you remember everything.

Keeping your reunion site tidy makes the cleanup easier, so I also include tips for keeping things tidy during the reunion, such as setting up areas for recycling (see Chapter 5) and diaper changing (see Chapter 6).

Determining How Often to Hold a Reunion

How often you hold your reunion depends entirely upon the location of your family. Large families who live close to one another can see each other regularly. For this type of family, a yearly reunion may be just the thing to bring the kinfolk together on a regular basis.

Families with members spread out across the country or around the world generally can't get together as often as those who live near one another due to budget restrictions and the demands of everyday life. For these families, a reunion every other year or every five years can do the trick.

Before you can make the decision for your family, you need to hold your first reunion and take it from there. Your first reunion is the testing ground from which subsequent reunions evolve.

An interesting side effect of regularly held reunions is that the number of family members in attendance grows from year to year, especially if the reunion is fun. Word gets around!

Staying in Touch

The reunion is over, the mess is cleaned up, and folks have gone their separate ways. Now you may be thinking of how to stay in touch with everyone.

Chapter 11 is full of ideas for family newsletters, Web sites, and other interesting things to make staying in touch easy.

Chapter 2

Playing Family Detective

• •

• •

*L*ong before you mail the invitations, you may find yourself in the role of family detective. Your job (if you choose to accept it) is to hunt down family members at large and lure them to the reunion location on the specified day at the proper time.

This task can prove difficult if your family is large and spread out all over the country. But with the wealth of information available on the Internet, finding people is easier than ever. Of course, you still have to do a bit of research, but as Sherlock Holmes says, "The work is its own reward."

Genealogists sometimes use a silly (but true) saying. It goes something like, "You know that you're a genealogist when you start looking at the graffiti on bathroom walls for surnames." The same idea applies to folks hunting down long-lost relatives. Sometimes, you find them in the strangest places!

In this chapter, I give you some tips and advice about playing the role of the family detective.

Locating Your Kinfolk

Tracking down the clan can be a challenge. As the years pass, children grow, old folks pass away, and people relocate, so knowing where to find everyone can leave you banging your head against the wall in frustration. (Don't bang too hard, because you'll give yourself a headache, or worse, you'll get a concussion and forget whom your relatives are!)

In the following few sections, I give you some trusty family-finding tips that you can start using as soon as you begin formulating your reunion ideas.

I must give you one quick caveat before you jump into this process. Some folks just don't want to be found, so if you find yourself facing some cold shoulders, respect their privacy and move on. Chances are, they may later regret their decisions not to participate in your family gathering.

Starting with your own brat pack

Although this seems like a no-brainer, you'd be surprised at how many reunion planners try to locate their missing relatives first, thinking that they can get the toughest part out of the way. However, starting with your immediate family can save you quite a bit of research.

Begin by making a list of immediate family members from your personal phone book or from your holiday-card list. These people shouldn't be too hard to find. Hopefully, you've been keeping track of new addresses and phone numbers as you receive them.

Networking with family members

Now you can track down other members of the pack through *networking,* which is the exchanging of information with others. Networking is an invaluable tool for trying to find family members, and it allows you to add information to your database of names, addresses, and phone numbers.

Start a family newsletter

While you have your ear to the ground tracking down the tribe, why not start a bimonthly family newsletter? A newsletter is a great way to keep family members up-to-date on what everyone else is doing, to help them celebrate their triumphs, and best yet, to remind everyone that a reunion is being planned!

Use the newsletter to provide news about your family history. For example, if you have an unusual last name, write an article about the origin of the name and include different variations of the name.

Give your newsletter a snazzy name that incorporates your surname. For instance, a family named Wheeler can call their newsletter the "Wagon Wheeler," or the Gibson family can call their newsletter the "Gibson Gazette."

You can download a desktop-publishing program from the Internet to help you create your family newsletter. But before you download, check out the programs on your computer. One of the programs included with your software may already have a desktop-publishing feature.

Call or write to the family members in your address book or on your holiday-card list. Ask them for the addresses and phone numbers of their children, cousins, aunts, uncles, and anyone else you want to see at the reunion. Although you may not have kept in touch with Aunt Sue or Cousin Timmy, other family members may know how to reach them.

Always ask for the *zip+4 code* (the five-digit zip code plus an additional four digits) when networking for addresses. If you can include this information in the mailing address, your mail can get to its recipient more quickly. Also, if you are planning a large-scale reunion for a few hundred people, you can check with your post office for bulk-mailing details.

If you need help drafting a letter, take a look at Figure 2-1. (This letter is also on the CD, so feel free to print a copy.) Keep your letter simple and direct, but not cold. Be polite and always let your family know that they're in your thoughts. If they think that you're just picking their brains for information, they may not reply!

The results of family networking may surprise you. For example, my husband wrote to his aunt in Minnesota and discovered that she had been keeping in touch with a cousin in Norway for years! By writing to this newfound cousin, my husband and I discovered branches of cousins that we never knew existed.

Folk-Finding on the Web

If your missing relatives have been spotted more times than Elvis but can't be located, or if you have exhausted all your immediate sources, you can try some creative sleuthing. The Internet is a great tool to use for tracking down branches of your family tree. If you have online access, you can easily use the people-finder Web sites that I provide in the next few sections. Be sure to try them all — if your kin doesn't pop up on one, they may on another — and follow the instructions given on each site. At times, you may feel like you're looking for a needle in a haystack, but keep in mind that persistence pays off.

If you don't have Internet access at home, check with your local library. Most libraries provide online access for their patrons. Keep in mind, however, that these computers are often best reserved ahead of time due to their popularity.

Date

Dear (insert name here),

We hope this letter finds you and your family well and happy. It has certainly been a long while since we've seen all of you! By now the children are as tall as can be and you're busier than ever.

As you may have heard, we are beginning to make plans to hold a family reunion sometime next year honoring Great-Grandpa Pennypacker's 100th birthday. We hope you and your family will be able to attend.

Because we all live so far apart and our lives are busy, we have lost track of several people. Can you help us locate the following misplaced cousins so we can let them know about the reunion plans?

(List the cousins here)

We'll send along another letter and more information as soon as we start making plans. We would like to get everyone's feedback.

We're thinking of you and hope to see you next year!

Until next time!

(Sign your names here)
(Your addresses here)

Figure 2-1:
Sample
letter of
request.

Consulting U.S. and Canadian finding aids

People-finder sites use different search styles to find information. Most sites check current address and telephone databases, and some sites feature reverse lookup. This method is helpful if you know the family member's phone number, but not his or her address. Most sites look up the *snail-mail address* (also known as a street or postal address) for a specific person. A few sites also look for an individual's e-mail address; however, I don't have much luck with these searches. Other sites look for specific information, such as school alumni or dates of birth. Try them all!

Getting to know everyone

Try getting a tidbit of personal information for each family member that you enter into your address database.

For instance, you may want to compile a list of everyone's birthdays to use in a family calendar that you plan to give out at the reunion. Or if someone has a unique talent, such as playing the ukulele or native folk dancing, add that information to the database! Listing everyone's occupation can also provide some interesting information. My family has a tendency toward engineering, art, and politics, and seeing all the family members who have these occupations "in their genes" is intriguing.

Use these common threads — birthdays, talents, and occupations — as headlines in your family newsletter. Everyone will be surprised to see family tendencies repeated in the younger generations. Plus, this information gives you something to write about if you suddenly suffer from brain drain or a bad case of writer's block.

Beware of searching by last name only. Unless you have an unusual name like Doodlefinger, the search may return thousands of names. Also, some searches have a limit on the number of listings returned. Try to limit your search to one state, or better yet, to one locale.

Here are some of the Web sites that I recommend using for your people search. You can also find hyperlinks on the CD to make getting to these sites a breeze. See the CD Appendix for information about the following hyperlinks:

- **555-1212:** www.555-1212.com. Searches for residential or business listings.
- **InfoSpace:** www.infospace.com. Searches for residential or business listings and e-mail addresses, features reverse lookup, and contains links to international search sites.
- **AnyWho:** www.anywho.com. Searches for residential or business listings.
- **BigFoot:** www.bigfoot.com. Searches for residential and e-mail addresses.
- **InfoUSA:** www.infousa.com. Searches residential and business listings and features reverse lookup.
- **Yahoo! People Search:** http://people.yahoo.com. Searches residential listings and e-mail addresses.
- **WorldPages.com:** http://worldpages.com. Searches residential listings for the United States and Canada.
- **SuperPages.com:** http://wp.superpages.com. Features residential and reverse lookup.
- **WhoWhere?:** www.whowhere.lycos.com. Searches residential listings and e-mail addresses.
- **Internet Address Finder:** www.iaf.net. Searches for e-mail addresses.

Searching for international information

This section contains only a partial listing of what's available on the Internet. To search for a country other than those I list, type "White Pages" followed by the name of the country in your favorite search engine. Also note that each country often has more than one site. If you can't find what you're looking for on one site, try another.

As with the sites in the previous section, I include hyperlinks on the CD to make visiting the sites quick and easy. No need to get finger cramps from typing in the following addresses:

- ✔ **WorldPages.com:** `www.worldpages.com`. Searches for business and residential listings in the U.S. and Canada and provides links to international directories.

- ✔ **World E-mail Directory:** `www.worldemail.com`. Provides residential listings and e-mail addresses worldwide.

- ✔ **Canada 411:** `http://canada411.sympatico.ca`. Provides White Pages in English and French.

- ✔ **Páginas Blancas Online:** `www.paginas-blancas.net`. Provides White Pages in Spanish.

- ✔ **teldir.com:** `www.teldir.com`. Provides links for residential and business listings as well as e-mail addresses from more than 170 countries around the world.

- ✔ **Les Pages Jaunes:** `www.pageszoom.com`. Provides Yellow and White Pages for France.

- ✔ **infobel.com:** `www.infobel.com`. Searches residential and business listings in Belgium, France, the United Kingdom, Spain, Denmark, Luxembourg, and the U.S.

- ✔ **Internet White Pages:** `www.whitepages.co.nz`. Provides White Pages for New Zealand and provides a World Directories link.

- ✔ **Australian White Pages:** `www.whitepages.com.au/wp`. Provides White Pages for Australia.

- ✔ **Swiss White Pages:** `http://tel.search.ch/`. Provides White Pages for Switzerland.

- ✔ **Greek White Pages:** `www.xrysosodigos.gr/scripts/samples/onform.asp`. Provides White Pages for Greece in Greek.

- ✔ **Pagine Bianches:** `www.paginebianche.it/pbol/home/index/html`. Provides White Pages for Italy in Italian.

- ✔ **UK PhoneBook.com:** `www.ukphonebook.com`. Provides White Pages for the United Kingdom.

Other useful search aids

There are several additional Internet sites that you may want to make use of when putting together your address list. Give these sites a try:

✔ **United States Postal Service:** `www.usps.gov`. If you're having trouble tracking down zip codes, this site can help. Type in the street address and the USPS does the rest.

✔ **Cedar:** `www.cedar.buffalo.edu/adserv.html`. Rewrites the address in the accurate format with the ZIP+4 code.

This is especially helpful if you're planning on doing a bulk mailing to the clan.

✔ **The Area Decoder:** `www.areadecoder.com`. New area codes are being added all the time. Use this site to help you find the correct codes for old ones that don't work any longer.

✔ **Westminster:** `www.westminster.ca`. Locates U.S. zip codes and Canadian postal codes.

✔ **German White Pages:** `www.teleauskunft.de/`. Provides White Pages for Germany in German.

✔ **PhoneNumbers.net:** `www.phonenumbers.net`. Multinational telephone-number finder.

Getting the Help of a Search Party

You may notice two types of search services — the ones that cost you and the ones that don't. Because I'm a cheapo, I prefer the ones that are free. However, if you don't mind spending the buckage, go ahead and pursue the fee-based services.

Before you hire a search service and spend your hard-earned cash to find the missing person, be sure to exhaust all your own sources. Chances are, one of your relatives already knows where the person is (because he or she isn't really missing, after all).

Search fees vary, depending on what you're looking for, the amount of information you provide, and the number of names to be searched. Some searches are available for less than twenty dollars, whereas others have a heftier price tag.

Most people-finder companies have a *no find–no fee* policy. This means that if they don't find what you're looking for, you don't have to pay. Be sure to ask about a company's policies before making a commitment. Write to the company or visit its Web site for pricing information.

When requesting a fee-based search, be sure to provide as much information as possible about your missing relatives. You should include their full names, dates of birth, last known addresses, current states of residence, and anything else that may be useful. Providing this type of basic information can help narrow the search results.

The following list includes Web and snail-mail addresses for some of the most popular fee-based search services. Although I don't usually recommend these services, they may come in handy as a last resort.

- **Searching for People.com:** www.searchingforpeople.com. P.O. Box 2601, Lutz, FL 33548. You give them as much info as possible, and they'll find your family. Works like a charm.
- **People-Finder.com:** www.people-finder.com. C/O Planet Investigations, Inc., 1070 Cleveland Street, Nipomo, CA 93444. This company will do the same as the preceding one. Just supply as much information as possible to help narrow the search.

You can also consult your local telephone directory for private detectives if you find yourself really desperate. But be prepared to drop a large chunk of change for their services.

More Creative Sleuthing Resources

Never rule out the public library as a source for sleuthing. Every library has a special section containing telephone directories for most areas of the United States and abroad. If the directory that you need isn't available, the library can order it through an interlibrary loan. The reference librarian can help you fill out the form.

Because directories are considered reference material, you can't check them out. Therefore, you have to allow yourself some time to search at the library. Be sure to bring a pad of paper, pencils, and some change for the copy machine.

Looking for alumni

If you know the high school that your missing relative attended, you can also try locating him or her on school alumni sites on the Internet. I suggest using two terrific sites:

- **Alumni.net:** www.alumni.net
- **Classmates Online:** www.classmates.com

On these sites, you can also search for schools by state and city. They also have a feature that allows you to search for an individual by name at graduation and by current name.

Due to privacy restrictions, you can't locate a postal address, an e-mail address, or a phone number on these sites. However, you can send an e-mail to your missing relative through the site systems. With a little luck, you may get a response.

Writing to the old homestead

Another idea for family gumshoeing is to contact former neighbors of your missing relative. Try addressing an envelope to the "current occupant" of the relative's last-known address and include a letter explaining whom you are and what you want to accomplish.

In your letter, ask the current occupant to give your letter to any neighbors who may know the whereabouts of your relative. Be sure to enclose a self-addressed stamped envelope so the neighbors can reply. Figure 2-2 shows you a sample letter.

Happy hunting!

Date

Dear occupant,

Please excuse the intrusion, but I am hoping you can help me. My Great-Aunt Annie Buckles lived at this address back in (year). Through the years we lost touch.

I have news I would like to pass along to her. A family reunion is being planned for next year in honor of Annie's grandfather, and we would like to let her know of these plans.

Is it possible that some of her old neighbors are still living in the area and may know how to contact her? If you have a moment, would you please ask them if they may know of her whereabouts?

Feel free to share my name and address with them. I have enclosed a self-addressed, stamped envelope to assist you with your reply.

Thank you very much for your help. It is much appreciated.

With kind regards,

(Sign your name here)
(Your address here)

Figure 2-2:
Sample
letter for
writing to an
old address.

Chapter 3

Calling on the Clan

• •

• •

*O*rganization is the key to planning a successful family reunion. Without organization, your reunion can easily turn into a fiasco. Remember, insanity is hereditary — you get it from your family.

In addition to keeping track of which folks plan to attend and whether they've responded to your RSVP, you also need to monitor available reunion sites, accommodations in the area, professional services, rentals, and, of course, the food and games that you plan to feature at the reunion.

In this chapter, I show you how to organize and store all your reunion materials. I also help you create committees that can help with the overall planning of your event. Getting other family members involved takes the pressure off you and makes the experience more enjoyable.

Organizing Your Information

As the official reunion coordinator (your new title), it's your job to keep everything organized. You need to come up with an effective way to keep track of the names and addresses of family members in addition to all the other important papers, brochures, and receipts that you collect as you plan the reunion. Loose papers stuffed in boxes and little pieces of paper stuck to the fridge with magnets are sure to get lost.

Starting a family file or notebook

I suggest using a file system or a notebook to organize and store your reunion information. For a file system, use hanging file folders and individual file folders to store your materials. Or you can set up a notebook, using a three-ring binder with two sets of eight tab dividers. You can purchase all these items at the office-supply store.

Be sure to store *all* reunion information — from address lists printed from your computer to brochures for potential reunion locations — in your file system or notebook.

Keeping track of your information

In the next few sections, you find out what to label your file folders or notebook dividers, and you get the lowdown on what to store in each folder. (See Figure 3-1 for an example.) I also give you some logs to help you keep track of your reunion information.

Figure 3-1:
How to label
your file
folders and
dividers.

You can find blueprints for many of the logs in this section on the CD-ROM. Be sure to print copies and place them in your folders (or notebook). You won't always be sitting in front of your computer when you need to record and/or review information.

Reunion preparation calendar

Keep a calendar in this folder to help you remember important dates, such as when you need to pay the advance to secure the reunion location, when you need to pay the caterer, or when you need to mail the invitations and finalize the menu. *Note:* Planning a family reunion takes a long time — a year or so is the average. You may lead a busy life in spite of the reunion, and without the calendar to guide you, you can easily overlook some of the most important things that you need to do.

Reunion-day schedules do not appear on this calendar. Because reunion-day schedules include everything from setting up to organizing games and activities to cleaning up, you should use a separate calendar for these things. You need to do so many things on the day of the reunion that these activities simply can't fit on a standard monthly calendar!

After scheduling all the upcoming dates, be sure to make copies of the calendar and distribute them to all the planning-committee members. (I talk about forming committees later in this chapter.) If everyone has a copy of the schedule, no one can make any excuses for not sticking to the schedule.

Addresses and phone numbers

If you've entered the information into your computer, print your address list or make a copy of your handwritten address list. If you've been adding family birthdays to the list, transfer these dates to your calendar (see the previous section). You want to keep this calendar up-to-date so you can prepare special correspondences, such as birthday and anniversary cards. I talk about these topics more in Chapters 9 and 11.

Committees and assignments

In this folder, keep lists of your committee members and their assignments. I provide two different lists to help you keep track of your committee members and their various responsibilities later in this chapter.

Invitations and RSVP log

Make a note of the date that you send out the invitations as well as the date that you receive the RSVPs. Doing so helps you plan for the number of people who will attend the reunion. Check out Chapter 6 to see what this log should look like.

Budget/expenses/receipts

After you and your committee members hash out all the important monetary details, store all your reunion budget information in this file (Chapter 4 contains a budget checklist that you can use). For example:

- ✔ If you plan to charge a fee or request a donation, keep a log of these payments in this file. Be sure to give a copy of the log to the correspondence committee so they know who may need a gentle reminder when it gets closer to crunch time.
- ✔ Put a large envelope marked *receipts* in this file. Use this envelope to keep all your reunion receipts safe and in one location.

See Chapter 4 for more budgeting information, including reunion-location costs, rental fees, and funding ideas.

Location information

You need another large envelope for this file so you can store brochures of potential reunion locations. Chapter 4 includes a Location Research Log that you can use to jot down information about each venue when you tour it.

Supplies and party rentals

Keep your supply lists and rental contracts in this folder. Supply lists include all the stuff that you need to buy, rent, or borrow for the reunion (see Chapter 4 for more details). Renting a dozen extra chairs or borrowing table tennis equipment doesn't seem very important at this point, but if you don't have your reunion needs written down and stored in the proper folders, you can easily overlook them later.

Be sure to place the receipts for all the purchased or rented items in your budget/expenses/receipts folder.

Sample menus and recipes

Although I include several sample menus in Chapter 5, you probably want to create your own. If you decide to host a potluck-style reunion, keep a "who's bringing what" log (also in Chapter 5) in this file. Knowing what foods people are bringing ahead of time ensures that you don't end up with one salad, a bag of chips, and 22 apple pies on the buffet table.

Vendors

Store vendor information and contracts in this file. Vendors may include the caterer, bartender, florist, photographer, and/or transportation company. In fact, I suggest that you keep information about any reunion item that requires delivery and setup by a vendor in this file. This includes rental portable toilets, tents, inflatable games, and/or other large-scale items not set up by you or your committee members (usually due to the vendor's insurance liability). Use the Vendor Checklist in Chapter 4 to keep track of your vendors.

Smaller rental items that you set up yourself, such as tables and chairs or buffet servers, belong in the supplies and party-rentals folder. This is a good thing — I doubt that anyone on the committee list is willing to haul and set up portable toilets!

Insurance and legal matters

If you plan to serve liquor, I urge you to consider extra insurance. I discuss insurance and liability in greater detail in Chapter 4. Keep anything of a legal nature, such as insurance documents, in this file.

Decorations and music

If you hire a disc jockey or other entertainment, keep the information in this file. That way, if you have any disputes over fees or if Coco the Clown shows up as Stanley the Stripper, you'll have your contracts safely stored in one location, ready to whip out at a moment's notice.

Keep your list of decorations (see Chapter 5) here, too. Also include notes on who's making the *sign-in board* (a list placed at the entrance to the reunion area so everyone attending can sign in).

Accommodations and maps

Store brochures from hotels and motels within 10 miles of the reunion site in this folder. Having these items in your file makes it easy to pass along room rates to your family members.

Also keep local maps and directions to the reunion site in this folder. You want to send the directions along with the invitations to prospective reunion attendees. And you can distribute local maps to everyone at the entrance to the reunion when they're signing in. By providing out-of-towners with local maps, you allow folks to explore the area at their leisure.

Games and activities

You don't want to forget about any of the great games or other activities that people suggest! Write them down and place them in this folder for easy reference. Be sure to bring this file with you to the reunion.

Also, you need to create a schedule for the reunion-day games and activities. In Chapter 7, you can find an Activities Checklist and Log to help you make this schedule, as well as tons of ideas for icebreakers and other reunion games and activities. Keep a copy of the schedule in this file and distribute copies to the activities committee.

Backup plans

Have a solid backup plan ready in the event of inclement weather. Store it in this folder. I discuss backup plans in more detail in Chapter 6.

Prizes and gifts

Are you planning to have T-shirts or ball caps printed for your reunion? Store the pricing and ordering information in this file. Be sure to include any fee due dates on your master calendar.

If you plan to give out prizes or certificates (see Chapter 7) during the reunion activities, keep a list of possible prizes in this folder.

Other or miscellaneous

You put the stuff that doesn't seem to fit anywhere else in this folder. Chances are, this folder will be the largest.

Getting the Clan Involved

Planning a reunion for a small group (fewer than 20 people) is relatively simple. Get a few volunteers from your immediate family, and you're set. But if you're planning a get-together for more than 20 people, don't even think of trying to plan this reunion by yourself. Planning a family reunion is a big job — no, make that a *huge* job. You will need help. As the reunion coordinator, you need to form committees, each with its own set of responsibilities.

The reunion coordinator is essentially "the boss" of all the committees. The coordinator has to be the tough guy (or gal) and make certain that deadlines are met and that everyone pulls their own weight. On some days, you feel like the top dog; on other days, you feel like the hydrant. The ups and downs are all part of the job. But keep in mind that the people on the committees are volunteers (not to mention your family members) and their time is just as valuable as yours — so be gentle.

Outlining some committee basics

Organizing a group of family members into committees is a terrific way to foster camaraderie and togetherness. The process can draw everybody closer together and strengthen bonds weakened by time and distance.

In fact, I recommend asking for the involvement of different generations of the family. Perhaps you can put the teens in charge of kids' games and the old-timers in charge of the family-history information.

For each committee to function properly, the members need to know their specific responsibilities as well as who else is on the committee. Each committee also needs a leader to keep the members and its responsibilities well organized and on schedule. This leader reports to the planning committee (see the next section for more details on the planning committee).

Here are a few other things to keep in mind:

- **Distance can be a good thing.** Committee members don't have to live near one another. Members can easily exchange information by writing, phoning, or sending e-mail. My preferred method is e-mail because it's instantaneous and cheap (unlike long-distance phone calls).

  Besides, long distance "committee-communing" is a great way to cement bonds before the actual reunion! Having committee members spread out in different areas also reminds everyone of the importance of keeping in touch with other family members and nurturing relations, no matter how many miles are spread out between them.

- **Psychology 101 may come in handy.** Take into consideration everyone's special talents when forming committees. For example, if Suzie has always been a party animal, put her in charge of the games. And if Uncle Bob is a stickler for organizing, put him on the planning committee. However, don't assign people with clashing personalities to the same committee. Doing so would be akin to asking for a kick in the rear.

  Also, don't forget Uncle Frederick (or Joe-Bob or Aunt Harriet). Just because you think that they won't be interested in helping doesn't mean that they aren't. Any one of them may turn out to be the best helper you ever had.

  You may also find that some folks are willing to serve on more than one committee. My feeling is that if these folks have the time and the energy for more than one job, let 'em have at it!

When working with your committees, remember that most people have an instinct (or perhaps I should say "tendency") to procrastinate. As the reunion coordinator, you need to make sure that each committee gets its stuff done on time.

I include two forms on the CD to help you organize the committees. The first form is a Master Committee List (see Figure 3-2). Use it to record the names, addresses, and phone numbers of each committee member. Doing so can prevent any confusion when you need to find out who's doing what.

The second form is a Committee Members and Responsibilities List (see Figure 3-3). Use this list to record the responsibilities of each committee as well as the due dates. You may want to print several forms from the CD because things change as plans are made. These lists guide the committees in their responsibilities, but keep in mind that nothing is ever written in stone.

Setting up the nitty-gritty committees

The number of people on each committee depends on its responsibilities. For example, the correspondence committee may require only two or three people to compile the address list and mail and keep track of the invitations/RSVPs. On the other hand, the cleanup committee may number five or more, depending on the size of the reunion and the amount of cleanup needed.

Use your best judgment and don't be shy about adding extra members to the committees when needed. Also, don't hesitate to move (or remove) committee members who don't follow through with their responsibilities. (See the section "Managing your committees," later in this chapter, for more details.)

Have an odd number of folks on each committee so you never have to deal with a tie when making group decisions.

The following list includes some common reunion committees and their responsibilities. For example:

- **The planning committee:** This is the most important committee and should be formed before any of the others. This committee selects the people for the other committees! It also sets the date, selects the location, sends out the invitations, and works out a budget. The planning committee also helps figure out which branches of the family to invite. Have at least three enthusiastic warm bodies on this committee. This is no place for the cooler slugs. You want people with energy and creative ideas to help you plan the reunion.

- **The menu committee:** Whether you're planning a simple potluck meal, a barbecue contest, or a catered bash, this committee is in charge of the eats. Members interview caterers, decide on a menu, or assign various potluck items.

✔ **The entertainment committee:** Ask the fun-loving folks to work on this committee. Let them come up with ideas for keeping everyone entertained. Options include games, music, and hired entertainers. (In fact, why not give them this book for some ideas!) This committee also makes the arrangements for T-shirts or ball caps, name tags, and buttons that you can give out or sell during the reunion. See Chapter 7 for more details on these items.

✔ **The family-tree committee:** A family reunion is an excellent time to add the kinfolk to the family tree. (If you're not already into genealogy, see Chapters 13 through 16 for information on getting started with this wonderful hobby.) This committee can also be responsible for creating keepsake items, such as a photo or video scrapbook of the event, an address list, or a family calendar. See Chapter 9 for details about these mementos.

✔ **The setup/cleanup committee:** In addition to setup and cleanup, this committee also takes care of picking up and returning rental items and setting up a recycling area. Everybody loves to help set up, but few people want to help clean up the mess afterward.

You can find setup and cleanup lists for your reunion on the CD. (I also include the lists in Chapter 10.) Be sure to give a copy of each list to the committee chairperson, and make certain that he or she assigns responsibilities to the committee members in advance.

✔ **The correspondence committee (optional):** The planning committee usually handles this task, but for huge reunions with 50 or more people, I also recommend having a correspondence committee. Planning large reunions can take up to a year because everyone needs to make arrangements to attend. The correspondence committee compiles the address list, sends updates on the status of the reunion in the form of postcards or newsletters, distributes invitations, and records the RSVPs.

If you are planning a small reunion, you can combine many of these committees.

Managing your committees

The people on your committees are average people. On some days, they function well; on other days, they're not worth a hoot. The same often applies to the reunion coordinator. I've been guilty of not being worth a hoot on more than a few occasions (shame on me!). Keep this idea in mind whenever you become frustrated with the reunion-planning progress.

So you don't fly into a tizzy and fire your committee members or cancel the reunion, I offer you some tips on dealing with common reunion-committee problems. First, I want you to take a deep breath, keep an open mind, and stay calm. Then you can better handle the situation in a mature, diplomatic manner.

Master Committee List

Name of committee _____

Committee chairperson _____ Phone # _____

Committee members with phone #

_____

_____

_____

_____

Name of committee _____

Committee chairperson _____ Phone # _____

Committee members with phone #

_____

_____

_____

_____

Name of committee _____

Committee chairperson _____ Phone # _____

Committee members with phone #

_____

_____

_____

_____

Figure 3-2:
Master
Committee
List.

Committee Members and Responsibilities

Name of committee _____

Responsible for _____

_____

_____

_____

Committee chairperson _____ Phone # _____

Committee members with phone #

_____

_____

_____

_____

Things to do   Date due

_____

_____

_____

_____

_____

_____

_____

_____

_____

Figure 3-3:
Committee
Members
and
Responsi-
bilities List.

No one wants to volunteer for anything

This is more common than any other problem. Folks love to participate in the actual event, but few want to involve themselves in the planning. This situation is much like the story about the little hen that wanted to bake some bread. No one would help her grow the wheat or grind it into flour. Nor would they help her mix, knead, or bake the dough — but all her barnyard pals wanted to eat the bread.

As the reunion coordinator, you must remember that you can't do the job alone. You need help from other members of the tribe. Get on the phone with some of the relatives and start talking. Tell your kin how much fun a reunion will be and wait for them to agree (which they undoubtedly will). Then say, "Great! I'd love to have you on the planning committee, and I'm adding your name right now! This is going to be so much fun!"

Repeat the process for all the committees. Eventually, you'll get those spaces filled! Remember that folks often don't know their own strengths until they're called upon to help.

A committee isn't following through on its responsibilities

This rarely happens, but it's still a possibility. After committee members get together and start gabbing, the plans work themselves out. By checking the progress of your committees frequently, you can usually spot trouble before it starts.

Start by talking with the committee head. Find out what the problem is. Did you allow enough time for the committee to complete its task, or is the committee too busy to fulfill its obligations? If you didn't plan enough time, add more people to the committee. More heads are better than a few.

However, when something goes wrong, the reason usually boils down to a clash of personalities within the committee. Your job is to figure out what went wrong and fix it before it's too late. This process may involve a change of the committee members or the committee head.

You're losing committee members

Some folks volunteer without realizing that they're making a commitment. Serving on a committee sure sounds like a good idea before the planning starts, but he or she may later discover that the time and energy involved is too great.

Let the person bow out gracefully, but ask him or her to find a replacement. Fresh faces often bring new ideas. Another thought is to assign the person to a less stressful post and move someone from another committee to fill the spot. Rotating committee members has its advantages. You keep the ideas flowing, and different folks get a chance to work together.

If the person is leaving due to a conflict with the committee head or other committee members, solving the problem can be a bit more complicated. Family dynamics are involved here, and sometimes, old wounds resurface at the strangest times. It's best to handle this situation by asking the unhappy person to serve on a different committee.

The committee head is too dominating

Some folks just can't handle leadership. Give the responsibility of committee head to someone else.

Everyone in a committee has an equal say, and everyone's input and opinion is important. The responsibility of the committee head is to keep the committee functioning, not to dominate it.

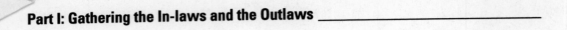

Part II

Getting into the Nitty-Gritty of Reunion Planning

The 5th Wave · By Rich Tennant

FAMILY REUNIONS WERE ALWAYS DIFFICULT FOR THE MITCHELLS HAVING SO MANY PROFESSIONAL BOXING REFEREES FOR FAMILY MEMBERS

In this part . . .

In Chapter 4, I explain the particulars of scouting out and selecting the perfect reunion location as well as working out a budget and setting fees for attendees. In Chapter 5, you can find ideas for fun reunion themes that'll really get your reunion started with a bang. I also tell you everything I can think of about renting supplies, hiring vendors, and feeding the crowd or hiring a catering service. Then, in Chapter 6, you can get some tips on finding accommodations for your reunion attendees and making backup plans — just in case your original plan doesn't work out.

Chapter 4

Figuring Out When, Where, and How Much

· ·

In This Chapter

▶ Selecting a date that suits everybody

▶ Choosing a location and booking your reunion

▶ Setting a budget and deciding on rental equipment

▶ Getting some easy insurance tips

· ·

*I*f you follow my advice in Chapter 3 and spread the work of planning the reunion around to different committees, you can formulate a vision of what you want the reunion to be like and relay this information to your helpers. Always be sure that the people on your committees share your vision.

Do you prefer an informal picnic for 15 to 20 of your closest relatives with music from a boom box, or a more elaborate get-together with a catered buffet, open bar, and live entertainment? Will the event last one evening, one day, or several days?

Clarifying your vision in the beginning helps to avoid confusion during the reunion planning. Use this vision (and the information that I provide in this chapter) to guide you in selecting the date, time, and place of the reunion, and to pinpoint any potential problems in advance.

Setting a Date

Most reunions take place during the summer months. This time of year is usually best because of favorable weather, children being out of school, and folks taking time off for vacation.

However, if you decide to schedule the reunion to correspond to a special event, such as a 50th wedding anniversary, you need to keep the following things in mind:

✔ If you choose to have your reunion sometime other than the summer months, try to schedule it close to a three-day weekend or during spring break. If you decide on a spring-break date, be sure to check with all the families who have kids in school because spring breaks can vary.

✔ If you schedule a reunion in mid-October, family members with school children probably won't be able to attend. The weather probably won't be nice either.

✔ If you schedule a reunion in the winter months, try not to schedule anything too close to major holidays, such as Christmas or Hanukkah. These are busy times of the year for most people, and their priorities may be elsewhere. Besides, have you ever seen a busy airport just before or after a major holiday? It's a zoo!

Determine your reunion duration

You can determine the duration of the reunion using some common-sense thinking.

One-day reunions are the easiest to plan and are the norm for families who live within driving distance of each other. These reunions are usually simple affairs, such as a picnic at the park or a backyard barbecue.

However, one-day reunions can seem like a bit of a waste to folks traveling across the country to get there. Imagine paying for plane tickets, boarding a crowded flight in a congested airport, renting a car to attend a one-day picnic, and maybe returning to a drab hotel. That doesn't really sound like a barrel of fun. If your family is coming from far and wide, consider holding a weekend reunion that lasts two days.

Multiple-day reunions do take more planning, of course. You must consider the cost of several nights in a hotel, and you should keep everyone occupied for more than one afternoon. For example, you may want to consider the following itinerary:

✔ Hosting a hospitality night for folks on Friday evening with snacks and drinks or a light supper.

✔ Holding the main reunion event (such as a dinner or a picnic) on Saturday.

✔ Having a casual, anything-goes day or even a family church service on Sunday.

Multiple-day reunions are the most enjoyable and memorable type of reunions. Spending two or more days with relatives that you rarely see is a treat!

Choose several options — Majority rules

When planning the date for your reunion, choose at least three possible dates that are a few weeks apart. After selecting a few potential dates, get some feedback from the rest of the family using the survey in Figure 4-1. Mail a survey to everyone on your guest list to find out which of your choices works best for each member of the family. Doing so helps avoid potential problems later — mainly the lack of attendees.

Dear cousins,

     In honor of Great-Grandpa Hooligan's arrival here in the states, we are considering holding our first-ever family reunion for Hooligan descendants and their families.
     We would appreciate your feedback to the following questions. Please mail this questionnaire back as soon as possible, but no later than (insert date here) so we may begin preparations.
     We hope to see your there!

                             With hugs from the planning committee,
                             (names and addresses of the committee members here)

We will plan to attend the reunion: yes   no

Which date works best for your family?   June 1   July 4   August 10 Other _____

To help with the costs of the reunion, we would be willing to spend or contribute this much as a family:
                              $25-$50 $50-$75 $75-$100   More _____

Total number in our family who would be attending: _____ adults   _____ children 0-12

We would be happy to volunteer for a committee or job: yes   no   maybe   unsure

Figure 4-1:
Sample reunion survey.

You can use your computer's mail-merge program to make preparing the survey envelopes a quick and painless task. Most computers come equipped with software that features some type of address book. All you have to do is select the addresses and click a button, and your computer prints the addresses on envelopes or labels. Printing addresses directly onto the envelopes is a bit more time consuming than labels because you have to stand at the printer and feed the envelopes through one at a time. I recommend the label approach if you have a lot of envelopes to address.

Your survey should ask the basics, such as the number of people attending and their preferred dates. You should also ask the following questions:

- What types of foods do they suggest?
- What types of games and activities do they want?
- Do they want to help plan the reunion?
- Do they prefer a one-day or multiple-day reunion?

You'll get a wide range of answers to your survey. Choose the ones that have a majority following. Sometimes, this doesn't include your top choice, so be flexible. The goal is to make sure that as many people as possible can get together and enjoy themselves — including you.

When you decide on a date, stick to it. Don't change the date to accommodate anyone, because the new date will inconvenience several others who have already made arrangements. Remember the old adage: If it ain't broke, don't fix it!

Location Is (Almost) Everything

Most small family reunions (20 people or so) tend to take place in the backyard of the family homestead or in a nearby park. Larger reunions tend to take place in rented halls, reserved park areas, and hotel facilities.

In fact, many factors go into determining your reunion location. For example:

- The number of people planning to attend and where they're traveling from
- The date and time of day of the reunion
- Your reunion theme
- How early you start searching for a location
- Types of activities (See the section "A busy clan is a happy clan," later in the chapter.)
- Your budget (See the section "Ka-Ching! Setting Up a Budget," later in the chapter.)

The rest of this chapter takes a look at several of these factors in greater detail. You find out what to look for when touring potential venues, when to reserve a site, and how to choose sites based on the activities that you want to do at your get-together.

Finding a venue and taking the grand tour

Finding a venue — or a place to hold your reunion — is simple. You open the phone book and make phone calls, find out about fees, and visit the sites.

Before you decide on a reunion location, take a good look at the place. Ask for the grand tour and take notes. I provide a Location Research Log on the CD to help you keep track of all the information that you gather on your location tours. Check out Figure 4-2 for an example.

Be sure to check out the facilities thoroughly. Is everything clean? Or does it smell like a bunch of guys have been cleaning fish in the main hall? Is there a kitchen that you can use, and does the facility supply small appliances, such as coffee makers? Is there a fee for using these appliances?

Where are the restrooms? Does the site have any recreational facilities? Is there access for disabled folks? Does the site allow for the serving of alcohol? What about insurance? Is adequate parking available? These are important issues that you need to clarify before you choose the site.

Reserve early or forever hold your peace

Reserving a spot at any public place, whether it's a park, campground, or hall, requires reservations up to a year in advance — or sometimes longer, if the spot is popular. No matter what site you choose, be sure to ask about the reservation requirements. Start with the following questions:

✔ How far in advance do I need to make reservations?

✔ What is the fee?

✔ Do you require a security deposit? How much is it?

✔ What is your cancellation policy?

Hiring an event planner

If you're thinking of hiring an event planner and taking the easy way out, I have one word for you — chicken! All kidding aside, these people can help you with all aspects of planning a reunion — from sending invitations to decorating to serving food and everything in between.

Event and party planners do their jobs well, but they don't come cheap. They put a tremendous amount of work and effort into your reunion and ask to be paid accordingly. You can find listings for these folks in the Yellow Pages or in Appendix B.

TIP

Always start your planning early! Eighteen months is the minimum for a large reunion; a year in advance is average. But if you're a procrastinator, give yourself at least six months for planning and reserving the location. If you wait any longer than that, you're pushing the limits.

Location Research Log

Name of site _____

Address _____

City / State / Zip _____

Phone / Fax _____

Contact person's name and title _____

Daily rate _____ Security / damage deposit _____

Maximum occupancy _____ How much notice required? _____

Kitchen facilities available?	Y N	Included in fee? Y N
Tables and chairs available?	Y N	Included in fee? Y N
Barbecues available?	Y N	Included in fee? Y N
Recreational facilities on site?	Y N	Included in fee? Y N
Clean, functional restrooms?	Y N	Electricity, hot/cold water available? Y N
Staff available for hire?	Y N	Shuttle for hire? Y N
Easy to find?	Y N	Plenty of parking? Y N
Alcoholic beverages allowed?	Y N	Music/dance area? Y N
Accommodations nearby?	Y N	Handicap accessible? Y N
Located indoors or outdoors?	_____	If outdoors, is it a covered area? Y N
Does it feel "reunion-friendly"?	Y N	Any adverse policies? Y N
Flexible cancellation policy?	Y N	Record additional comments below.

Comments:

_____

_____

_____

_____

Figure 4-2:
Location
Research
Log.

A busy clan is a happy clan

You want to have a variety of activities at your reunion so folks can get to know new faces as well as mingle with people they haven't seen in years. When selecting a location, check to see what types of activities are available because you may want to add them to your activities list (see Chapter 7). For example, some indoor facilities offer swimming pools, shuffleboard areas, volleyball courts, billiards, and other nifty activities.

Likewise, outdoor sites may feature tennis and basketball courts or areas for rousing games of softball or touch football. Beachside reunions can easily accommodate sandcastle contests, beach volleyball, and other beach games.

If you or a family member has a backyard with a swimming pool, consider having a pool-party reunion. Make sure that the backyard can accommodate the crowd. Most pools (except the blow-up, kiddie variety) take up a lot of space, leaving little room for people and barbecue equipment.

If you select a beachside location or a site with a pool, remember to appoint a lifeguard to keep the little ones safe. Teenage family members make terrific lifeguards!

The bottom line is that if you plan to have lots of activities for everyone, you can select just about any spot for your reunion. But if your list of activities is a little slim, be sure to choose a site that offers a wide range of things to do. In Chapters 7 through 9, I give you tons of ideas for games and activities to keep the whole clan amused — inside and out.

Narrowing Your Options

No matter what type of site you choose for your reunion, you'll find both good and bad things about it. I haven't run across a perfect site yet, and I probably never will. In this section, I give you the strong points and pitfalls of common location options.

Before selecting a location as your reunion site, take a look around and compare your options.

The backyard

Using your backyard as the reunion site can be a wonderful thing, especially if you (the reunion planner) have run all over town making arrangements for the big bash. Now you get to cool your heels at home in the yard.

Backyard pros

- ✔ It's cheap, close, and available.
- ✔ Guests can linger long into the evening.
- ✔ You make the rules regarding pets and alcoholic beverages.

Backyard cons

- ✔ People continuously come in and out of your house, and you can expect lines at the bathroom.
- ✔ In the event of bad weather, the house may be too small to accommodate a large crowd.
- ✔ Parking can be a problem.
- ✔ Neighbors may not appreciate the noise.

A local park

A local park sounds like the perfect spot for a family reunion. There's plenty of space and fresh air, and lots of outdoor stuff for the kiddies.

Park pros

- ✔ Costs are minimal.
- ✔ It's close to your house.

Park cons

- ✔ The party has no place to go in the event of bad weather or extreme heat.
- ✔ The restrooms may not be close to the picnic site, making it difficult for the elderly or parents of small children to use them.
- ✔ Some park shelters have a sink, but no kitchen facilities.
- ✔ Noise (especially loud music) from other parties may be bothersome.
- ✔ Most parks want everyone out by sunset.
- ✔ Some parks don't allow alcoholic beverages or pets.
- ✔ This location may be close to your house, but far from everyone else's homes.

A hotel ballroom

Hotel ballrooms are another option for family-reunion planners. Personally, I think that they are better suited for weddings and conventions, but I believe in the adage "different strokes for different folks."

Hotel ballroom pros

- ✔ It's indoors (which means air conditioning), so you don't need to worry about the weather.
- ✔ Restrooms are close by.
- ✔ You can hire the hotel to do the catering.

Hotel ballroom cons

- ✔ It's expensive. Renting a hotel ballroom can cost hundreds of dollars a day.
- ✔ There are no outdoor recreation activities.
- ✔ You need to have all your family members out of the building at a designated time — no chance to linger.
- ✔ Absolutely no pets are allowed, and children are expected to behave as adults.

The local church hall

If you have a church in your area that has a nice-sized hall, it can be a terrific option for a reunion site.

Church hall pros

- ✔ It's reasonably inexpensive, especially if you are a church member.
- ✔ Kitchen facilities, tables, and chairs are usually available, and so are outdoor areas for games.
- ✔ You can count on plenty of parking.
- ✔ Weather is not a problem.

Church hall cons

- ✔ The site is not available Sundays due to church activities and is often booked for weddings on Saturdays, so you need to set the date 14 months or so in advance.
- ✔ Loud parties and pets are usually a no-no. Alcoholic beverages may not be allowed either.

A grange hall or community center

Grange halls and community centers offer nice large indoor areas for reunions, often providing kitchen facilities and tables and chairs.

Grange hall/community center pros

- These locations are inexpensive to rent.
- Most provide kitchen facilities for an extra fee (very minimal).
- Parking is plentiful, and weather is not a factor.
- Restrooms are close by.
- Some locations have outdoor facilities, such as basketball or shuffleboard courts and pits for sand volleyball.
- Grange halls usually allow you to remain after dark.

Grange hall/community center cons

- These locations don't allow pets.
- Grange halls are often in rural areas, so guests have a longer drive back to their hotels.
- Some grange halls are old and may be a little musty.
- Some grange halls may be available only to members. The rules vary, so be sure to call and ask first.

A campground

Holding a reunion at a beautiful campground can be very enjoyable, especially if your family likes the outdoors.

Campground pros

- You don't need to worry about hotel accommodations. The clan stays together as a group.
- Reunions can take place over the course of several days.
- The kids love the camping experience.

Campground cons

- Weather can be a problem.
- Some folks are lousy campers and prefer to stay in a hotel.
- Pets may not be allowed.
- Other campers can be noisy, or the campground may have a noise curfew of 10:00 p.m.
- Restrooms can be a hike from the site. Some campgrounds have pit toilets.
- Some campgrounds don't provide showers.

The family farm or homestead

If you're lucky enough to have a large family homestead or farm that's been passed down through the generations, you may have the perfect reunion site. Your family members can even camp at the site, saving them the expenses of a staying in hotels.

To help shuttle folks from the house to the field or barn, consider keeping a pickup truck (also known as a motorized wheelbarrow) handy to move people and supplies back and forth.

Family farm/homestead pros

- You don't need to worry about the noise level or nosy neighbors.
- A field provides plenty of parking and lots of space for outdoor activities.
- You can rent party tents in the event of bad weather — if you have a barn, that's even better.
- Family members can even camp at the site.
- Your family can enjoy lots of fresh air.
- The reunion can last for several days.

Family farm/homestead cons

- The location may be out in the middle of nowhere.
- If the reunion site *is* out in the back forty and the nearest restroom requires a hike back to the house, you need to rent some toilets.
- Family members who don't enjoy camping likely won't find hotels close by.
- Nearby farm animals may give off an objectionable odor.

Making a vacation out of it

If budgets allow, you may want to plan a vacation-style reunion at such locations as Disney World in Orlando or a beach resort in Maui. If your family consists of a bunch of soft city folk, a reunion at a dude ranch or a national-park campground may be a nice change of pace. A cruise may be a good option, too, as long as your family isn't prone to motion sickness. When planning a vacation-style reunion, consult a travel agent to locate the best package deals, or call the intended resort for information. Many of them are more than happy to help you arrange your reunion plans.

When your family members are spread out across different states, selecting a reunion location can be more challenging. Having a *central* location to which everyone can migrate is always best, because no one feels like they've been singled out because they live on the other side of the continent. If you plan on having a reunion every few years, another option is to rotate location each time. Doing so gives everyone a chance to show off his or her hometown and play host to the clan.

Ka-Ching! Working Out a Budget

So many factors influence your reunion budget that deciding where to begin can be difficult! I recommend charging a small fee, even for potluck and *BYO* (Bring Your Own) reunions, because expenses always crop up and the host shouldn't bear the entire burden. A fee of $5 to $10 per family should suffice. (See Chapter 5 for more details on BYOs.)

Creative funding for family reunions

Family reunions can be expensive events. But you can take some of the sting out of things by holding fundraising events before or during the reunion (especially if you want to make reunions a regular feature in your clan's life).

Some ideas to consider for reunion fundraising during the planning stages include multiple-family garage or yard sales, auctions, car washes, and raffles. For fundraisers during the reunion, consider creating family reunion memorabilia, such as baseball caps, recipe books, or group photos to sell to family members. Chances are, everyone will jump at the opportunity to own a piece of the reunion!

For a yard sale or auction before the reunion, have each family member contribute one or two items of value — not just junk. This event is a fundraiser, so you don't want to find yourself dumping everyone's leftover garbage.

For fundraisers during the reunion, you can give out surprise bags filled with candy or other items, family calendars featuring everyone's birthday, reunion cookbooks, homemade crafts,

or family T-shirts. Raffles are an entertaining way to raise money, too! Raffled items can include bottles of wine from local vintners, movie tickets, or anything else you can think of. If you have quilters in your family, ask them to make a raffle quilt.

Although these fundraisers are meant to defray some of the reunion costs, they're not meant to take the place of charging a fee to attend. Instead, use the funds to help lower the per-person charge. Any fundraising done during the reunion should be used to reimburse the reunion planner who usually pays for lots of stuff out of his or her own pocket.

Besides covering the costs of the reunion, the money collected at a family fundraiser can go toward a scholarship fund for college-bound family members, making reunion funds available to folks who couldn't otherwise attend school due to budget restrictions. Or you can always put the money into a special account and hold it until it's time to plan the next reunion.

Vacation-style reunions (see the sidebar " Making a vacation out of it," in this chapter) are the most expensive. For this type of get-together, I recommend the "everybody for themselves" approach.

Use the results of your family survey (see Figure 4-1) to help set the budget.

Getting your expenses down on paper

Although something as simple as a backyard barbecue doesn't seem like much, you *will* find yourself spending hard-earned buckage to plan it. Large-scale reunions cost even more. You need to plan your budget accordingly.

This budget is the toughest part of reunion planning, so you need the help of your planning committee (see Chapter 3). To start the budget-setting process, hold a meeting with everyone (in person, by conference call, or over the Internet using a chat room or instant messenger service).

The Reunion Budget Checklist shown in Figure 4-3 (and included on the CD) can help you keep track of projected and actual expenses. Print copies of the checklist, give one to each member of your planning committee, and keep a copy in your budget folder (see Chapter 3). In the rest of this section, I break down the form for you section by section so you get a better idea of the budgeting process.

A word to the wise: Keep track of every penny that you spend or plan to spend when planning the reunion.

Facility rentals

You don't need facility rentals if you hold the reunion at the family homestead or in your backyard. But if you plan to hold your reunion at any other location, you need to plan for the fees. Fees can range from nothing more than a refundable deposit at a local park to several hundred dollars plus a refundable damage/cleaning deposit at a hall or a hotel. The more people you plan to invite, the larger your site needs to be. This often translates to a larger budget, too.

If you have not yet visited any potential reunion sites, you can fill in an estimated cost by calling around to different facilities in your area. Be sure to ask about the maximum occupancy of the site to determine if the area is large enough for your reunion. Average the costs from the different phone calls and use this number as your estimated rental fee. You determine the actual fee based on the final site selection.

Reunion Budget

	Estimated	Actual
Facility rental	_____	_____
Refundable deposit		< _____ >
Telephone	_____	_____
Postage	_____	_____
Copies	_____	_____
Transportation	_____	_____
Linens		
Tablecloths	_____	_____
Napkins	_____	_____
Table skirting	_____	_____
Utensils		
Plates	_____	_____
Cups and glasses	_____	_____
Dinner and cocktail napkins	_____	_____
Silverware	_____	_____
Serveware (salad tongs, serving spoons, etc.)	_____	_____
Rentals		
Tables	_____	_____
Chairs	_____	_____
Grills	_____	_____
Chafing dishes	_____	_____
Beverage dispensers	_____	_____
Tent	_____	_____
Dance floor	_____	_____
Lighting	_____	_____
Toilets	_____	_____
PA/AV rental	_____	_____
Other	_____	_____
Food		
Appetizers	_____	_____
Meat/cheese trays	_____	_____
Salads	_____	_____
Bread	_____	_____
Vegetables	_____	_____
Meat	_____	_____
Desserts	_____	_____
Other	_____	_____

Figure 4-3:
Reunion
Budget
Checklist.

(continued)

(continued)

Reunion Budget

	Estimated	Actual
Beverages		
Coffee and tea		
Soda/juices	_____	_____
Bar (Beer, wine, spirits)	_____	_____
Entertainment		
Disc jockey	_____	_____
Bartender	_____	_____
Karaoke	_____	_____
Games	_____	_____
Rented games	_____	_____
Popcorn machine	_____	_____
Disco ball	_____	_____
Bubble machine	_____	_____
Photographer	_____	_____
Decorations		
Signs	_____	_____
Centerpieces	_____	_____
Miscellaneous	_____	_____
Stationary/Printing		
Survey cards	_____	_____
Invitations	_____	_____
Announcements	_____	_____
RSVP cards	_____	_____
Questionnaire	_____	_____
Directory forms	_____	_____
Special Items		
Gift bags	_____	_____
T-shirts	_____	_____
Cookbooks	_____	_____
Other	_____	_____
Special Items		
Charcoal	_____	_____
Ice	_____	_____
Film	_____	_____
Total cost of reunion		_____

Family communication

Factor in telephone, postage, and copy costs. If you are making long-distance phone calls to committee members or other kinfolk, your budget depends on how gabby you are. If you figure 10 to 15 cents per minute for calls, you'll probably have at least 6 to 10 hours of talk-time after everything has been finalized. If you're sending a bunch of reunion information by mail, you'll have postage and photocopying fees to consider.

Transportation

Transportation costs are tricky to determine. These costs may include your gas and mileage while checking out potential sites and accommodations, or you may choose not to factor in this expense. (I usually don't count traveling costs. My view is that if I'm hosting the reunion, I have certain responsibilities that I don't worry about). If you choose to factor in these costs, estimate them to be approximately 12 cents per mile.

Also be sure to factor in transportation costs like shuttle service and parking fees to and from the reunion site.

Linens/utensils/rentals

Next come linens, utensils, and rental items. Linens and utensils can be purchased or rented. For ease of cleanup, opt for disposable paper or plastic items. If your reunion vision is on a grander scale, you can choose fancy rented stuff. Estimate the costs for these items by visiting a party-supply store and making notes of the prices. (You can also see the sidebar "Common reunion rentals," in this chapter, for more tips.)

When it comes to utensils and tableware, plan for two dinner plates, one dessert plate, two sets of utensils, and ten drinking glasses per person. Although ten glasses per person may seem like a lot, you need this many because as soon as everybody sets their glasses down, they all look alike and folks will immediately go scrambling for new glasses. Estimate the number of tables needed according to the head count (see Chapter 5 for details).

Food and beverages

Estimating the cost of food and beverages depends on the type of reunion you're planning. For example, if you're planning a potluck meal, you need only to plan for basic items, such as chips and dip or snack trays, along with basic beverages. You and your kinfolk will be bringing the bulk of the menu items.

To make the menu planning simple, I always recommend that the reunion planner provide the beverages. You can chill them in ice chests before the clan arrives. Warm pop or beer isn't very refreshing.

Common reunion rentals

Here's a list of commonly rented reunion items and their approximate fees. Prices vary depending on local rates and the amount of time you rent the item. Before adding them to your budget, call your local rental and party centers for current pricing.

Tables (depending on size)	$5–8 each	Lecterns	$20–50
Chairs	$0.75–1 each	Projectors	$20–30
Plates/utensils/ glassware	$2–3 per place setting	Barbecues (gas/propane/ charcoal)	$30–40 each
Linens (per table)	$5–20 per table	Popcorn maker or hotdog machine	$20–40
Small appliances or coffee makers	$8–12 per appliance	Pizza oven	$40–50
Hot pads or warming plates	$3–5 each	Snow-cone/ cotton-candy machine	$40–50
Chafing dishes	$14–20	Bubble machine	$15–20
Foldaway beds	$10–15	Portable (chemical) toilets	$60–70 each
Party tents/ canopies (in case of rain)	$60–180 (depending on size)	Floodlights on stands	$10–15 each
Karaoke system	$50–80 (depending on quality)	Raffle drum	$14–16
		Beer/margarita dispensers	$40–90
Portable dance floor	$140–150 (depending on size)	Dunk tank	$165
		Bingo	$20–30
Mirrored disco ball (if you're into flashbacks)	$30–45	Mini-golf	$100–125
		Human bowling	$300–400
		Inflatable toys	$125–175 (depending on toy)

If you plan to provide the food yourself, you need to budget for it. Call or visit your local supermarket or deli for estimated prices. You can use the food estimates in Chapter 5 to guide you. If you're planning a catered reunion, call or meet with local caterers and talk to them about sample reunion menus. Have them give you an estimated cost per person. You can write this number in the space marked "Other" under the food heading in Figure 4-3.

Entertainment

Before filling in any information in the entertainment section, talk to your activities committee and find out what they have in mind for games and activities. Ask them to provide a list of needed items — everything from rentals and game materials to balloons and kiddie pools. Next you have to estimate the costs for these items by figuring how many of each item you need. Figure one or two balloons per child. Rented activities are simple: Just call the party-rental store and ask about the fees and deposits.

Photographer or videographer

If you plan to hire a photographer to take pictures or a videographer to videotape the reunion, include these fees in your estimated reunion costs. Call around for the best deal.

In fact, use the Vendor Checklist in Figure 4-4 (and on the CD) when talking to any prospective vendor. This goes for photographers, caterers, party planners, and DJs.

Decorations

Include decorations for the reunion on your budgeting sheet. Banners, centerpieces, and streamers all need to be factored in. This stuff costs money!

Stationery and printing

Stationery and printing costs are usually nominal and include invitations, postcards, and welcome packets. You can print these items on your computer and have copies made, or in the case of invitations, you can purchase preprinted items and fill them in yourself. Estimate the costs for these items on a per family basis.

Special items

Special items — such as gift bags, T-shirts, or family recipe books — are optional. Many families ask reunion attendees to prepay for these types of items. Order the number needed plus a couple extras, just in case someone decides that they want one later. The cost for preparing these items varies greatly. Call around for estimates. Gift bag costs depend on what you decide to put in them.

Vendor Checklist

Vendor Name _____

Address _____

City / State / Zip _____

Phone / Fax _____

Contact person's name and title _____

Amount of deposit _____ Date due _____

Gratuities _____

Total amount due _____

Does the vendor provide a written contract?   Y N

Is the vendor insured / bonded / licensed?   (Lic# _____)   Y N

Does the vendor provide reliable references?   Y N

Does the vendor have a flexible cancellation policy?   Y N

Does the vendor have a professional appearance / demeanor?   Y N

Other itemized costs:

_____ $ _____

_____ $ _____

_____ $ _____

_____ $ _____

Comments

_____

_____

_____

_____

Figure 4-4:
Vendor
Checklist.

Other necessities

And don't forget the other necessary items, such as film, charcoal, and ice.
I include a space at the end of the budget checklist (see Figure 4-3) for these
items. Film can also include disposable cameras and developing costs.

After you get your reunion-budget estimates, get together with the planning committee again and make the financial decisions. Getting the estimates ahead of time makes this task much easier. After selecting the final location, rental items and other necessities, include the fees in the "Actual" column in Figure 4-3. That way you can have a clear picture of how much the reunion is going to cost!

Although you don't really need to have a separate bank account for small reunions, it can be very helpful for larger ones. Keeping the reunion monies separate from household funds eliminates any confusion.

Borrowing what you need

Also consider borrowing what you need. Other family members, friends, and neighbors may have supplies that can save you money as well as time. Lots of people own folding chairs and tables, barbecues, electric coffee dispensers, and hotplates, and they'll be happy to let you borrow them.

To help organize what you need to borrow, rent, and purchase, I suggest using the lists on the CD (see Figures 4-5, 4-6, and 4-7 for examples). Use these lists to get an idea of everything you need, and then start asking around.

Be sure to return all the borrowed items promptly and in their original condition. You may need to borrow them again for the next reunion!

Pondering insurance issues

The general rule is, if you plan to gather people together in a group, regardless of the occasion and what's being served, you should consider extra insurance. This is called *host-liability insurance,* and you can purchase this coverage as an add-on to your homeowner's policy. The minimum dollar amount that I recommend is $500,000. The insurance rates vary by state. Check with your personal insurance agent for information about your particular situation.

Liquor and liability

No one wants to see reunion guests face down in their macaroni, and no host wants to be held responsible for the actions of intoxicated guests. At last count, 42 states and the District of Columbia have laws that hold liquor servers liable. Other states are in the process of drafting similar legislation.

Stuff to Rent			
Item name	How many	Quoted price	Deposit

Figure 4-5:
Stuff to
Rent List.

Rental center _____ Phone _____

Stuff to Borrow		
Item name	Picked up	Returned

From whom? _____ Phone _____

Figure 4-6:
Stuff to
Borrow List.

Stuff to Buy			
Item name	*How many*	*Price each*	*Total*

Figure 4-7:
Stuff to Buy
List.

What this means is that the host — whether in a private home or a fancy hotel — is potentially liable for drunken guests. Because you are the host, you may be liable for damages, injury, or death caused by drunk drivers that you served at your reunion.

After speaking to several attorneys and insurance representatives, here's what I recommend: Contact your own homeowner's insurance agent. She can explain the liability laws for your state or area and recommend a separate policy called *host-liability protection,* or she may suggest purchasing an add-on to your existing policy, known as a *rider.* Your agent's recommendation depends on your circumstances, for example:

- ✔ **BYOBs:** In some states, a BYOB (Bring Your Own Bottle) party is exempt from the liquor liability laws. At a BYOB, the guests bring their own liquor, wine, or beer.

   What makes this party different is that you are not *providing* the liquor. I recommend checking with your own insurance agent, just in case your state laws differ from the others.

- ✔ **Professional bartending services:** If you plan to hire a professional bartender, make certain that this contractor has the appropriate liquor-liability insurance and that your reunion is covered by this insurance. Ask to see a "Certificate of Insurance" that lists you as an additional insured.

   Because you're contracting out the furnishing and serving of beer, wine, or alcohol, you are theoretically transferring the risk to the bartending service and are not be liable for unruly guests.

No matter what the circumstances, do not serve liquor or other alcohol to any guest who

- ✔ Is obviously three sheets to the wind (intoxicated).

- ✔ Has a health-related issue, especially pregnancy.

- ✔ Is a minor (under the legal drinking age).

- ✔ Is the designated driver.

Reminders about rentals

Party-rental companies also offer you insurance for rental items. This insurance can apply to everything from tables and chairs to lighting and popcorn machines. The fee is usually small and manageable.

For small disasters (such as a flaming turkey melting a plastic table), the extra coverage that you take out through your insurance agent should suffice. However, if the fire spreads to all the tables and eventually burns down every one of them — plus the chairs, the china, the disc jockey's equipment, and all the portable toilets — your added insurance may not be enough. Use your own judgment when you're offered the optional insurance.

You may also want to call your credit card company if you use your card to rent equipment. Your company may offer rental insurance to cardholders automatically.

Setting Up Sensibly

After you choose your reunion location (see the section "Narrowing Your Options," earlier in this chapter, for ideas), you'll need to make certain that all the necessary items and professional services arrive and are placed in their proper spots.

Keeping track of everything on one sheet helps you make certain that nothing important is forgotten or left behind. Figure 4-8 lists the majority of the items that you may need to include during your reunion setup. (If you want a copy, you can print this list from the CD-ROM.)

Decorations and Setup Checklist

Outside of location
_____ Directional signs
_____ Transportation
_____ Parking
_____ Traffic director
_____ Party tent rental
_____ Strong people to carry things

Entrance
_____ Welcome sign/banner
_____ Sign-in table
_____ Sign-in board
_____ Pens/pencils
_____ Name tags
_____ Welcome packets
_____ Handouts/programs
_____ Balloons
_____ Welcoming gifts/goodie bags
_____ T-Shirts
_____ Official greeting persons (at least 2)

Inside Reunion Area
_____ Tables and chairs
_____ Other seating
_____ Lecturn
_____ Microphone
_____ Sign to restrooms
_____ Music
_____ Dance area
_____ Kiddy table
_____ Buffet tables
_____ Bar/beverage table
_____ Dessert table
_____ Barbecue grills
_____ Family history table
_____ Family tree board
_____ Photo mural
_____ Ceiling treatment
_____ Themed decor
_____ Lighting
_____ Flags

Guest Tables
_____ Centerpieces
_____ Linens
_____ Condiments
_____ Other

Hired Help
_____ Caterer
_____ Disc jockey
_____ Bartender
_____ Entertainment
_____ Photographer

Activity Items
_____ Rented games
_____ Portable toilets
_____ Kiddy table
_____ Kiddy activities
_____ Blow-up pool
_____ Activity table
_____ Games/equipment
_____ Music system/music
_____ Piñata
_____ Candy
_____ Prizes
_____ Family memorabilia

Necessities
_____ Plates and utensils
_____ Cups and glasses
_____ Napkins
_____ Ice chests
_____ Ice
_____ Extension cords
_____ Duct tape
_____ Charcoal
_____ Lighter fluid and matches
_____ Hotpads/potholders/aprons
_____ Tongs/spatulas
_____ Disposable cameras
_____ Extra film
_____ Camera batteries
_____ A/V equipment
_____ Trash cans and extra bags
_____ Recycling bins
_____ Aluminum foil
_____ Plastic wrap
_____ Tape and push pins
_____ Diaper-changing area
_____ Post-reunion survey
_____ Directory forms
_____ Recipe forms
_____ Family history forms

Figure 4-8:
Decorations
and Setup
Checklist.

Chapter 5

Planning for a Barbecue, Buffet, or Blowout

● ●

In This Chapter

▶ Selecting a theme for your reunion

▶ Deciding on decorations

▶ Managing menus for hungry kinfolk

▶ Choosing party music

● ●

After you meet with your committees (see Chapter 3), select a date and location, and set the budget (see Chapter 4), you get to do the most enjoyable part of reunion planning — decide on the grub.

Sharing a meal with loved ones allows your family members to enjoy one of life's treasures — food. To make the reunion food memorable, consider creating a theme. In this chapter, I discuss various ideas for reunion themes, including decorations, food, music, and other things to set the mood for a good time. I also include a potluck planning chart and a music list to help you plan your menu and create an enjoyable atmosphere.

If you're planning to serve alcoholic beverages at your reunion, you may want to consider having transportation available to return folks to their hotels and homes. The combination of fun and alcohol can often cause folks to over-imbibe. Your family's safety and the safety of others is a very important concern when alcohol is served.

Picking a Reunion Theme

Whether your reunion takes place in a hotel ballroom or in the backyard, it should have a theme. The theme gives the event a unified character and promotes involvement among the attendees.

I include a few sample menus to go along with each theme in this chapter. (If you need more theme ideas, especially tips for ethnic-related themes, check out Chapter 20. You can also find more sample menus and décor ideas in that chapter as well.)

If you prefer to come up with your own reunion theme, you can use the ideas in this chapter as springboards. In fact, I recommend talking with your planning committee about theme ideas. Someone on your committee may already have a terrific idea for a theme.

Throwing a birthday bash

Honor the old-timers with a group birthday party. Select the oldest family members in attendance and put birthday hats on their heads. Pin birthday badges on their shirts and let them share their life stories with the family.

For this theme, use lots of brightly colored tablecloths and accessories. Place a balloon centerpiece on each table and sprinkle a little bit of confetti at each place setting. Load a huge cake full of candles. Don't forget to include the cake when planning your budget (see Chapter 4).

In lieu of "real" presents, ask everyone to bring a *white-elephant gift* (basically, a piece of junk that no one wants) for each birthday honoree. Be sure to give attendees a week or two of advanced notice so that they have time to find the perfect piece of junk for the honoree. If anyone needs ideas for this type of gift, tell them to visit a few garage sales or junk stores — which are full of potential gifts. The sillier the gift, the better. Singing fish are always a hit.

Activities for this reunion theme include birthday-party basics, such as Pin the Tail on the Donkey and relay races. Another fun activity is to *roast* the honorees. To do this, have folks stand and say something silly about the honorees. This can range from telling funny old memories to giving goofy toasts. Be sure to let the attendees know about the roast in advance so they come prepared with fun facts.

To make this theme even more entertaining, contact family members before the reunion and ask them to send you photos of the honorees at different ages. Use the pictures to create storyboards that detail the honorees' lives.

Here's a sample menu for a birthday-themed reunion:

- **Burgers and dogs with buns and condiments:** A staple for any birthday bash.
- **Assorted salads:** Supplement the meal with potato salads and other favorites, including Confetti Macaroni Salad (on the CD).

- ✔ **Include tasty party snacks:** Set out chips and dips (on ice), and other finger foods like chopped vegetables.

- ✔ **Build-your-own baked potato buffet:** Provide a large tub full of hot baked potatoes in aluminum foil and include lots of accompaniments, such as steamed broccoli, grated cheese, chili, chopped onions, crumbled bacon, and ham cubes.

- ✔ **Cake and ice cream:** Place a fire extinguisher near the cake as a gag.

- ✔ **Pop, beer, wine, and other simple beverages:** Be sure to provide lots of ice. (Party punch is optional.)

Honoring the old country

Unless you are a Native American, your ancestors came from another country. Although your family may now be part of the huge American melting pot, you can celebrate and honor the "old country" by using it as a theme for your reunion.

Select tableware, ethnic music, and games that reflect the culture of your motherland, and keep books about the old country on hand so family members can find out more about their heritage. Consult with old-timers in the family about the music, games, and books. Chances are, some of them have these items, or they may remember ethnic games and songs that they can share with the rest of the family.

Of course, food is a major component of the old-country theme. By featuring traditional foods from your country of origin, you not only enjoy a lovely feast, but you also pass on a little something to the youngsters about their origins.

If you're really into the theme, have everyone dress in traditional costume. Ask an older member of the family to teach traditional dance or folk crafts to the kids.

Roping 'em in for a hoedown

Everybody loves a hoedown! A crazy, casual, jeans-wearing attitude prevails, and the smells coming from the chuck wagon are deeee-licious. Dressing in denim, checkered shirts, cowboy hats, and boots adds to the entertainment.

Country music, red and white checkered tablecloths, and hay bales used for bench seating complete the atmosphere. If the reunion is in a large private location, rent a dance floor so your kinfolk can really kick up their boots. If your budget is a bit more modest, clear an area of the reunion site for dancing. Pop some classic country dance tunes into the boombox and grab a partner.

How to be a super-duper barbecuer

Barbecuing is a favorite way to prepare foods for large get-togethers, such as family reunions. But if you're prone to scorching chicken or burgers, you can use these tips to make sure that your foods are cooked to perfection. (If you need more help, check out *Grilling For Dummies* by Marie Rama and John Mariana, published by Hungry Minds, Inc.)

✔ Douse charcoal briquettes with a little starter fluid and allow them at least 20 minutes to fully catch fire. Notice I said a little fluid and a lot of time? Don't drown the coals, because the starter fluid can affect the taste of the food. No one likes wieners that taste like they were marinated in a gas can.

✔ If you're starting a lot of coals at once, such as a whole 20-pound sack, pile the briquettes in a mountain at the center of the barbecue. Be sure that the base of the barbecue is not clogged with old ash and that the vent holes are open. These steps allow the coals to catch fire evenly.

✔ After igniting the coals, place the grill over them to help burn off any old residue from previous barbecues. Then clean the grill using a wire barbecue brush.

✔ Don't place meat on the coals until they are glowing and have turned gray. Attempting to cook your meat before the coals are ready only blackens the outer surface of the meat, leaving the inside uncooked and giving it an unpleasant, charred taste.

✔ In case of flare-ups, have a spray bottle filled with water handy. This is helpful for putting out small grease fires and for keeping the meat moist. Larger flare-ups may require a sprinkling of baking soda to kill the flames.

✔ When cooking marinated meats, never reuse the marinade that the raw meat soaked in, unless it has been boiled thoroughly. The marinade can harbor bacteria. Barbecue sauces should be added only at the end of cooking, so the sugars don't turn black.

A *cow-chip-throwing contest* (Frisbees sprayed with brown paint and thrown at a bulls-eye painted on the lawn) makes an amusing and appropriate game.

Be sure to choose a menu that reflects a chuck wagon type of theme. Here's a sample menu to get you started:

✔ Baked biscuits

✔ Assorted types of chili (You can even have a chili cook-off!)

✔ Barbecued meats (How 'bout a barbecue contest, pardner?)

✔ Assorted green salads or good ol' potato salad and cole slaw

✔ Pasta salad made with wagon-wheel pasta

✔ Assorted casseroles and main dishes

✔ Macaroni and cheese

- ✔ Veggies and dip
- ✔ Corn on the cob
- ✔ Assorted pies and ice cream for dessert

Enjoying a beach-blanket barbecue or clambake

If you live near the sea — or better yet, have oceanfront property — host a seaside reunion for your kinfolk. You can plan activities for all the generations, such as beach combing, sandcastle building, and digging for clams. If you live by a lake or river, you can adapt the theme to suit your location.

A few sun umbrellas, a nice campfire, blankets, beach chairs, food, and family are all that you need. Let Mother Nature take care of the décor! A steaming pot of homemade clam chowder or soup helps warm swimmers after their dips in cold water. Here's a sample menu to get you started:

- ✔ Lots of snacks (Swimming makes people hungry!)
- ✔ Vegetables for dipping
- ✔ Clam chowder or other soup
- ✔ Steamed shellfish
- ✔ Assorted fish and seafood, grilled or baked
- ✔ Assorted salads
- ✔ Assorted casseroles or other main dishes
- ✔ Campfire-roasted corn on the cob (See the sidebar "How to roast whole corn in a campfire," in this chapter, for details.)
- ✔ Pies and cakes for dessert

Feasting at a low-budget luau

A Hawaiian theme is popular for summer reunions. The food and drinks (complete with little umbrellas) are refreshing. Family members can deck out in shorts, T-shirts, and, if a pool is available, bathing suits! To add some humor, the hosts can wear grass skirts.

To create the mood, set a few potted palms in strategic locations, and use pineapples as centerpieces. Just for fun, include a few pink lawn flamingoes and a blow-up pool for the kids. Check with your local music store for Hawaiian or luau music to add to the ambiance. Be sure to give everyone hugs and leis at the welcome table to break the ice.

How to roast whole corn in a campfire

If you've never roasted corn in a campfire, you're missing a special treat! These ears go fast, so make a few extras and keep plenty of melted butter on hand. Follow these steps if you want your family to enjoy sure-fire corn:

1. **Soak unpeeled corn in salted water for two hours.** If you're soaking a lot of corn, you may want to use a large pail or bucket. Use about ½ cup of rock or sea salt to each gallon of water.

2. **Place a brick (or bricks) on top of the corn to keep it submerged.**

3. **Remove the corn from the water.**

4. **Using insulated gloves or long tongs, place the corn 4 to 6 inches from the hot coals.**

5. **Roast the corn for 10 minutes, turning often.** Letting the husks catch fire now and then is okay — it adds to the flavor. Don't worry — the corn will not burn if you soaked it according to Step 1!

6. **Using insulated gloves, peel back the husks and remove the silk.** The silk should come off easily. Leave the husks attached to the corn as handles for eating.

7. **Serve ears of corn with melted butter.**

Here are a few food ideas for a luau, but I bet you can think of more goodies that would be perfect for this theme:

- ✔ Roasted meats, especially a pig
- ✔ Fruit salads with lots of pineapple
- ✔ Fresh fruit platters with a sweet dipping sauce
- ✔ Rice dishes studded with colorful bits of fruits or vegetables
- ✔ Pineapple upside-down cake for dessert

For the truly ambitious reunion planner, consider roasting a whole, dressed pig using a special rub. I don't mean dressing the pig in a tuxedo or ball gown before roasting. Instead, dressing includes butchering and cleaning (done by your local meat merchant) and then rubbing a dry mixture of herbs and seasonings into the meat before roasting. This method is not for the timid.

You can choose from several ways to roast a whole pig, from digging a hole in the ground and lining it with rocks, known as pit-roasting to building a spit roaster with a rotisserie (only for small pigs — 30 pounds or less) or renting a giant barbecue.

You can find pig-roasting directions in specialty cookbooks or on the Internet. Check with your relatives, too. Uncle Joe may have some experience with this type of thing. Keep in mind that whole pigs take a long time to cook, so be sure to start roasting the night before the reunion. You want the meat to be so tender it melts in your mouth. Gosh, I'm starting to get hungry.

Estimating tortilla chips and dip

Tortilla chips and salsa go together at a fiesta like peanut butter and jelly do in a sandwich — they're made for each other! Use this guide to help estimate the munchies. For every 20 people you need the following items:

- Two large or three medium bags of tortilla chips
- 3 cups of salsa
- 2 cups of guacamole

Reveling in a southwest fiesta

Families of Hispanic descent often have fiesta-style reunions. Even if you're not Hispanic, you can still enjoy the south-of-the-border flavors and colors of a fiesta!

Mexican food, guacamole, chilies, and salsa are the order of the day at this type of event. Small piñatas make great centerpieces, and a large one stuffed with candy and ready for breaking is every child's delight. Hire some mariachis to play music or put some fiesta-style CDs or tapes in the boom box. You can find plenty of specialty tunes at your local music stores.

Some menu suggestions for a fiesta-style reunion include the following:

- Carne asada, carnitas, or other roasted meats
- Enchiladas, tamales, tacos, and burritos
- A big pot of *frijoles* (beans)
- Guacamole dip, jalapeños, sour cream, and chopped onion as condiments
- *Pan dulce* (dome-shaped sweet rolls with a shell design on top, usually with a sugar topping) for dessert

Another great (and easy) idea is to set up a "build-your-own burrito bar." Stock the table with plenty of giant flour tortillas, refried beans, different salsas and fillings such as sour cream, shredded meats, chopped tomatoes, guacamole, and other items. Don't forget the jalapeños!

Perusing other theme ideas

Perhaps none of the previous themes tickled your fancy. In that case, here are a few other ideas to consider for your family reunion:

- ✔ **Campground safari:** Gather the clan at a nice campground and pretend that you're on a safari. The kids will love it.

- ✔ **Southern fish fry:** Does your family like to fish? Great! Send them out to catch dinner. Fry the catch in a traditional southern style with all the accompaniments. Don't forget the hush puppies.

- ✔ **Northern bean bake:** Folks from the Boston area love bean bakes. Outdoor games and activities will trigger hearty appetites. Keep some Beano on hand.

- ✔ **Lakeside or homestead campout:** If you're lucky enough to have a lakeside retreat or family homestead available for the reunion, take advantage of the natural surroundings and create a family retreat. Potluck meals mean everyone gets a chance to relax.

- ✔ **Picnic in a park:** Easy, laid-back, and fun! No need for decorations or a theme! Think of it as quality time with the tribe.

The recommendations that I give in this chapter are just suggestions. I'm sure that you can think of many more themes. Be creative and come up with a theme to suit your own family.

Feeding the Masses

If you're planning on doing most of the cooking yourself, you're either a glutton for punishment or just plain nuts. But you're also in luck. In the appendixes in the back of this book, you can find terrific reunion recipes provided by the Betty Crocker kitchens.

If you're feeling a little less ambitious, you can always enlist the help of your family members (or even some folks outside the clan) to prepare your reunion feast. The next few sections give you ideas for getting folks involved in potlucks and BYOs, as well as tips on hiring a catering service.

Planning for potlucks

The most common form of group comestibles is a potluck feast — which is the cheapest and easiest way to feed a crowd.

For potluck meals, every attendee must bring a contribution to the buffet table. You get a wide variety of items from a wide variety of cooks. (You can even swap recipes with some of the other gourmets in your family at the reunion.) Some folks may even bring along old family favorites that you haven't had since you were a child. What a treat!

Hosting a potluck for a crowd does require a bit of preplanning. On the CD, you can find a Potluck Tracking List like the one in Figure 5-1. This list can help you keep track of who's bringing what. The feast can be a real bummer if everyone brings salads and nobody remembers dessert!

Potluck Tracking Sheet

Type of dish	*# Servings*	*Who's bringing*	*Type of dish*	*# Servings*	*Who's bringing*
Appetizers/Snacks			**Bread/Rolls/Buns**		
1.			1.		
2.			2.		
3.			3.		
Salads			**Desserts**		
1.			1.		
2.			2.		
3.			3.		
4.			4.		
Vegetables			**Beverages**		
1.			1.		
2.			2.		
3.			3.		
Meat Items			**Condiments**		
1.			1.		
2.			2.		
3.			3.		
Main Dishes			**Other Goodies**		
1.			1.		
2.			2.		
3.			3.		
4.			4.		

Figure 5-1:
Potluck
Tracking
List.

To simplify the potluck process, you may want to assign each branch of the family a different item. For instance, your Aunt Tilly and her grown children can handle the salads, while Uncle Hubert's clan can bring main dishes.

However, some family members often want to bring special potluck items that they've made for years. Whenever possible, try to accommodate them.

Figuring out how much food to provide can be a challenge. A few family members always require more than the normal amount of food. If your nephew Clyde is a 7-foot-tall linebacker, he likely consumes enough food for a couple people. The same rule goes for beverages. But there are also family members that will require less food than the normal adult, such as children and some seniors. My advice is: Don't worry about it. When it comes to potluck meals, there's *always* more than enough food!

Use the following lists to help you figure quantities of common reunion items. Keep in mind that this information is merely intended as a guide — nothing is written in stone. I give amounts based on 50 attendees. You can easily double or divide the amounts.

Appetizers

Reunions, just like all parties, need lots of appetizers and snack items. This gives folks something to munch on while they're waiting for the main meal. Here are some appetizing ideas:

- 2 pounds of nuts
- 8 large bags of chips
- 4 cups of dip
- 5 pounds of cheese
- 5 pounds of assorted cold cuts
- 3 boxes of crackers
- 1 quart of pickles

Accompaniments

You can never have too many salads or vegetable dishes! Consider the following:

- 3 gallons baked beans
- 20 pounds of potatoes
- 50 to 60 ears of corn
- 60 rolls or 5 loaves of bread
- 2 pounds of butter or margarine

Also choose two or three of the following items:

- ✔ 6 quarts of fruit salad
- ✔ 6 quarts potato or macaroni salad
- ✔ 25 melons (cantaloupe, watermelon, and/or honeydew)
- ✔ 1½ quarts of salad dressing
- ✔ 12 heads of lettuce
- ✔ 8 quarts vegetable or pasta salad
- ✔ 1 gallon of fresh steamed vegetables

Meats and main dishes

Be sure to keep the meat chilled in your cooler until it's ready to cook, and pull out only as much as you can cook at one time. (For more hints on food safety, see the sidebar "Common food-handling safety tips," in this chapter.) Use the following list for figuring out meats and main dishes for the masses:

- ✔ 20 pounds of meat (like hamburger) or poultry
- ✔ 25 whole chickens, average size
- ✔ 1 15-pound whole turkey with 1 pound of cranberry sauce
- ✔ 15 pounds of hotdogs with 15 packages of buns
- ✔ 3 gallons of soup

Desserts

And now for the best part of the meal — dessert! Some folks may not like chocolate, so be sure to include a variety of items. For example, you can plan for the following:

- ✔ 10 9-inch pies
- ✔ 3 quarter-sheet cakes
- ✔ 3 dozen brownies
- ✔ 2 gallons of ice cream (if you have a freezer available)

Ice cream isn't a practical dessert for a picnic unless you have found a nifty way to keep it frozen (which I have not been able to do). Instead, substitute a few dozen cookies for the ice cream.

Be sure to have plenty of ice on hand so folks can refresh their drinks! You can store fresh ice in separate coolers (from the beverage coolers) and refresh the beverage coolers as necessary. Be sure to check your ice stash regularly — it melts pretty fast. If it looks like you're running low, send someone to the local mini-mart or corner grocery store for a fresh supply.

Opting for BYOs

You can also plan *a Bring Your Own* (BYO) event. BYOs can range from *Bring Your Own Beverage* (the classic BYOB) to Bring Your Own Everything (BYOE).

BYOE guests are expected to pack their own picnics, complete with food, beverages, plates, cups, and utensils. If you decide to host a BYOE, be sure that your guests understand what the term means so they don't leave the reunion disappointed and mighty famished.

Using a catering service

If your reunion is large and you have a nice-sized budget, you may want to hire a professional caterer to handle the food. Hiring a caterer allows you to spend most of your time mingling with your guests rather than worrying about the buffet table.

Common food-handling safety tips

When preparing the foods for your family reunion, you need to keep a few things in mind to avoid food-borne illnesses — especially during the summer months when the hot sun beats down on your picnic feast.

Keep in mind that harmful bacteria begin to multiply after they reach 40 degrees Fahrenheit. You can't always determine by sight or smell that food is spoiled. The following guidelines can help prevent the clan from getting Montezuma's revenge.

- Be sure to keep cold foods cold and hot foods hot.

- Don't let cold foods sit without refrigeration for more than 2 hours. If the weather is hot, refrigerate cold foods immediately after serving.

- Store beverages and foods in separate coolers. The lids to the beverage coolers tend to be opened more often, allowing the cold air to escape.

- Take only as much meat out of the cooler as you can cook at one time. Keep the remainder in the cooler until you're ready to cook it.

- When making chicken and pasta salads, make certain that all ingredients are thoroughly chilled before combining them.

- Be sure that your hands and utensils are clean before handling food.

- Transfer marinated meats to a clean platter — never reuse the platter that held raw meat and marinade without thoroughly washing it.

- Keep an antibacterial liquid soap handy for guests to use before eating.

You can hire different types of catering services ranging from menu planning to event organizing. Catering fees vary depending on the services provided. When asking for quotes, make certain that you let prospective caterers know exactly what services you want. In fact, before calling caterers and asking for quotes, you need to know a few things up front. If you don't know the answers to the following questions, hold off on calling a caterer until you do. (You can save yourself and the caterer a lot of frustration.)

These questions work for caterers coming to your reunion site and for caterers provided by the site, such as a restaurant or hotel ballroom. For example:

1. **What is your budget?** Knowing how much you can afford to spend helps narrow the menu and the types of catering services available. Don't expect prime rib on a hamburger budget. (See Chapter 4 for more details on budget-planning tips.)

2. **How many people will you be feeding?** Add 10 people to this number so you have a little extra in the event of unanticipated guests or really hungry kinfolk.

3. **How do you want your guests to be fed?** Do you want the caterer to prepare individual portions for each guest, or do you want the caterer to provide a buffet table? Serving a catered buffet meal is a practical and inexpensive choice for a reunion. Plus, guests can mingle and make their own food selections.

4. **What else is the caterer expected to provide?** You may need to provide the tableware and centerpieces, so if you don't specify this in advance, you may end up with a buffet table filled with food but no plates or utensils. Not a happy situation!

After you answer all the questions, call for quotes. Be sure to check with each caterer regarding insurance, cancellation policy, gratuities, and payment schedule. If you hire a caterer, remember to get a written contract so you have proof of the expected services. Most caterers expect a 50 percent down payment at the time of the contract, with the remaining 50 percent to be paid on the day of the event.

Gettin' the Grub

When the chow is finally ready, your kinfolk need to find plates and chairs. So, in this section, I give you some tips on keeping the traffic flowing to avoid chow-line gridlock. I also give you details on choosing table accommodations so everyone can eat and drink without knocking elbows.

Traffic flow is an important element in a family reunion chow line. It keeps folks from tripping over each other as they try to get from the jiggly carrot salad to the honey mustard. Here are some tips to keep the traffic flowing smoothly:

✔ **Start the chow line at one end of the buffet table.** Make sure that you keep the plates on one end of the table so your tribe recognizes the starting point. It's pretty hard to dish up the beanies and weenies without plates!

✔ **Be sure the buffet starting point has enough room for a line to form.** You don't want a batch of people cramming together scrambling for plates. Organization is the key.

✔ **Place the napkins and utensils at the end of the line.** This keeps everybody from having to juggle more than just full plates until they reach the end of the line.

✔ **For large groups — 75 people or more — form a double-line buffet.** This setup is the same as a single-line buffet, but with identical foods set out on opposite sides of the table. A double-line buffet can quickly get a big group through the chow line. See Figure 5-2 for a few buffet-line options.

✔ **Place the beverages on a separate table at least 5 feet away from the buffet line.** This prevents the plate balancers from crashing into the beverage-cup jugglers.

✔ **Place the desserts on a separate table, too.** Doing this keeps Gramps and the kids out of the chocolate cake and apple pie until their meals are finished. Granny and the moms will thank you.

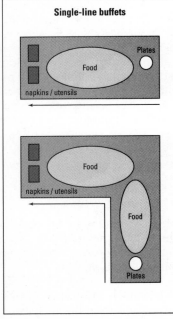

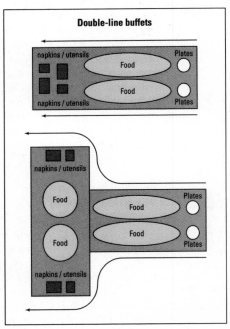

Figure 5-2:
Buffet-line
options.

a   b

Setting the Mood with Music

The right music can really make a reunion. Whether you are thinking of hiring a professional disc jockey or placing a family member in charge of the boom box, select music that is upbeat and fun.

When hiring a professional disc jockey, you should ask him several important questions before making a decision. For example:

- Do you use professional equipment? (An amateur system can sound awful.)
- Do you provide a written contract?
- Are you insured?
- Do you have a backup system in case of emergency?
- Have you done other family reunions?
- Can you provide three qualified references?
- How long have you been a disc jockey?
- Can you dress according to the reunion theme?
- Will you take requests?
- Do you like to interact with the audience? In what manner?
- Can you help us plan or carry out scheduled activities? (It's helpful if the DJ can make announcements and help coordinate activities.)
- Do you have a demo tape? (It's best to see how they operate ahead of time.)
- Do you have a list of music?
- Can we provide a list of music that we want to play?

If you plan on assigning a family member the task of DJ, give him or her a play list with a variety of music choices. You don't want to spend the day listening only to the DJ's favorites. Select a mix that appeals to everyone.

You can purchase CDs or cassettes that feature variety mixes. For example, you can buy compilations that feature dance hits from the 40s onwards. Alternatively, you can pick several CDs and borrow a boombox that can shuffle and play multiple CDs. Play a bit of this and a bit of that, and keep everybody happy.

If you want to plan your music list in advance, check out the song list in Table 5-1. These songs are popular party tunes. Add your own favorites, too!

Table 5-1	Top Party Songs
Title	**Artist(s)**
"We are Family"	Sister Sledge
"YMCA"	Village People
"Love Shack"	B-52's
"Getting Jiggy Wit It"	Will Smith
"Shout"	Isley Bros/Dynatones/Otis Day
"Celebration"	Kool and the Gang
"Conga"	Miami Sound Machine
"Wanna Be"	Spice Girls
"Electric Slide/Boogie"	Marcia Griffiths
"Any Man of Mine"	Shania Twain
"Whoomp! There it Is!"	Tag Team
"In the Mood"	Glen Miller
"Unforgettable"	Natalie/Nat King Cole
"Runaround Sue"	Dion
"Unchained Melody"	Righteous Brothers
"Play that Funky Music"	Wild Cherry
"La Bamba"	Los Lobos
"It's Raining Men"	Weather Girls
"Wooly Bully"	Sam the Sham & The Pharaohs
"Chattahoochee"	Alan Jackson
"Old Time Rock N' Roll"	Bob Seger
"Jump, Jive & Wail"	Brian Seitzer Orchestra
"(You Shook Me) All Night Long"	AC/DC
"Brown Eyed Girl"	Van Morrison
"Start Me Up"	Rolling Stones
"Tequila"	Champs
"Brick House"	Commodores

Title	Artist(s)
"MMMBop"	Hanson
"Twist and Shout"	The Beatles
"Respect"	Aretha Franklin
"Get Down Tonight"	KC and the Sunshine Band
"Pretty Woman"	Roy Orbison
"I Will Survive"	Gloria Gaynor

Making Your Reunion Earth-Friendly

You're going to generate a lot of garbage at your reunion (no, I don't mean Uncle Ned, the thrice-married tattooed biker). Dispose of your reunion trash in an earth-friendly manner by setting up a recycling area. Provide covered bins lined with trash bags and marked with the labels Cans, Bottles, Paper, Plastic, and Garbage.

After the reunion, pull the bags from the bins and take them to the local recycling center. You'll feel like you've done your good deed for the year. (For more tips on cleaning up after the big event, check out Chapter 10.)

Chapter 6

Preparing for the Family

· ·

In This Chapter

▶ Distributing invitations and collecting RSVPs

▶ Securing accommodations for out-of-towners

▶ Formulating some back-up plans

▶ Preparing for people with special needs

▶ Readying for emergencies

· ·

*A*t this stage in your reunion planning, things are moving along. Your committees are busy making arrangements, and you've come to a family consensus on the date and location. Congratulations!

If you've planned your reunion in sync with Chapters 1 through 5, your reunion should take place in about three months. Now you get to send out all the invitations and wait to see who's coming to supper. But, before you do, I want to go over a few things to keep your plans running smoothly. In this chapter, I tell you about creating invitations, figuring out where to put everybody, and making backup plans in case the unexpected happens.

Handling Invitations and RSVPs

In Chapter 2, I tell you how to find all your kinfolk and how to prepare your address list. Now you and your planning committee get to finalize the guest list and prepare the invitations for mailing. In this section, I give you several invitation options — and some other nifty ways of spreading the word about your upcoming reunion.

You need to mail the invitations three months before the reunion to give everyone time to plan their trip.

Deciding between store-bought and homemade

You can purchase pre-made invitations with cute matching envelopes from a party-supply store. Although they're handy, these cookie-cutter invitations are small and impersonal. You don't get much room to include the festive information that'll make the tribe come running to the reunion, either. So, let me offer a suggestion — make your own invitations.

You can make your own invitations quickly and easily by crafting one master invitation and having color copies made to send to relatives. At any craft-supply store, you can find a broad assortment of decorative papers, stickers, rubber stamps, and press-on lettering that makes creating personalized invitations a snap.

On the CD, you can find the basic reunion invitation shown in Figure 6-1. You can use this as a guide for what to include, but do try to personalize your reunion invitation.

Alternately, you can buy a nifty stationery-maker program for your computer. This type of program includes a variety of built-in templates. You simply choose a style of invitation from the list of sample templates, add your own wording, and the program does the rest. Most of these programs also include lots of party-related clip art and other goodies, such as different fonts and sample papers for your printer. You can easily create colorful, professional-looking invitations with the click of a mouse.

However you decide to create your invitations, be sure to include the following:

- ✔ A description of the reunion
- ✔ The date, time, and location of the reunion
- ✔ A map to the reunion site
- ✔ The contact person's name, address, and phone number
- ✔ The cost per family and the payment procedure
- ✔ A self-addressed RSVP card
- ✔ The theme and whether guests should bring anything special, such as a potluck item or some extra chairs

When corresponding with family members, keep the tone light-hearted and polite. In addition, be sure to tell them how much you're looking forward to seeing them at the reunion. As the reunion planner, your tone can help increase the level of anticipation in your family members.

Come climb the family tree!

Join us for the first-ever (your family name here) family reunion!

When: _____ Time: _____

Where: _____

Join us for fun, family and food!

Our reunion theme is _____
Put on your fun reunion duds and join the party!

Please RSVP to:

Name: _____

Address: _____

Phone: _____

E-mail: _____

Cost per family: $ _____ **Please send with your RSVP**

For more information, contact the person listed above, or visit the Web site at: http://www.(insert name here).

Figure 6-1:
Sample family-reunion invitation.

Whether you make the invitations yourself with paper, pens, and stickers or use a computer program, gear the art on the invitation toward your theme. The art you choose can really add a frolicky feeling to the invitations. This gets the invitees excited and looking forward to the event. A touch of fun is the most important thing that you can add to the invitation — no one wants to be left out!

Mighty nice mapmakers

I suggest including a map with your reunion invitations. You can scribble your own map on a piece of paper, have copies made, and tuck it into the invitation, or you can print professional-looking, detailed maps from your computer by using an Internet map site.

If you use a site on the Internet, follow the directions listed. Basically, you just type in the address, state, and zip code for the site or area, and the site does the rest. One site even lets you add gas station stops to your map. Pretty neat stuff!

Several useful map sites include the following:

- `MapQuest.com`
- `MapBlast.com`
- `Maps.yahoo.com`
- `Qwestdex.com`

For example, if you plan a western hoedown, you can add cows, boots with spurs, and covered wagons to the invitations. For a luau theme, you can add hula dancers, tropical fish, and pineapples. Invitations for a seaside theme include seashells, crabs, boats, and beach umbrellas. The possibilities are endless — be creative!

Keeping track of the takers and the bailers

After you create, address, and stamp your invitations, you're ready to send them out the door. Be sure to send them out no less than three months before the reunion to give your relatives time to plan whether they can attend.

Now you get to hold your breath and wait to see who's going to make it, and who's going to bail out on you. If your invitations are lively and fun, you should start getting the RSVPs back almost immediately. If you aren't getting back many RSVPs after a few weeks, send out a reminder to your relatives. Do this no less than one month in advance so you still have time to adapt your plans, if necessary. For instance, if only 20 folks are coming to the reunion rather than the anticipated 50, you need to alter your figures before you arrange for chair rentals or catering.

In terms of the reminder, you can send a simple postcard that includes wording that goes something like this: "A few weeks ago, you were sent an invitation to our family reunion. We're excited to hear whether you'll be joining in the fun, so don't forget to RSVP! Please call or write if you can't find your invitation or if it didn't get to you."

ON THE CD

To keep track of the *takers* (the nice folks who plan to attend) and the *bailers* (the folks who aren't going to show), you need to have an Invitation and RSVP Log like the one shown in Figure 6-2 (and included on the CD).

Invitation and RSVP Log				
Family name	Invitation mailed	RSVP	Rec'd	Number attending

Figure 6-2:
Invitation
and RSVP
Log.

Page _____ of _____   Total number attending

Key phrases for successful invitations

To get the folks excited about the reunion, consider adding the some of the following phrases.

Come celebrate your family.

Do you remember when?

Join us for our first-ever family reunion.

Bring the family.

The more interesting the invitation, the bigger the crowd!

Come climb the family tree.

In honor of . . .

Join the clan for fun and frolic.

Family, Fun, and FOOD.

For each invitation that you send, record the family name and the sent date. As the RSVPs come in, record the date you received it and the number of people attending. Doing so helps you get an accurate head count.

Give your invitees two to three weeks to respond to your invitation. If a few weeks go by and you still have few RSVPs, send the slackers postcards reminding them about the reunion. Be sure to tell them that you can't get an accurate head count without their RSVPs. If you still don't get replies, assume that they're not coming.

Always add 10 percent more people to your head count. Some folks have a tendency to show up even after sending in their RSVPs stating that they can't make it or that only two of them plan to attend. These people may bring along their neighbors, their kid's friends, and whomever else they happen to pick up along the way. Plan for them — this will happen.

Creating a Reunion Web Site

While you're busy preparing the invitations, give some thought to creating a reunion Web site. A Web site is a nifty way to keep everyone informed about the reunion. Think of it as an electronic newsletter. Be sure to include the *URL* (or Web site address) on your invitations so folks can visit and get the latest information for the reunion.

If you're not up to creating the Web site yourself, enlist the help of a computer-literate niece, nephew, or grandchild. Kids love doing this type of stuff, and they learn about it in school. (My daughters, without any help from me, had their first Web sites built by the time they were 10.) Plus, youngsters can get excited about the reunion by helping out.

Your Web site should include interesting news about family members and exciting reunion activities to look forward to. You can even include a list of people who plan to attend the reunion and a list of people who haven't responded yet. (A Web site is a great way to get the stragglers to turn in their RSVPs.) Other possibilities for your Web site include a suggestion box for food, games, or activities, a copy of the family tree, directions to the reunion site, and family recipes.

Be sure to update the Web site often! Keep your kin coming back to the site with fresh news, photos, and announcements.

The reunion Web site doesn't need to be elaborate or expensive. In fact, dozens of sites on the Internet allow you to create a free Web site. (You have to put up with a few bits of advertising from the sponsoring site, but it doesn't cost a cent.)

The following list includes several good sites for you to explore. All these sites are completely free of charge, but they require you to register as a member. Each site gives you page-layout options, page wizards — helpful guides for planning the site — and hit counters so you can see how many folks have visited your site. You can also add a guest book and use some of the site's clip art or import your own. This is a great feature if you want to add family photos to the Web site. (I talk more about all these topics in Chapter 11.)

The following list explains the amount of space in *megabytes* (MB) that each site allows. Don't worry — it takes a lot of material to use up 20 MB! Check out one or more of the following sources to create your own family Web site.

- **Free Web Space:** www.freewebspace.com (20MB)
- **Yahoo! GeoCities:** http://geocities.yahoo.com (15MB)
- **Cybercities:** www.cybercities.com (25MB)
- **FreeServers:** www.freeservers.com (20MB)
- **MSN Homepages:** http://msnhomepages.talkcity.com (30MB)
- **A Free Home:** www.afreehome.com (50MB)
- **MegaSpace:** www.megaspace.com (50MB)
- **FreeWebSpace, Inc:** www.free-web-space-inc.com (100MB)
- **Dreamwater:** www.dreamwater.com (50MB)
- **About.com:** www.freehomepage.com (20MB)
- **Angelfire:** http://angelfire.lycos.com (30MB)
- **Easyspace:** www.easyspace.com (25MB)
- **ProHosting:** http://free.prohosting.com (50MB)

Keeping in touch with kin online

The Internet can be a wonderful tool for planning your reunion and for keeping in touch with everyone. The Internet makes it simple to keep in touch by providing opportunities not only for creating Web sites, but also for e-mail correspondence and for live chats with your family members.

Using e-mail for correspondence is practical. If you're already connected to the Internet, all you need to do is send e-mail to other family members who are also connected. It doesn't cost extra — and with the cost of postage going up regularly, e-mail has a definite advantage over post.

You can use e-mail to keep in touch with your committee members (see Chapter 3), exchange reunion ideas with family members, or just touch base with folks you don't often get to see. E-mail can be instantaneous, or it can be delayed, usually by a few minutes.

Internet chat rooms are also a terrific way to communicate with your relatives because you "chat" in real time. As soon as you click the "send" button, your relatives can read what you just wrote because you are essentially in the same "room" on the Internet. It all happens in the blink of an eye.

I recommend two chat downloads: Yahoo! Messenger and AOL Instant Messenger. To use the chat facilities, you need to download a small piece of information — and so does everyone else you want to chat with. By having everyone on the chat system at once, you can chat live by typing what you want to say and then pressing the send button. The only other that thing I recommend is having really quick fingers! (If you want more information about e-mail or chatting online, check out *The Internet For Dummies,* 7th Edition, by John R. Levine, Carol Baroudi, and Margaret Levine Young, published by Hungry Minds, Inc.)

See Appendix B for some Web sites specifically designed for family reunions. Many of these sites even post a free announcement about your upcoming get-together.

Getting There and Staying Put

As the official host, you're going to have folks coming in from all four compass points for the reunion. Your guests need a place to stay and a way to get to and from wherever everybody's going. In the next few sections, I give you my tips for accommodating the tribe.

Finding accommodations

Out-of-town guests need a place to hang their hats during the duration of the reunion. Accommodation choices include local hotels and motels, campgrounds for guests who bring gear, or the sofa at your house.

Personally, I don't recommend the latter. You have only so much room to spare, and with all the commotion generated by the upcoming reunion, you need your space. You can't relax and catch your breath if you're catering to the needs of houseguests. Put everyone up somewhere else. This arrangement is good for your guests, too, because they don't have to worry about snoring, running out of hot water, or intruding on anyone's privacy.

Before selecting the hotel or motel, take the tour, just like you do for the reunion location (see Chapter 4). You want to be sure that the place is clean and friendly and that it offers rooms for smokers and non-smokers and provides helpful in-room goodies — such as kitchenettes, cable television, and extra blankets.

You also want to see if the hotel or motel provides any recreation facilities (namely, a swimming pool) onsite for the kids. In addition, be sure to ask about the accommodation's pet policy just in case Granny brings Fifi and Fido along for the adventure.

Use the Accommodations Checklist on the CD (see Figure 6-3 for an example) to rate each location. Print a copy and take it with you to each place you visit. Fill in the checklist while you take the tour so management takes notice of your organization, which can make them more eager to work with you. After all, no one likes to work with a disorganized group.

To help the reunion attendees save money, ask local hotels and motels if they can offer group rates for your reunion. Most lodgings are more than willing to work with you if your group is large enough. They often reserve a block of rooms in one area (usually along the same hallway or on the same floor) specifically for your group. This keeps all the noise and commotion corralled in one location. (Families can be a rowdy bunch.)

If you're going to add campgrounds to your places-to-stay list, be sure to check out the facilities as well. Auntie Martha was never much of a camper, and she'd be mighty unhappy if all she found were pit toilets and cold-water showers after Uncle Joe pitched the tent.

Dorm facilities are another option that may be available if you live near a college or university — especially if your reunion takes place during the summer months when school isn't in session. Check with the college administrators for more information on dorm availability.

Accommodations Checklist

Name of site _____

Address _____

City / State / Zip _____

Phone / Fax _____

Contact person's name and title _____

Price for single - double bed _____   Price for single - king bed _____

Price for double - king bed _____   Price for double - two beds _____

Kitchenette available?	Y N	Included in price? Y N
Cable channels?	Y N	Included in price? Y N
Shuttle to / from airport available?	Y N	Included in price? Y N
Is it clean?	Y N	Does it smell good? Y N
Non-smoking rooms available?	Y N	Is the staff helpful and friendly? Y N
Pets accepted?	Y N	Restaurant on site? Y N
Shuttle to reunion site available?	Y N	Close to shopping? Y N
Easy to find?	Y N	On-site laundry facilities? Y N
Recreational facilities on site?	Y N	Heated pool or spa? Y N
Are these group rates?	Y N	Extra beds or cribs available? Y N

Comments:

_____

_____

_____

_____

_____

Figure 6-3:
Accom-
modations
Checklist.

Transporting the tribe

Many of your reunion attendees will arrive by their own means — car, van, motor home, bicycle, or their own two feet — whatever they choose. But you will have some attendees who need transportation.

Folks flying in from other areas will more than likely rent cars for the duration of the reunion, but you'll have a few people who will need transportation from the airport. My suggestion is to recruit other family members for this task. Assign folks with vehicles to pick-up duty! You can use the same approach for getting people to and from the reunion site.

However, if the reunion site lacks parking, consider hiring a shuttle service. These folks can provide buses or vans that pick up the clan at one location (such as a large parking lot) and shuttle everyone to the reunion site and back again.

Preparing for the Unexpected: Making a Back-up Plan

Nothing in life is ever certain — not even when it comes to reunions. The weather can turn nasty, your list of attendees can suddenly triple in spite of the number of takers indicated on the RSVPs, your caterer may be sucked into a huge black hole, or your disc jockey may run off with the local beauty queen *and* your deposit.

So, you need to have a few back-up plans to deal with the unexpected. In the next few sections, I go over some common reunion pitfalls and give you some easy ways to deal with them when (or if) they occur.

If you decide to charge a fee for attending the reunion, relatives may ask if you have a cancellation policy should the reunion get disrupted. This can be a touchy subject. My advice is this: After a family has paid, they've committed, so there should be no cancellation option. The task of being reunion coordinator is a volunteer one — you're not a business. The money is being spent on the reunion for everyone's enjoyment.

Weather forecast: Night, followed by day

Planning for inclement weather isn't a problem if your reunion is indoors. However, an outdoor reunion can become a disaster. Remember the old saying: Climate is what you expect, but weather is what you get.

Before the reunion, contact your local branch of the *USMS* (United States Meteorological Service) and ask if they can provide you with an approximate ten-day forecast. A few days before the reunion, ask for another one. You can find the USMS phone number in the phone book in the area for government listings. If you don't have a USMS branch in your area, contact your local TV news station.

Another option is to check out the Weather Channel Web site at `www.weather.com` or your local newspaper's Web site. Most newspapers have their weather column clearly listed on their home page.

If the weather is likely to be a wee bit wet, rent a party tent from the local rental center and set it up the night before the reunion. Party tents are also helpful in the event of intense sunshine because they are white and deflect heat. They also have clear vinyl windows, so you don't feel like you're camping out under the dining room table.

Party tents come in a variety of sizes. Get the biggest tent that your budget allows, and make sure that it can accommodate the number of guests. Having too much room is better than packing everyone in like sardines in a can. If your group is really large, get a couple of tents and set them up so the doors face each other, allowing guests to easily move from one tent to the other.

I give you pricing averages for party tents in Chapter 4. You can also call your local rental centers for cost information. Be sure to ask about the setup and takedown fees so you're not surprised when you receive the final bill for payment!

The caterer doesn't show

I have some good news and some bad news. First the bad: You've already put down a deposit on the food, but there's no grub at the reunion. Everyone is hungry and threatening to eat Fifi and Fido. Grandma is mortified and threatening to leave because her pets are being eyed as food. To make matters worse, the caterer was supposed to bring all the plates and utensils.

Now for the good news: You haven't paid the balance of the catering fees (except the deposit), because he or she didn't show up with the grub. The caterer gets the final payment *after* the party.

Send a trustworthy group of family members to the local fried chicken joint to bring back buckets of cluck with all the trimmings. Chinese food or pizza is a hit, too. Be sure to have them grab plenty of paper napkins, plastic forks, and any other items that they may need when they pick up the grub. Come to think of it, you may want to keep a supply of paper napkins and plastic utensils in the trunk of your car, just in case.

These times will try your patience, but they can also turn into the times of your life!

The reunion location relocates to Kansas

Sometimes, bad things happen. Tornadoes, bad weather, hurricanes, earthquakes, fires, or floods can send your reunion plans down the drain. Clicking your heels together a few times while wearing ruby slippers can't really help you much.

If your reunion location becomes a "goner," contact local churches, restaurants, or the YMCA. Most of these locations have large common areas for parties and get-togethers. If you tell them your sad story, you may get the location for a discount or even for free.

After finding a new site, give your army of family members a new map and meet them at the new location. Party like nothing ever happened.

The guest of honor bailed on you

Guest of honor failed to show? Pick another one!

Have each person write his name on a piece of paper and toss the paper into a hat. Whoever gets picked is the new guest of honor. Make up some impromptu stories about the new honoree's life (true or false — just have fun with it) and roast 'em! That was easy.

Grumpy Gus shows up

Variety is the spice of life, but somehow a jalapeño grew on your family tree. So how do you deal with a grumpy relative?

I suggest several ways to handle soreheads, but feel free to come up with a few of your own:

- **Pull the offending person(s) aside and have a talk.** Find out if something specific is bothering them and see if you can help correct it in some way. If he or she has a problem with one of the attendees, suggest avoiding that person altogether. Then explain that everyone is there to have a good time and enjoy each other's company. Sometimes, giving the grump a little attention is the perfect remedy.

- **Have several people pull the offending relative aside and have a talk.** If enough people bring the bad behavior to the offender's attention, he or she may stop behaving like a jerk.

> ✔ **Ignore the person.** After having her comments repeatedly brushed off, the hint may hit home. If her demeanor doesn't change, tell her that you don't appreciate her making negative comments in front of everyone.
>
> ✔ **Ask the person to leave.** Use this tactic only as a last resort. Remember, you're all family!

Planning for People with Special Needs

Some of your reunion attendees have special needs that you need to consider. In this section, I give you some of these needs and what you, as the reunion coordinator, can do to make these people more comfortable.

Mature folks or those with disabilities

The elderly and handicapped need unrestricted access to the reunion site and the hotel. Be sure to inquire about these items as you tour potential facilities. The Location Research Log in Chapter 4 (and on the CD) has a space provided specifically for this purpose.

Everybody needs to use the outhouse now and then. If you expect handicapped individuals at your reunion, be sure to rent portable toilet facilities that are handicap accessible. These facilities are also helpful for the elderly and for the parents of small children.

I give information on toilet-rental fees in Chapter 4. Although handicap-accessible toilets cost a few dollars more to rent, they are more spacious than regular portable toilets, making them ideal for young children who still need a little help when using the restroom.

Little ones

Parents of young children can always use a break. They appreciate a little time away from the youngsters to engage in meaningful adult conversation. To help facilitate this break time, how about setting up a childcare area? Be sure to do it in a safe location away from the barbecues and water areas. Enlist several preteens to babysit the little ones. You may have to pay the teens a small fee to babysit, but it's money well spent.

Another idea for keeping the kids entertained is a "kiddie table" with stuff for the under-8 crowd. Some items to consider including are the following:

- ✔ Art supplies (paper, crayons, and finger paints)
- ✔ Coloring books
- ✔ Storybooks
- ✔ Puzzles
- ✔ Blocks
- ✔ Goodie bags
- ✔ Games and other nifty items

One more thing that I recommend doing for parents of young children is to set up a diaper-changing area. The area doesn't need to be elaborate. Include a padded table (a towel is sufficient padding), a covered trash can, a box of diapers, and some baby wipes.

That's all you need. Your other guests will thank you for not having to watch (and smell) while Mommy changes junior's diapers on the picnic table.

In case of emergency

A child falls and scrapes her knee. Another youngster gets a blister on his heel. Uncle Ned gets too close to the barbecue (again!) and needs some burn cream on his pinky finger. These emergencies aren't dire, but they are painful and require attention.

To help reunion attendees weather their boo-boos, you should provide an emergency kit. Put your own kit together with an assortment of bandages, some antibacterial cream or spray, anti-itch spray, aspirin, acetaminophen, antihistamines for sudden allergies, sunscreen, syrup of ipecac, gauze bandage with tape, scissors, and tweezers for splinters. You should also include a few clean plastic bags for ice packs. (Use ice from the coolers.)

You can also purchase a first-aid kit from the drug store, but it includes only the basics, such as bandages, ointments, and gauze.

Keep your kit under one of the tables, ready to use at a moment's notice. And of course, if you have a serious emergency, call 911.

Part III
Keeping Everyone Busy

The 5th Wave   By Rich Tennant

"We really shouldn't wait so long for the next family reunion."

In this part . . .

Because family interaction is what reunions are all about, this part gives you some ideas about how to facilitate communication during the reunion. Check out Chapter 7 for some great icebreakers to get your kinfolk laughing and talking. Then go to Chapter 8 for a look at dozens of fantastic games designed to keep your family involved and engaged throughout the day. Finally, Chapter 9 provides some tips about unique ways to preserve your family keepsakes.

Chapter 7

We're All Here ... Now What?

*I*f this is your first reunion, you may feel like a fish out of water. You're nervous because you want everything to go off without a hitch, and you're tired from all the pre-reunion preparations. You haven't seen most of these people in decades, and you can't even remember some of their names without a hint.

A little voice in the back of your head is telling you to run as fast as you can before anyone notices you. Chill out, my friend! Break the ice and get to know each other. That's what this reunion is all about.

In this chapter, I give you lots of tips to make everyone feel welcome and to get everybody mingling, including yourself!

Rolling Out the Welcome Wagon

First impressions can set the mood. Greet your guests with a bang!

Every reunion needs a welcoming committee. This group is made up of friendly folks who greet everyone as they arrive for the reunion. You don't need to assign this duty in advance. Instead, ask the first few who arrive on reunion day or several close family members who are giving you a hand to act as the welcoming committee. After all, the first folks to arrive are usually some of the most excited to start the reunion!

Your welcoming committee needs to be stationed at the entrance to the reunion site. Set up a table with a few chairs to keep the committee comfy. Brief them on their responsibilities (smile, greet, shake hands, and smile some more). Make sure to place a large welcome banner or sign near the entrance to the reunion.

Other nice (but not essential) things to have at the welcome table include

- ✔ A *welcome packet* containing brochures for local sites of interest, coupons from local businesses, and a map of the area from the local Chamber of Commerce.
- ✔ A reunion schedule, if events are planned for certain times of the day.

Have a person from the welcoming committee (called the greeter) point out the important locations, such as restrooms, places to dump purses and jackets, and where the least-favorite relations are hanging out (just kidding!). Oh — tell the guests where the food is, unless you like having a ton of leftovers.

A clipboard on the table holds the Attendance List (see Figure 7-1). Ask a person assigned to the welcoming committee to make certain that everyone signs in so you can keep track of head count. If your reunion is a large one and lots of folks are meeting each other for the first time, have someone from the planning committee prepare name tags for everyone and lay them out on the welcome table. Family members can look for their own tags and pin them on before entering the reunion area.

You may also want to consider having some goodie bags and balloons for the kids. These bags can contain special treats, games, crayons, or other activities to keep the wee ones busy. A basket of mints within reach of attendees and the welcoming committee kills dragon-breath before introductions are made.

At the welcome table, give everyone a Family Directory form, shown in Figure 7-2 (and also on the CD), to fill out. You can include one of these forms in the welcome packet, if you want. Put a basket on the welcome table so folks who get their forms filled out right away can turn them in.

You use these forms to help coordinate the next reunion and to provide family members with their own copy of the family directory. It's a nice way to encourage everyone to keep in touch after the reunion. *Note:* If someone prefers not to be listed in the family directory, she can check the specified box on the form.

The entrance to the reunion is also a perfect location to post a message board. Place a small corkboard or dry-erase board on an inexpensive folding easel so family members can leave messages for each other. Be sure to provide dry-erase markers or tacks.

Attendance List

Name of family	Number attending	Your hometown

Figure 7-1:
A sample
Attendance
List.

Family Directory Information

☐ Check here if you don't want your information included in the Family Directory

Name _____

Address _____

City / State / Zip / Country _____

Telephone _____ E-mail address _____

Birthday (year optional) _____ Occupation _____

Hobbies and special interests _____

Branch of the family tree _____

Name of spouse _____ Birthday (year optional) _____

Spouse's maiden name _____ Wedding anniversary date _____

Spouse's hobbies and special interests _____

Your children   Birthdays
_____
_____
_____
_____
_____
_____
_____
_____
_____
_____

We're all nosey - How did you meet your spouse?
_____

Please send a 3x5" or 4x6" photo of you with your family so we can include it in the directory. Smile really big!

Figure 7-2:
Family
Directory
form.

Say cheese!

At the sign-in table, you may want to have a basket of single-use cameras marked with the date of the reunion and your name. Place a sign near the basket asking guests to feel free to take photos at any time. This is a great way to get candid shots from different people's perspectives! A few cameras placed on tables are also a nice touch. To let everyone know what the cameras are for, attach a note to each camera saying something like, "Help us capture reunion memories! Feel free to take pictures throughout the day and then leave the used camera on the table when all pictures have been taken, and we'll pick them up."

Introducing Yourself

At the start of the reunion, introduce yourself and give a brief talk on family fun facts or your reasons for holding the reunion. If the reunion honors an individual (or a couple), have him stand and tell the group all about himself.

If the reunion is being held to honor your ancestors, tell a little bit about them. People interested in finding out more about their ancestors can check out the family-history table, where they can also find family group sheets to be filled out for their own families. I explain these sheets in Chapter 13.

The introduction is also a wonderful time to acknowledge your helpers and the people on the committees for working so hard to make the reunion a success (see Chapter 10 for details). If you find yourself short on reunion-day helpers, now is also the time to ask for volunteers. If no one raises a hand, assign duties to able-bodied folks who look like they need something constructive to do.

Your next job is to warm everyone up by having them participate in entertaining activities to help them get acquainted.

Warming 'em up with Icebreakers

Many people at the reunion are going to feel like strangers. They haven't seen the rest of the family in a long time and may have lost touch. Perhaps they've never met, or they're bringing new spouses. As the host, your job is to provide ways to break the ice and get people mingling.

You can choose from many activities to get your guests warmed up. I give you several options in the next few sections. Use the Activities Checklist and Log in Figure 7-3 (and on the CD) to help you and your entertainment committee keep track of what you intend to do. This way, you won't forget any important activities, such as family bingo!

Activities Checklist and Log

Name of activity _____

When played _____

Materials needed _____

_____

_____

_____

Name of activity _____

When played _____

Materials needed _____

_____

_____

_____

Name of activity _____

When played _____

Materials needed _____

_____

_____

_____

Name of activity _____

When played _____

Materials needed _____

_____

_____

_____

Figure 7-3:
Activities
Checklist
and Log.

Playing Guess that Baby

One of the easiest and most popular icebreakers for a reunion is a photo board. Place it just inside the reunion entrance (but don't block the entrance).

Before the reunion, ask everyone to send in baby pictures of themselves. Then paste the photos to a large foam board. Guests can look at the photos, guess who the people are in the pictures, and note the often-remarkable family resemblances. Plus, everybody loves to look at baby pictures!

Turn it into a game by numbering each photo, handing out a numbered sheet of paper, and asking people to identify the family member in each photo. The one with the most correct answers wins!

If the photos need to be returned to their owners, use a dab of rubber cement instead of glue. This makes the photos easy to pull off the board when the reunion is over.

Gettin' silly

An amusing way to get people talking is to dole out rewards based on silly facts. The rewards can be as simple as paper award certificates or buttons to pin on shirts, or they can be as elaborate as movie tickets or a bottle of wine. (Check out Chapter 8 for more award ideas.)

Give out awards based on the following trivia:

- ✔ Who's the youngest attendee?
- ✔ Who's the oldest?
- ✔ Who traveled the farthest to get to the reunion?
- ✔ Who's missing the most teeth? (Teething babies aren't included.)
- ✔ Who has the most unusual first name?
- ✔ Who's the most prolific? (How many kids did you say you have?)
- ✔ Who arrived the latest?

And here's a fun game for the ladies at the reunion. It gets everyone laughing and giggling before they even get in the door. Place a bathroom scale at the reunion entrance. When each gal signs in and picks up her name tag, have her weigh her handbag. The gal with the heaviest purse wins!

Engaging in some name games

Everyone is familiar with name games. They're easy, fun, and guaranteed to get people laughing. Here are a few different games to loosen everyone up.

My name is . . .

Have each person stand in turn, state his or her name, and say the origin of the name. You'll find that some people are named after family members and ancestors, but others have a funny story behind their name. Who would have known that Aunt Sarah was actually named after the pooch of her mother's best friend?

My name is Gary — It rhymes with Hairy

Ask folks to stand and state their name followed by a rhyming noun. Some of the answers will be quite creative!

Line 'em up!

Another entertaining name game is to ask everyone to line up alphabetically by first name. Watch the confusion as everyone tries to figure out where they belong in line. This one is great fun! Now that everyone's giggling, stretch the game out a little bit further by asking them to line up again based on height. Then have them line up according to their birthdays or from youngest to oldest. Make sure that no one trips Granny.

We're the Walleyes from Walla Walla, Washington

To find out more about everyone and where they're from, have an entire family group stand, state their names and where they're from, and tell what branch of the family they belong to. Then have the individuals within that group tell everyone an interesting fact about themselves. Perhaps Jane plays the tuba, and maybe Billy is double-jointed. There's bound to be someone else who can relate! Be sure to have someone take a picture of each group while they stand and blush.

Finding Out More about Your Kin

This section includes some more great games to help everyone discover more information about each other. Some games are short and quick, and others can take a bit more time, depending on the number of people attending your reunion.

The scavenger hunt

The object of this icebreaker is to find people who fit certain criteria. Create a playing sheet by compiling a list of silly facts or questions with a space for a signature after each one. Pass one sheet out to each guest. See Figure 7-4 (and check out the CD) for a sample sheet.

Have each person ask the reunion attendees to sign on the line that best describes them. The rule is that you can have only one name per line!

Human Scavenger Hunt

Find one person who best describes each statement and have them sign name on the line.

Can balance a spoon on nose _____

Likes brussel sprouts _____

Speaks another language _____

Has a belly button that's an outie _____

Wears false teeth _____

Can dance like a chicken _____

Unable to boil water without burning it _____

Has your same last name _____

Lives in the same state as you _____

Has green eyes _____

Drives a truck _____

Is wearing boots _____

Is over the age of 70 _____

Is under the age of 18 _____

Likes pumpernickel bread _____

Eats ice cream from the container _____

Drinks directly from the milk jug _____

Has braces on teeth _____

Can roll tongue _____

Plays musical instrument _____

Is wearing the biggest ring _____

Figure 7-4:
Scavenger
hunt sheet.

The toilet paper caper

Bring a couple rolls of TP to the reunion. Without giving any instructions, start passing around the rolls and tell each person to take as much toilet paper as they think they need.

Next, have everyone tell everyone else one fact about themselves for each section of toilet paper they took. You may want to grab a soda or a hot dog because this may take a while!

You can also play the same game with a bowl of chocolate-covered peanuts. Instruct the group not to eat any before their turn is played. Chocolate and peanut lovers beware!

Truth and lies

Ask everyone to think of one true tidbit and two false things to say about themselves. Then have the group decide which statement is the truth. You may discover that your tribe has some hidden talents and occupations!

I'd like to introduce . . .

This game is a fun one. Have everyone introduce the person sitting to their right by stating his or her name and an interesting fact about that person. If they don't know the person's name or anything about them, they can make it up.

Balloon bust

Give everyone an uninflated balloon, a small piece of paper, and a pencil. Ask each family member to write down his or her first name and favorite hobby on the piece of paper. Have everyone fold the papers into small wads and insert them into their balloon. Now have everyone blow up their balloons and tie them. Be sure to help those who have trouble tying the balloon.

Ask everyone to toss their balloons in the air and bat them around for a while, hitting whichever balloon comes near them (it need not be their own). This is a great way for the adults to relieve tension, and the kids think that it's terrific, too.

After about 5 or 10 minutes, have everyone grab someone else's balloon and pop it. Unfold the paper and ask everybody to locate the person on the piece of paper. If you accidentally burst your own balloon, trade the piece of paper with someone else.

Pocket and purse scavenger hunt

This game is a hoot! Have everyone pull the following items out of their purse, wallet, or pants pocket:

  ✔ The most useless item

  ✔ The most revealing item

Now ask everyone to explain how the most useless item ended up in their pants pocket or purse and what they find to be the most revealing about the second item.

Dividing Up into Teams

When you feel confident that the ice is broken and people are moving and active, you can divide the group into teams for playing games later. You can do this in many different ways, but I give you a couple of hints in this section.

For example, you can assign people to a red or blue team. Place an equal number of red or blue lengths of ribbon in a hat or basket. Ask each family member to close his or her eyes and pick one piece of ribbon. Then have everyone staple their ribbons to their name tags. You need to borrow a few staplers for this task — it's always best to have several. See Figure 7-5 for an example.

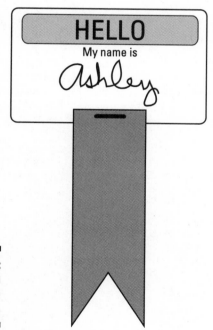

Figure 7-5:
Team ribbon stapled to a name tag.

Alternatively, you can have everyone choose from a basket full of pin-on badges. Party-supply stores are great places to find plastic fire and police badges that are perfect for identifying team members.

Try your best to assign spouses to opposing teams and to separate children from parents so everyone gets to know other family members.

Now pass around the snacks and liquid refreshments to get everyone ready for the big games. Yee-haw! Let the fun begin!

Chapter 8

Bridging the Generation Gap with Games

- -

In This Chapter

▶ Making merry with the kinfolk

▶ Playing games indoors and outdoors

▶ Handing out prizes and awards

- -

In addition to the theme (see Chapter 5), games set the tone for the reunion. Frankly, a reunion without games is boring. If you use the icebreaker ideas in Chapter 7, you can get everyone warmed up and ready for more fun. Bring on the games!

In this chapter, I show you how to keep everyone active and amused. I provide many games that are multigenerational, which means that everyone can participate. I include a number of games that the older folks and people confined to wheelchairs can play, too! You'll see a "Fun for Everyone" icon next to these games.

Getting the Group Involved

Now you get to shake the family tree and watch the nuts fall out! Games and activities can really bring the clan together. Good, clean fun (and a little dirt, too) helps everyone relax and brings out everyone's personality.

While playing games, you're sure to discover surprising tidbits about each family member. Perhaps you didn't know that Aunt Emma was so competitive or that Cousin Billy hates to get his feet wet.

The fun and games are the domain of the entertainment committee, but as reunion coordinator, you have lots of input. Encourage your committee to choose an assortment of games, keeping in mind the skill levels of the various participants. The goal is to get all the generations involved. Don't leave anyone out of the fun!

The family Olympics

Races, relays, and contests are picnic standbys. They encourage teamwork and friendly competition — and they're just plain fun. In this section, I explain some of my favorites.

Beach-towel volleyball

This game is a blast! You can play it at the park, at the beach, or in the backyard — anywhere you can set up a volleyball net, in fact. In addition to a net, you need 12 team players, six large beach towels, and one volleyball.

To play, two groups of two hold on to opposite sides of beach towels — one hand on each corner, for each team. The serving team places the volleyball in the towel, lowers the towel, and then raises it quickly, flinging the ball over the net. The opposing teams try to catch the ball in their towels and fling it back over the net. When the ball drops or goes out of bounds, rotate the teams by having the third 2-person group come in while one group steps out for a rest, and then serve again, as in standard volleyball.

Keeping score isn't really necessary. Just be sure to rotate team members so everyone gets a chance to play.

You can also play this game with four players per team and one large blanket per team. Each team member holds one corner of the blanket, and the group tries to catch and fling the ball over the net, as in the beach-towel version.

Family-Friendly Competitions

Many of the games included in this section require a *judge* to help keep the games fair. Choose a family member who you think can remain impartial, and ask her to be the official judge. Remember, the judge has final say, so don't argue over the outcome.

Backwards crab walk

This game requires some agility, so get the youngsters in your family to participate!

Position the racers at the starting line. Sit them down just behind the starting line with their backs facing the finish line. Next, have them raise themselves onto their arms and legs like crabs. Then the judge yells "Go!" — and they race to the finish line.

This game is tough, but great for laughs!

One and three-legged races

These races have been around forever, but they're still as fun today as they were eons ago.

For a one-legged race, bind each person's legs together with tape or a strip of fabric. For a three-legged race, bind the inside legs of two people together with tape or a strip of fabric.

Position the players at the starting line. When the judge shouts "Go!" the participants race (or hop) to the finish line

Group get-up

This game is as much fun to watch as it is to play. In fact, Granny will be rolling off her rocking chair with laughter.

This activity requires two to four teams of three to six people. At the starting line, each team stands and makes a circle with the team members' backs facing in (so they're facing out). Next, have them all sit down and then link arms.

When the judge yells "Go!" the teams scramble to their feet and race to the finish line — all without unlinking their arms!

Pass the pretzel

For this game, you need pretzels and one or two packages of disposable chopsticks (available at oriental markets and kitchen stores).

At the starting line, provide each team (you can have any number of teams, with each one having at least six people) with a bowl of pretzels — no snacking allowed! At the end of the line, provide an empty bowl for each team. This is where the teams will put the passed pretzels.

Separate the pairs of chopsticks and give each player one chopstick. Each person holds a stick with one hand and places the other hand behind her back (you may need to tape her hands back there!). When the judge yells "Go!" each team passes the pretzels from stick to stick until the team reaches the empty bowl. If someone drops the pretzel, it goes back to the starting bowl, and the team has to start all over again.

At the end of one minute, the team with the most pretzels in their bowl wins!

The clan carnival

Although relay races and individual games (such as family bingo) are great fun, carnival games with fewer competitive factors are nice to have, too! Carnival games let everyone hang loose and enjoy themselves at their own pace.

Hoop toss

This game is suitable for everyone! To play, you need two hula hoops, two lengths of rope, and an equal number of beanbags or tennis balls for each hoop. Four to six balls per hoop are usually sufficient. You also need a few beanbag or ball chasers, and a few extra balls in case some get lost.

Hang the hula hoops from the ceiling using the ropes. Have an equal number of players line up for each team. The person at the front of each line tries to throw the beanbags or balls through the hoops. Teams get one point for each bag or ball that makes it cleanly through the hoop.

To make the game fun for all ages, you can mark off throwing distances for various ages. For adults, a distance of 8 to 10 feet is appropriate. Youngsters and the elderly may need a throwing distance of 3 or 4 feet. Just for laughs, make the teenagers stand back one foot for each year of age. Their parents will get a kick out of it.

Catch that fruit!

Some of the games that I include in this chapter are a little bit unusual and may require some skill, such as eye-hand coordination. Catch that fruit is one of them.

For each team (have as many as you'd like), you need three people, one piece of fruit (such as an apple, a pear, or a peach), a skewer, tape, and two 5-foot lengths of clean, narrow twine.

Prepare the piece of fruit by tying the twine to one end of the skewer and forcing the skewer and clean twine through it. Remove the skewer so that only the twine remains — like "fruit on a rope." Next, two team members take opposite ends of the rope, holding the fruit up at mouth level.

The third person from each team places her hands behind her back so she can't cheat — lightly tape her hands if necessary! When the judge yells "Go!" this person gets to try to eat the fruit.

Folks with loose or false teeth should not play this game — chances are good that they'll lose them!

The family scramble

Everyone can participate in this event! Gather the group together and ask people to line up as quickly as possible, according to the following criteria:

- ✔ Age
- ✔ Height
- ✔ Birthday (month and date, not year)
- ✔ Alphabetically by first name

Where are grandpa's teeth?

This game is similar to "Doggy, doggy, where's your bone?" but with a silly twist. You can get wind-up, chattering teeth at gag and party stores.

Have the participant sit with his back to everyone. Next, hide the chompers somewhere in the group. To eliminate the gross-out factor, place the teeth in a plastic bag or, better yet, use some mechanical wind-up teeth from the party store.

Have everyone sing "Grandpa, grandpa, where's your teeth? Someone stole them from your cheeks." The person in the chair then has three chances to guess who has them. If he is correct, the person who has the teeth is next in the chair. If incorrect, the person keeps guessing. Usually, however, the guilty party gives herself away by the silly look on her face.

Kick-the-can ice cream

This isn't necessarily a game, but it's an activity that kids and grandpas really enjoy. A mixture of yummy items is placed in a can, which is placed inside a larger can filled with ice that is kicked around for a while. The result is a small amount of ice cream made with a whole lot of fun! This recipe is enough for three batches.

For the materials, you need a 1-pound coffee can, a 3-pound coffee can (both with lids), rock salt, and crushed ice. To make the ice cream, mix together 2 quarts of whole milk, two cans of sweetened condensed milk, one 4-ounce package of instant vanilla or chocolate pudding, and 1 cup of sugar.

Place the ice cream ingredients in the smaller can and leave one inch of head space at the top of the can. Place the lid on the can and tape it down securely with duct tape or some other strong tape. Put the smaller can inside the larger can and put the rock salt and ice around it. Place the lid on the larger can and tape it down securely.

Now let everyone kick the can around for about 30 minutes! Afterward, open the outer can carefully and rinse off the inner can with cold water to remove salt residue. Then open the inner can and share the ice cream with the kinfolk!

Family bingo

Here's another game that everyone can participate in, regardless of age. Plus, you can reestablish ties and acquaint yourself with unfamiliar folks.

To play, give everyone pens or pencils and bingo sheets like the one in Figure 8-1. Next, each player must find a person to match the criteria for each box and then get his signature in the appropriate square. A person can sign a sheet only once.

The first person to get a line filled diagonally, vertically, or horizontally and then yells "Bingo!" wins the game.

Has blue eyes	Knows all the words to the *Brady Bunch* theme	Is your cousin's husband	Has been to other family reunions	Is under 10 years old
Can stand on one leg while patting head and rubbing belly	Was born in the same month as you	Likes broccoli	Is under 3 feet tall	Is artistic
Can play an instrument	Watches the 11:00 p.m. news	FREE	Has the same last name as you	Is your aunt or uncle
Has served in the military	Owns a dog	Is more than 6 feet tall	Has been to the Grand Canyon	Can drive a tractor
Is more than 60 years old	Works on the family history	Drives an SUV	Owns a farm animal	Knows how to waltz

Figure 8-1:
Family bingo
sheet.

A splashin' shindig

Because most family reunions take place during the summer, the weather can be hot. Cool down the clan with water games! The following games are terrific for all ages.

Hole in the can

This game is a relay in which everyone can participate. Have teams form two lines of 6 or more people per line.

At the beginning of each line, place a 5-gallon bucket filled with water and a smaller can or bucket with several holes punched in the bottom. Make certain that the can or bucket has plenty of holes.

At the end of each line, place another 5-gallon bucket to serve as the receiving bucket. Have each team select an able-bodied "runner," and place this person next to the receiving bucket.

When the judge shouts "Go!" the first person in each line dips the holey bucket or can into the water-filled bucket and passes it along the line until it gets to the receiving bucket. The person at the end of the line dumps whatever water is left in the can into the receiving bucket and passes the can to the runner.

The runner then takes the can to the beginning of the line, and the process is repeated all over again for one or two minutes, depending on the number of people on each team. The larger the team, the longer the time limit.

The team with the most water in the receiving bucket at the end of the allotted time limit wins the game!

Floating treasure

Assemble a collection of 20 to 30 small items that can float. You can use corks, small toys, fishing bobs, or any other inexpensive items. On the bottom of five of the items, place a mark or sticker to indicate that the items are "treasures." Fill a small kiddie pool with water and toss in the floaters.

Next, line up the clan and let each person pull one of the floaters from the water. Whoever picks a floating treasure wins a prize.

To make this game even more entertaining, toss 40 floaters in a larger wading pool, blindfold each participant, and let him wade into the pool to find a treasure.

Water balloon volleyball

This game is not for the meek — or for anyone who doesn't want to get wet!

You need a volleyball net, a couple empty buckets (inexpensive disposable paper painting buckets from the home improvement center work great), and a whole lot of water balloons.

Give each team a large bucket or box filled with water balloons and hand an empty bucket to each team member.

To play, a team member serves the balloons from the back of the court by hurling them over the net. The receiving team members then try to catch them in their buckets. After ten minutes, the team with the most filled water balloons wins!

Table-tennis target game

This is a fun team game. To play, you need eight empty 1-liter bottles, eight table-tennis balls, two tables, and two teams. Line up four of the bottles on each table — one table for each team. Place a ball on top of each bottle. You also need two judges.

Give a participant on each team a filled water pistol. The trick is to shoot the balls off the bottles within the allotted time — 30 seconds works well. After each participant's time is up, she hands the pistol to the next person in line and places the balls back on the bottles. The judges must make certain that the game is played fairly, so place a judge from the opposing team at each table. The team who knocks off the most balls wins!

Shaving cream shoot-off

This is a great game for older family members to participate in, especially on a hot day!

To play, select two nice folks who want to "have a shave." Place each person in a chair and cover his face with shaving cream. Next, select six other folks to be the "shavers," having 3 shavers per chair. Give them each a small filled water pistol.

When a judge yells "Go!" each team shaves the person in the chair by shooting off the shaving cream with the water pistols. The first team to squirt off all the shaving cream wins!

Over-and-under water relay

Divide the group into two teams and line them up. At the beginning of each line, place a bucket filled with water and a paper cup. At the end of each line place a bucket.

Have each team select a "runner" and place this person next to the receiving bucket. When the judge shouts "Go!" the team member closest to the water-filled bucket fills the paper cup and passes it to the next person by reaching over her own head. The next person in line passes it to the following person under his own legs.

The entire line repeats the over-and-under routine until it reaches the last person. This person dumps the remaining water into the empty bucket and hands the cup to the runner. The runner then brings the cup back to the end of the line, and the over-and-under process starts all over again.

The team with the most water in the receiving bucket at the end of two minutes wins!

More entertaining stuff

Just in case I didn't give you enough ideas for activities, here are a few more to consider. Remember that having activities keeps everything lively, but do give sufficient "breaks" in between so folks can catch their breath.

Blindfolded shoe shuffle

For this game, you need blindfolds and family members willing to take off their smelly shoes. Each team selects six to eight players who remove their shoes and get blindfolded.

To play, the players form a circle. Toss the shoes into a pile in the center of the circle. Next, someone mixes up all the shoes in the pile.

Then everyone tries to locate their own shoes by feel — and smell, if necessary.

Broom hockey

This game is an old favorite and can be played in a large hall, on a tennis or basketball court, or in the parking lot. I've also played it on an ice rink wearing tennis shoes!

To play, divide your clan into teams and give each player a broom. Select one person from each team to be goalkeeper. Place cardboard boxes on opposite ends of the playing area — the boxes are the goals. Then, settle on a time limit — 10 to 15 minutes is sufficient.

Now toss in a tennis ball for the puck and let the fun begin! The team that has made the most goals by the end of the allotted time wins!

Be sure to rotate players in and out of the game so everyone gets a chance to play.

Dress the mannequin

Before the reunion, ask the older family members to bring funky clothing, shoes, hats, and accessories from their closets.

At the reunion, gather the clothing and other items. Select teams of six people and designate one person from each team as the "mannequin." You can pick a male or a female — they just have to be a good sport!

When the judge yells "Go!" each team has one minute to dress the mannequin. The rest of the family gets to judge the dressing contest. The funniest and most creative mannequin wins!

Know your kin

Was Uncle Henry a secret agent in the war? Was Granny a fashion model? Everyone has a secret that no one knows about (or at least very few folks know about). This game can uncover those funny secrets.

Have everyone write their names down on a piece of paper and place all the papers in a hat or box. Next, have everyone draw a name from the hat. Sometime during the reunion, each person secretly interviews the person named on her piece of paper and tries to find out one secret about that person.

When everyone is seated during mealtime, each person tells the clan the secret, and everyone must guess who that person is!

Scavenger hunt

This game keeps the kids amused for hours, giving the adults a much-needed respite. The rules are simple: Everyone has to find everything on the list and then return to show their booty. This can be done individually or in teams, depending on the number of kids participating.

Some of the items on the list can be found on other reunion attendees. These items should all be returned to the owners after the game has ended. Other items, such as golf tees, must be secretly hidden at the reunion site in advance.

Give each participant a plastic shopping bag and send her on her way with the list shown in Figure 8-2.

Scavenger Hunt List

Pine cone

Chewing gum, chewed or unchewed

Leaf from a ? tree (you name the tree)

A feather

A paper clip

A tube of lipstick

A penny from the current year

A golf tee

A bottle cap

A business card

An empty candy wrapper

A hat or cap

A comb or brush

A coupon

A pickle

A rock with a face on it

A plastic spoon

A bug

A toothpick

An empty film canister

A potato or tortilla chip

A napkin with lipstick on it

An empty bag, bottle, or can (helps with the cleanup!)

An elderly person
(This is a kick for the elderly. They love being chosen!)

Figure 8-2:
Scavenger
Hunt List.

Opting for Rental Activities

For really big games, check out your local rental center or party-supply store. Because these games are expensive to rent and often require a lot of room, they're usually rented only for large reunions. However, I have also seen some of these items rented for kiddie birthday parties, so anything goes!

For a daily fee, you can rent really neat items, such as the following:

- **Dunk tank:** Put Uncle Piccolo in the hot seat, throw a few balls, and watch him swim with the fishes.

- **Karaoke machine:** Set it up, plug it in, and let the tunes begin. If you're really lucky, you'll get the dogs howling, too.

- **Dance floor and disco ball:** A portable dance floor and disco ball can get your relatives dancing like Fred Astaire (or Jerry Lewis, depending on their personalities!).

- **Bungee bull ride:** Not your 70s bar ride anymore! This game has the "bull" suspended by bungee cords over an air-filled surface. Four people tug the lines to start the wild ride. The object is to stay on the bull as long as possible. This game is as much fun for the spectators as it is for the participants.

- **Inflatable golf:** A miniature golf game that everyone can enjoy. Watch out for Granny — she may try to stick her ball in the hole when no one's watching.

- **Inflatable obstacle course:** Tons of fun packed into an inflatable monster. You can rent various versions and layouts, featuring climbing walls, crawl tubes, and other obstacle course necessities with a safe, well-padded environment.

- **Human bowling:** This game is not for people prone to motion sickness! In human bowling, a lucky (or unlucky) teammate is trapped into a ball-shaped metal cage and rolled like a bowling ball. The object is to knock down the huge balloon pins at the end of the lane. Don't try this one after dinner.

- **Rodeo roper:** A perfect game for a western-themed reunion! The rider saddles up on a life-size fiberglass horse with no legs and tries to lasso a moving calf (also with no legs) while it races down a metal track.

- **Inflatable toys:** Although expensive, these items are terrific if you're having a lot of children at the reunion. You can find many different types of inflatable toys, from simple toys that everyone jumps in (much like an enclosed trampoline) to elaborate ones with slides and tunnels. A compressor keeps the toy inflated.

- ✔ **Sumo wrestling:** Two people wear inflatable sumo suits and try to knock each other out of the ring by bumping bellies. (The arms are filled with air, making them impossible to bend, hence the belly-bumping.) This game is amusing for both the participants and the spectators.

- ✔ **Inflatable slides:** This activity can keep the kids busy for a while. The slides are available in different sizes and guaranteed to bring out the kid in everybody — even Cousin Archibald.

- ✔ **Double or single-shot basketball:** This game is a favorite at carnivals and large parties. A metal and vinyl frame is set up with a hoop or hoops at the opposite end. Players score by shooting their balls through the hoop(s). Some versions also feature timers and sound effects.

- ✔ **Game shows:** Yes, you can even rent game shows. The games resemble such favorites as *Jeopardy!, Name that Tune, Family Feud,* and others. If you're thinking "board games" think again — these games come complete with 6-foot spinning wheels and light-up answer boards.

- ✔ **Other games:** Also available for rent are trivia games, foosball tables, and the old standby — bingo.

If you want more information (including ideas and expenses) on rental items, check out Chapter 4.

Doling Out Awards and Rewards

With all these games, you need some prizes or awards. They don't need to be elaborate or expensive items — just stuff that can keep everyone motivated, especially when the winners wave their prizes in the jealous faces of other team members. (I include more information on prizes in Chapter 10.)

Setting up a clan casino

If your family is stinking rich and money is no object, set up a casino! You can rent roulette wheels, inflatable slot machines, and blackjack and craps tables. In fact, some rental companies even allow you to rent the dealer! Check with your local party-rental store. (**Note:** Adding a few cash-based casino games is a great way to raise seed money for the next reunion!)

But even if your family isn't living on Easy Street, a casino can still be a lot of fun. Instead of using cash, give everyone a pile of plastic poker chips, which can be redeemed for prizes. (See the section "Doling Out Awards and Rewards," in this chapter, for prize ideas.)

Here are some ideas for prizes:

- Candy bars
- Baked items, such as cupcakes or cookies in a pretty container
- Bottles of wine for the of-age crowd
- Gift certificates (hopefully donated) to local restaurants
- Boxes of candy corn
- Toys, books, or crayons for the kids
- Interesting books for adults
- Family-history software for would-be family historians
- Movie videos
- Disposable cameras

When selecting prizes, be sure to keep the various age groups of the reunion attendees in mind. Try to keep a selection of items in case someone wants to make a trade for a more age-appropriate item.

Secret prizes

These prizes are always a hit, because no one knows what they are! Some prizes can surprise and delight the winner, and others can make the recipient roll with laughter. The game winner gets to choose from a pile of wrapped items ranging from very small to very large in size. Sometimes, the biggest boxes contain the silliest items.

Here are some ideas for secret prizes:

- Junk gifts
- Mouthwash
- Golf balls and tees
- Polka music CD
- Insect repellent (especially handy for a campground reunion)
- Packets of flower seeds
- Houseplant fertilizer
- Small games, such as jacks or a jump rope
- A toothbrush
- Toothpaste (or denture cream, for laughs)
- Gag gifts from the party-supply store

Keep your family members in mind when selecting the prizes — especially if they have a sense of humor. I'm sure that you can think of more items to add to the prize list.

Award certificates

An even cheaper, simpler route than giving prizes is to make paper award certificates for the reunion game participants. This method is especially helpful when rewarding an entire team! Simply give one printed award to each team member, or give one to the entire team.

If you give the award to the team as a whole, count the number of awards that each team has received at the end of the day. Then you can reward each team member with a small prize or individual certificates.

You can find many computer programs that create certificates, or you can make your own certificates using a word-processing program and adding clip art. You can use the sample award certificate in Figure 8-3 as a guide, or you can print the sample from the CD and use it as is.

You can also find ready-made certificates, ribbons, and emblems at office-supply and educational-supply stores. They come in a wide range of colors and styles and are easy to use. Just fill in the blanks, and you're done.

Certificate of Award

Given to: _____

Date: _____

Event: _____

Your family acknowledges your unique style and outstanding performance during the reunion games.

Congratulations!

Figure 8-3:
Sample
award
certificate.

Chapter 9

Establishing Family Traditions

Your family reunion brings together several generations and gives family members the chance to enjoy each other's company. This event is not only an ideal time to establish or renew family traditions, but it's also the best time to pass on your family history and record stories from the old-timers in the family.

In this chapter, I give you some ideas and tips for sharing and preserving your traditions as well as some nifty ideas for creating new ones.

Making Your Memories Last a Lifetime

The older generations have a habit of slipping away when you least expect it. While you have the old-timers together, record their personal histories to share with future generations. The older people in your family have a lot to share, and they're more than willing to tell their stories.

Reliving the glory days

If you have a guest of honor or just have a lot of interesting folks at your reunion, ask them to stand and tell the family about their childhoods or about memorable events in their lives. Reminiscing is a great way to get everyone interested in the family history. You (or another family member) can discreetly take a few notes mentally or on paper so the stories of the older generations can live on.

I love it when my older relatives tell stories about their childhoods. I had no idea that my grandmother fed my aunt mud pies! Who knows what interesting tidbits you can discover?

Telling the family story

If you or someone in your family has been researching the family history for years, ask that person to tell the family story. Provide a podium and bulletin board for visuals, such as a blown-up version of the family tree (see the sidebar "Showing off the family tree," later in this chapter, for more details).

The family history presentation is often an emotional time during the reunion. Some folks reminisce, and others find out information about ancestors and family traditions. To keep the sentiment going, honor the oldest family members by asking them to stand and share brief stories with everyone.

Celebrate your family history and encourage the younger generations to cherish it.

Recording an oral history

A great way to record a person's oral history is to get it on tape. You need a tape recorder, a microphone, and some blank cassettes. You can also use a video camera, but that method can make some folks uncomfortable.

Choose a quiet place away from the noise and bustle of the reunion activities, and provide a nice comfy chair for the interviewee. Roll the tape and begin the interview by asking the person when she was born. Ask her to tell a little bit about her birthplace. Was it a small town or a farm? Or was it in a taxicab on the way to the airport?

Next, have her reminisce about her childhood, adolescence, and early adulthood. A few good subjects to bring up are attending her first day of school, learning to drive a car, traveling to the city, and hearing about the birds and the bees.

You can make a list of questions, but I have found that I rarely stick to a list. I let the person being interviewed lead the conversation. The interview naturally progresses into the person's adult life.

Let the interview happen — don't force it. If you notice the person is uncomfortable with certain questions, move on to the next one. Be sure to allow the person plenty of time to tell her tales.

Setting up a family museum

Before the reunion, gather pieces of family memorabilia from your relatives. Some items that I suggest are old photographs of ancestors, veteran memorabilia, diaries, old passports, and handcrafts. Ask everyone to contribute something — they will get their items back after the reunion. Set up your "family museum" in a special location at the reunion. I recommend placing it near the bulletin or photo boards.

If you have any old "mystery photos," bring them along and place them on the museum table. Tack a note to each mystery photo asking if anyone can identify the person shown in the photo — it works like a charm.

Putting on a play

Here's an activity to entertain the younger family members. Ask them to create a play or skit that tells a story about your family.

For example, if your ancestors arrived by boat from the old country, a nautical reenactment can be great fun! If your ancestors traveled west by wagon train along the Oregon Trail, use this idea as your theme. And feel free to get creative with props and foreign accents.

Filling in the records

In Chapter 7, I mention placing family group sheets at the entrance to the reunion. These sheets are given to each family to fill out. Each sheet has a space for everyone's name, date and place of birth, marriage, and if applicable, death (see Chapter 13 for a sample).

Be sure that you remind the clan to fill out these sheets at the reunion. I'll tell you more about family records in Chapters 13 and 14. At this point, don't worry about blank entries — just get what you can from everyone.

Showing off the family tree

I like to have a huge, blown-up version of the family tree mounted to a foam board at reunions to show how far back the family history goes. The display always draws a crowd — folks like to see their own names when climbing the family tree!

Keep a pen handy — hang it from a piece of string tacked to the board. Family members can use it to fill in any blanks, add new babies to the tree, or make any necessary corrections.

Name that ancestor

Years ago, I had an old photograph that my immediate family and I couldn't identify, so I brought it to the family reunion. When I showed the photograph to my family members, someone immediately made an identification — it was the sample picture that came in the original frame. You can imagine how red-faced I became!

Sometimes, family members may be hesitant about giving personal information. This is understandable. But if you explain your purpose in collecting the information (which is, of course, to preserve the family history for future generations) and make a few small concessions, the process may go much more easily. Later, when you have had the time to compile the information and create a family history binder (see Chapter 14), offer to send the hesitant family member a copy. I promise the binder will pique their interest!

For instance, let people know that leaving off their year of birth is okay. Although this is definitely an important piece of information, you can probably pick someone else's brain for it. Chances are, you have a nosey aunt who knows the exact year that everyone was born!

Be sure to collect everyone's completed forms before the end of the reunion. Place a special helper in charge of this task.

Creating Reunion Keepsakes

There's an old saying that goes, "We all have photographic memories, but some of us forget to bring film." To help capture the memories of your family's special day, consider creating a reunion keepsake. Because a reunion is a special gathering, you want to record the event in every possible way — through photographs, videos, and special keepsakes that linger long after the barbecue has cooled and everyone has gone home. In the next few sections, I share some great ideas for reunion keepsakes.

Posing for a family portrait

Snag a nonfamily member to take a group photo. Get everyone in the picture. You can usually find someone nearby who's more than willing to lend you a hand — ask the caterer, a park ranger, or a stranger passing by with her dog to snap the photo.

As the reunion planner, you'll more than likely be the person responsible for developing and distributing the group photo. You can do this inexpensively by having duplicate copies made at your local processing lab. The more copies you have made, the cheaper the price.

However, if you're considering having an enlarged print made — say 8x10 inches or so — it can get expensive. Consider asking family members to pay a small fee to cover the cost of having their copy made and the cost of postage (if you have to mail it to them). A couple of bucks should suffice.

Making a photo or video scrapbook

People love to snap pictures — what better place to do this than at a family reunion? If you come from a family of shutterbugs, ask your relatives to help you take photos for a family scrapbook.

Ask folks to have duplicates made of their snapshots, or better yet, ask them for the finished rolls and get the film developed yourself. Make sure that you order double prints so you can send your relatives a complete set of prints. Another option is to have a few disposable cameras stashed throughout the reunion. Ask family members to snap pictures and then return them to you at the end of the reunion.

After the reunion is over and life gets back to a normal pace, get the film developed. Sort through the photos and choose your favorites. Place the photos on heavy 8½-x-11-inch paper using a small dab of rubber cement (which allows you to remove the pictures easily). This is the step where you can be as creative as you want, adding borders, stickers, mementos and artwork to the pages. Next, take the sheets to your local copy center. If you're taking orders for scrapbooks from the reunion attendees, have enough color laser copies made of the pages to fill everyone's order — plus a few extra. Place the color photocopies in pretty binders and send them on their way.

If you're planning on making a video scrapbook, assign one or more people who own a video camera the task of recording the reunion. You can also rent video cameras at your local rental center. If you have bucks to burn, you can also hire a professional videographer (see Chapter 4 for more information).

Personally, I prefer having family members tape the reunion footage. It's economical and fun. You'll see what I mean when family members perform for the camera because they know the person behind it. Let the family videographers tape whatever strikes them as fun and interesting. Different people have differing perspectives and this adds character to the videos.

After the reunion, watch the videos and find out where the best shots are. Take the videotapes to a local editing house (look them up in the phone book under "video") and have folks there combine your favorites portions of each tape into one tape. You'll have to stick around because the person transferring the video needs you there to show them what to transfer and what to leave alone.

When the video scrapbook is finished, you need to make copies. You can find many places that make videotape copies for a fee. In fact, the fee is often lower than the cost of buying a bunch of blank videotapes and making copies on your own (by sitting on your living room floor and working with two VCRs).

To offset the costs of videos or photos and binders, charge a small fee for copies of the scrapbooks. Take orders at the reunion — most family members want copies of their own.

Compiling the family recipe book

Okay, so you really didn't like Cousin Ethel's lima bean and yogurt soufflé. But someone else may have loved it — certainly Cousin Ethel is fond of it. To help spread Cousin Ethel's love for whipping up this tasty-if-not-unusual treat, consider compiling a family recipe book.

Before the reunion, encourage family members to bring along their favorite recipes — especially recipes passed on by previous generations. My recipe file includes recipes for my father-in-law's baked beans, my grandpa's favorite pickle recipe, and the cookies my mother-in-law baked for my husband every Friday after school. These are my favorite family treasures!

After you gather all the recipes at the reunion, you can later type them into pages using a word-processing program on your computer. Add a few pieces of clip art, and print copies. Then place the copies in small binders or report covers and send the recipe books to everyone who ordered one — and everyone who didn't request a book but contributed a recipe. Include a copy of the family portrait, too! (See the section "Posing for a family portrait, earlier in the chapter, for details.)

To help offset the costs of paper, copies, binders, ink, and postage, I recommend charging a small fee for the recipe book.

Designing Other Unique Mementos

In addition to the memorable items previously mentioned in this chapter, how about providing or selling some other family goodies. Remember, if you're going to be selling these items, let everyone know in advance so they can come prepared with cash. If you're planning on including them in the reunion fee, you need not worry about it.

Donning survival gear

Have some T-shirts or buttons printed that say something snappy. Perhaps something like "I survived the first annual Jones family reunion."

You can make your own buttons or T-shirt iron-ons on your computer using special kits, which you can find at craft stores and office-supply stores.

Constructing a family birthday calendar

After gathering everyone's family group sheets (see the section "Filling in the records," earlier in this chapter), you can assemble a family birthday calendar. But because the calendars can't be ready by the end of the reunion, you need to take orders. Be sure to ask everyone who orders a calendar for a small prepaid fee to cover the costs of paper, postage, and copies.

You can use a calendar-maker program on your computer (the tidiest method) or a blank store-bought calendar that you fill in neatly by hand (if you have a calligrapher in the family, draft her for this task). Send a copy of the completed calendar to everyone who requested one.

Preparing birthday cards

This activity involves the whole group. Bring several boxes of birthday cards to the reunion and have everyone sign them.

After the reunion, refer to your family birthday calendar or your family history information and send a birthday card to everyone who attended the reunion.

The recipients not only laugh when they see their own signature, but they also reminisce about signing the cards with family members and get excited about holding another reunion!

Creating a time capsule

After the reunion is over, gather up photos, a copy of the invitation, a brochure from the location, and other memorable reunion items and place them in a box. Ask a family member to keep the box in a safe location where it won't be misplaced. Don't open the box until the next reunion, so you can see how people have changed.

Making a quilt

Making a quilt is like making a time capsule, especially when it's reunion oriented. You can use the quilt to help finance the next reunion by selling raffle tickets at the current reunion and placing the money raised in a separate reunion bank account.

Here are some tips for making a special handicraft:

- ✔ **Transfer reunion photos to fabric and stitch them together.** Photo transfer paper is available at most fabric or craft-supply stores. To use this paper, coat your original photo (not a photocopy) with a special solution and place the photo face down on the specially prepared fabric. Complete directions are found in the photo-transferring kit. Remember, however, that the original photo will no longer be useable. If it's a photo you want to keep, have a second print made at your local photo lab.

- ✔ **Make a handprint quilt.** Have everyone dip their hands in acrylic paint and press them onto the fabric. Then have everyone sign their names underneath their handprints using a permanent marker.

- ✔ **Create a community quilt.** If you have a lot of stitchers in your family, ask them to contribute a reunion-themed block for a quilt. If you need more quilting tips, check out *Quilting For Dummies* by Cheryl Fall (that's me!), published by Hungry Minds, Inc.

Be sure to gather volunteers to help you assemble the quilt. It's a nice way to continue the sense of kinship.

Part IV
After the Reunion

The 5th Wave By Rich Tennant

"Uncle Bud says Aunt Ronnie and the kids are getting hungry again. You'd better push over another garbage dumpster."

In this part . . .

In Chapter 10, you get some quick and dirty guidelines (pardon the pun) for cleaning up the mess after your reunion. (If everyone pitches in, it won't take long — I promise!). In Chapter 11, I give you some ways to keep in touch with the clan after your reunion. And in Chapter 12, you can get ideas on using your reunion-planning strategies to organize other events.

Chapter 10

All's Well That Ends Well

. . . .

In This Chapter

▶ Thanking your family

▶ Rewarding your helpers

▶ Leaving the reunion site clean and tidy

▶ Returning the accoutrements

▶ Finding out what everyone liked and didn't like

. . . .

Your head may hurt, and your bones may ache from playing games. But somehow, you've survived your family reunion. In fact, the event was a great success. What a sense of accomplishment! You schmoozed with all the cousins, aunts, and uncles and reacquainted yourself with their spouses. Hey, you even discovered that Sally's husband George is not as bad as you'd thought, even if he did spill pudding on you at their wedding. Everyone had a great time, and now everyone is even talking about continuing the reunion tradition.

In this chapter, I tell you how to end the reunion gracefully, poll the family for advice, and reward the many deserving helpers.

Speech . . . Speech: Thanking the Clan

As the reunion winds down and the ending draws near, you should give a family speech. You're the host, so one of your duties is to stand up and thank everyone for coming. After all, your reunion was a success thanks to the folks who attended — the people make the party. But give your speech *before* Cinderella turns into a pumpkin — don't wait until half the people have headed for home.

If you're inspired, tell everyone about your favorite part of the reunion. Did you almost pass out laughing during the games? Did grandpa's pre-dinner toast make you weepy? Or was it just the flood of wonderful old memories that ran through your head throughout the reunion? ***Note:*** Avoid being long-winded, because you may lose their interest.

Let others have their say, too. Everyone had a great time and wants to share their favorite moment. You and your family members may shed a tear or two, but that's fine. It's your family.

Rewarding a Job Well Done

After the thank-yous and the speeches, you need to award the game winners with prizes and certificates. (See Chapter 8 for award and certificate ideas.)

I strongly recommend giving each committee a special certificate to honor a job well done. Also give a little something special to each committee member and helper. Chocolate is always good. Aspirin may be helpful, too — after all, reunions require a lot of effort, so some folks may get headaches.

Sending Everyone Home

Say farewell to everyone — except the cleanup committee! You need these folks to hang around a little bit longer. But do send home all the nonessential people. Home can be a local hotel or any other guest accommodation.

If you hire a van or shuttle service to deliver the folks to and from home, call the service about an hour before the reunion ends so the driver(s) can arrive on time. If the shuttle has to make several trips, send the elderly and families with young children home first. They're probably tired and deserve a little R and R.

Ask folks who are able-bodied and awake to stay behind and help with the cleanup. The more people who are willing to help, the more quickly you can get the job done. Notice that I said *help* with the cleanup — this does not mean sitting in chairs *watching* the cleanup.

Cleaning Up the Mess

I know that it's late and you're tired, but you still have the cleanup ahead of you. Every great party has its share of cleanup. Bummer!

Dirty barbecues, trash, and leftovers need to be taken care of. Plus, you need to return all the tables and chairs to the rental center. Hopefully, the members of your cleanup committee are still standing.

So now is the time to speak in short sentences containing few syllables. Try saying, "tables, fold 'em. Chairs, stow 'em." They'll get the idea. Just point their tired noses toward the mess.

Knowing when and what to delegate

As the reunion coordinator, you're responsible for leaving the reunion site in the same condition that you found it — if not better. But don't try to do the entire cleanup by yourself. It's simply too much for one person to handle. (After all, even superheroes have helpers!) This was a family event, so everyone should pitch in.

Hopefully, the cleanup committee worked out its strategy in advance, assigning each member certain responsibilities. If not, use the list in Figure 10-1 (and on the CD) to dole out cleanup responsibilities. With the cleanup committee's help, your job as reunion coordinator boils down to supervising, using the list in Figure 10-1 as your guide.

The more people you have helping, the better. But you'll likely find that these people are the same folks doing each and every task. Bless them. Praise them. Kiss their feet and tell them what you need them to do.

Here's a list of tasks that you can assign to a person or group of people. Be sure to check the items off your list when they're completed.

- **Cleaning up the entrance and welcome area:** Take down the welcome banner and remove any items left on the sign-in table and give them to the coordinator. Remove directional signs and clean up the parking area. This task includes picking up trash and replanting any trees that Uncle Bob ran over.

- **Packing up (and storing) all equipment:** Fold and stow all tables, chairs, and tents. Stack them in one location so nothing gets left behind.

- **Dealing with decorations:** Take down all decorations, including centerpieces, streamers, balloons, and props. Take down the displays, including the family museum, any photomurals, or a podium/lectern and return them to their owners or give them to the reunion coordinator. Round up all the film and disposable cameras (if applicable) and guard them so they don't end up in the trash bin. Remove the sign for the restrooms.

- **Gathering up the toys and games:** Tidy up the kiddie area. Drain the wading pools and dry off anything wet. Deflate the inflatable items. Save all the great artwork created by the kiddies.

- **Scouring the cooking area:** Clean barbecues and cooking equipment. Clean the sink and counter tops. Disinfect everything that came into contact with food — especially raw meat. Scrub, scrub, scrub.

- **Saving leftovers:** Place the leftovers in ice chests and return anything that does not belong to the reunion coordinator to its owner. Snacking is encouraged (and makes for fewer leftovers), so share the goodies with the rest of the cleanup committee.

✔ **Taking care of the garbage:** Clean up the recycling area and get everything ready to go to the recycling center. Gather trash on the ground and around the reunion area. Bundle up the trash and the recyclables and load them in the designated vehicle. Ask a nice, helpful committee member to drop the bundles off at the recycling center.

✔ **Handling any final details:** Sweep or vacuum the floor. Make certain that nothing is left in the refrigerator or the oven. Gather up any items left behind and place them in a lost-and-found box. Give the lost-and-found box to the reunion coordinator. Lock the door and get the heck out of Dodge.

Returning rentals and loaners

Gather together all the items that need to be returned to the rental center or party store. Place them in the designated vehicles, which belong to you, your helpful committee members, or other generous helpers.

Before pulling away from the curb, take inventory. Make certain that all the rented items are going back to the store. If you forget or lose anything, you'll be charged for it.

If the rental center or party-rental store is still open when your reunion ends, return the items to the store. If the store has closed, load the items in your vehicle or a helper's vehicle and take them to a safe, secure location and return them in the morning. Make certain that you have a person poised and ready for this job.

For an additional fee, your rental center may offer a delivery and pick-up service. This service can cost anywhere from under $10 to $50, depending on the items being picked up and delivered. The smaller the load, the smaller the price. Check when making your arrangements because this service can save a tremendous amount of time and effort during the reunion.

Return all borrowed items to their owners or place them in your vehicle or a helper's vehicle to be returned the following day. Be sure to return all the borrowed items in as timely a manner as the rentals. Don't leave their owners wondering when you'll bring their stuff back — you may need to borrow it again for the next shindig.

Knockdown and Cleanup Checklist

Outside of location
_____ Directional signs
_____ Transportation back to accommodations
_____ Parking lot cleaned up
_____ Tent taken down
_____ Strong people to carry things

Entrance
_____ Welcome sign/banners removed
_____ Sign-in table taken down

Inside Reunion Area
_____ Tables and chairs cleaned
_____ Tables and chairs stacked
_____ Other seating removed
_____ Lecturn removed
_____ Microphone removed
_____ Sign to restrooms removed
_____ Dance floor removed
_____ Barbecue grills cool and clean
_____ Family tree board removed
_____ Photo mural removed
_____ Ceiling treatment re-packed
_____ Themed decor removed
_____ Lighting removed
_____ Flags removed

Guest Areas
_____ Centerpieces removed
_____ Linens stacked
_____ Condiments removed
_____ Floor swept or vacuumed
_____ Other

Kitchen Area
_____ Counters cleaned
_____ Sink cleaned
_____ Oven empty
_____ Fridge empty

Hired Help
_____ Caterer paid
_____ Disc jockey paid
_____ Bartender paid
_____ Entertainment paid
_____ Photographer paid
_____ Space rental paid

Activity Items
_____ Rented games removed
_____ Portable toilets removed
_____ Blow-up pool drained
_____ Activity table cleaned up
_____ Games/equipment put away
_____ Family memorabilia stored

Necessities
_____ Ice chests drained and cleaned
_____ Extension cords stored
_____ Duct tape removed
_____ All dishes/utensils clean/stored
_____ Hotpads/aprons cleaned
_____ Tongs/spatulas cleaned/stored
_____ Cameras/film rounded up
_____ A/V equipment removed
_____ Trash cans emptied
_____ Food wrapped and stored

Paperwork
_____ Post-reunion survey handed out
_____ Directory forms handed out
_____ Recipe forms handed out
_____ Family history forms handed out

Final Stuff
_____ Trash/recycling removed
_____ Final check for belongings
_____ Rented items being returned
_____ Door locked

Figure 10-1:
Knockdown
and Cleanup
Checklist.

Settling money matters

As the chief boss, you are also responsible for paying and sending off any hired help. They usually don't leave until you pay them. But if they participated in some of the liquid festivities, you may have to call in Cousin Bubba, the family bouncer!

Use the checklist in Figure 10-1 to make sure that you have taken care of any hired-help fees. You may also want to bring along your contracts in case any questions or disputes arise after the reunion has ended.

Determining What Worked — and What Didn't

No reunion is perfect. Unfortunately, you can't do much about bad weather, no-show vendors, or accidents. But you can do something about minor problems, such as poor catering service and unpopular food items. Thus, you need to review and evaluate the things that you *can* change in order to better plan the next reunion.

To get a better idea of what everyone enjoyed and what they didn't care for, you need to get some feedback from the gang. However, your family members may not be willing or able to communicate their opinions to you directly. The Post-Reunion Evaluation Form shown in Figure 10-2 (and included on the CD) is where the reunion attendees can express themselves openly.

Make sure that everyone at the reunion fills out this form. Hand out copies to all the reunion attendees after your thank-you speech (see the section "Speech. . .Speech: Thanking the Clan," earlier in this chapter). Place a basket on a centrally located table so folks can drop off their completed forms.

The simple rating system is based on five criteria: great, good, fair-to-middlin', so-so, and horrible. Hopefully, your guests will stick to the first two options!

Your reunion attendees can briefly explain their ratings in the lower section of the evaluation form. I also provide a space for additional ideas and suggestions.

Post-Reunion Evaluation Form					
Please help us plan the next reunion by filling out this form. Be honest!					

Name _____

Address _____

City / State / Zip / Country _____

Phone / E-mail _____

How would you rate the reunion overall:	Great	Good	Fair-to-middlin'	So-so	Horrible
How was the food?	Great	Good	Fair-to-middlin'	So-so	Horrible
How about the games and activities?	Great	Good	Fair-to-middlin'	So-so	Horrible
How do you rate the reunion planning?	Great	Good	Fair-to-middlin'	So-so	Horrible
How was the reunion site?	Great	Good	Fair-to-middlin'	So-so	Horrible
How would you feel about regular reunions?	Great	Good	Fair-to-middlin'	So-so	Horrible
How was the length of the reunion?	Great	Good	Fair-to-middlin'	So-so	Horrible

What did you like best about the reunion?

_____

_____

What did you like the least?

_____

_____

What would you like to see done differently at the next reunion?

_____

_____

_____

Additional suggestions and ideas:

_____

_____

_____

Figure 10-2:
Post-
Reunion
Evaluation
Form.

Wrapping It Up

Before leaving the reunion site, take a good look around. The site should be sparkling clean with nothing left behind. Your checklist shouldn't contain any blank spaces, and you should be able to account for all rented or borrowed equipment. Yes, you are the last to leave!

If your reunion takes place on a Saturday and if your family is faithful, get everyone together the following morning for church services. Attending church with your family is an inspiring and memorable way to end the weekend, strengthening family bonds in the process.

Chapter 11

Keeping in Touch and Gathering Feedback

*A*fter the cleanup is over and you have a chance to rest, start thinking about maintaining the lines of communication within your family. Don't let everyone distance themselves from one another all over again!

In fact, while you're basking in the reunion afterglow like a snake on a hot road, you may want to consider ways of keeping in touch with everyone so the next reunion is easier to plan. In this chapter, I explain some of the ways to keep your family close, even across the miles, until your next reunion.

Following Up with the Family

After the reunion, send follow-up letters or postcards to the reunion attendees. The purpose of the follow-up is to thank everyone for coming and for participating in the reunion activities.

The follow-up letter doesn't need to be elaborate — a simple postcard is sufficient. But if you do choose to go the letter route, enclose a copy of the group photo (see Chapter 9). Everybody loves photos!

Mailing the family to the family

An even better idea is to have postcards made of the family photo. Any photo-processing house — including the local drugstore photo lab — can order these postcards for you. The price per postcard varies depending on the number of postcards that you need. The more you order, the cheaper the cost per postcard, ranging from 25 cents each on up.

The reverse side of a photo postcard is the same as a typical postcard. The left side has a space for a handwritten note, and the right side has a space for the address and postage.

In your note, be sure to remind the stragglers to send in their family directory sheets (see Chapter 7), family group sheets (see Chapter 13), or post-reunion evaluation forms (see Chapter 10). And don't forget to add the closing remark "See you again next time!"

Unless you plan on sending out a couple hundred postcards, don't worry about writer's cramp. But if you have a large number of notes to send, you can send copies of a handwritten letter or send copies of a letter prepared on your computer.

E-mailing postcards

If everyone provides e-mail addresses on their family directory sheets, you can send electronic postcards over the Internet. You can find several Web sites that allow you to upload photos and attach messages. I recommend the following:

- **Electronic Greetings:** www.arkworld.com/pete/greetings
- **123 Greetings:** www.123greetings.com
- **Yahoo!Greetings:** http://greetings.yahoo.com

Sending out thank-you notes

Your volunteers work hard to help you plan and pull off the perfect reunion. You should not only thank them personally toward the end of the reunion, but you should also send them written thank-yous.

Be sure to write something that expresses your feelings of gratitude. Some folks may remember your kind thanks and recognition and then volunteer to help you again when the next reunion rolls around. And you're planning to organize another one, right?

Reviewing the Post-Reunion Evaluations

After you send off the thank-yous and follow-up letters, you get to review the post-reunion evaluations (see Figure 10-2 in Chapter 10 for a look at this form). These evaluations help you pinpoint the successful and not-so-great aspects of the reunion so you can better plan the next one.

The most important part of the evaluation is the overall rating. Hopefully, everyone circled *great* or *good*. But, if the reunion attendees didn't circle one of these options, the reunion probably wasn't up to snuff. Read through your evaluations to find out what you should do differently next time.

Here's a look at some of the questions on the evaluation:

✔ **How was the food?** Because most people (myself included) love to eat, the reunion food is often the one thing that your kinfolk remember most. If you hired a catering service and the food was not rated very highly, you definitely don't want to use the same caterer at your next reunion! If the food was potluck or BYO (see Chapter 5), that's a touchy issue. Perhaps you should consider ordering pizza for the next reunion.

✔ **How were the games?** Did you have enough — or too many — games or activities at the reunion? Were the games too vigorous for some attendees? Did you have enough activities for the children?

Athletic families may go for active games, such as relays, volleyball, and touch football, whereas reserved families may prefer laid-back games, such as bingo or trivia games. Sometimes, you can't decide on the activities until you see the clan in action. After you see how your family participates — or doesn't — you can plan accordingly.

✔ **How did everyone rate the reunion planning?** If everyone had a terrific time and gave the reunion high ratings, Madame Cheryl, the psychic author, sees another reunion in your future. Consider hosting a second reunion in a year or two. However, if folks rated it poorly, perhaps you should consider passing the baton to someone else for the next reunion.

✔ **Did everyone like the location?** Hopefully, the ratings indicate that the location was clean, comfortable, and easy to find. If the location garnered some so-so comments, try to isolate the problem and find a solution. For example:

• If the reunion was held outdoors, perhaps the weather had something to do with it. Consider holding the next reunion indoors.

• If the reunion took place indoors, such as in a hotel ballroom, perhaps the location was too formal for your family. If your kinfolk are relaxed types who enjoy a laid-back atmosphere, maybe a park is a better location.

✓ **What about the length of the reunion?** The length of the reunion may have been too long, not long enough, or just right. If the reunion took place over a couple days, consider shortening the next reunion.

My favorite comment is that the reunion wasn't long enough. If people had such a great time, maybe the next reunion should be longer!

✓ **What did everyone like best and least about the reunion?** Pay close attention to everyone's comments and suggestions, especially comments about what family members would do differently.

Save your reunion evaluations so you can refer to them when you begin planning the next family shindig.

Keeping in Touch with the Clan

After you familiarize and reacquaint yourself with all your cousins, aunts, uncles, nieces, nephews, and all their spouses, I'm certain that you don't want to lose touch with them again! With the proper nurturing, these relationships can last a lifetime.

Keeping in touch with everyone enables you to collect updated information on family members, such as new addresses or new additions to the family tree. In this section, I give you some ideas to keep everyone in everyone else's business — every family likes to gossip!

Starting a family newsletter

Because families are often spread out geographically over large areas, staying in touch can be difficult. But if you create a family newsletter, you can keep everyone up-to-date. Through the family newsletter, everyone can share in family triumphs.

If you're the only person working on the newsletter, keep it brief. Sending out a single-page newsletter once or twice a year is a good start.

As other family members become interested in the newsletter, ask them to volunteer. With the help of your kinfolk, the newsletter can grow considerably. If you eventually gather enough information to fill several pages, you may want to consider sending out the newsletter on a quarterly basis.

Add lots of interesting tidbits to your newsletter, such as photos or other funny items. To make your newsletter visually appealing, make copies of it on special paper. You can find decorative papers at office supply stores, stationery stores, and variety stores or drugstores.

Creating a family logo

A family logo adds a unique touch to family newsletters, postcards, Web sites, and so on. If your family has an unusual last name, you can make a logo that represents the name. For example, if your last name is Bacon, you can design a curly tailed pig with the name "Bacon" written across its side in bold letters. If your last name is Wheeler, you can create a logo shaped like a wagon wheel. For my last name, Fall, I created a logo featuring a leaf blowing in the wind, with the name "Fall" in the center, written in a pretty, wispy script.

If you can't think of an idea for a family logo, poll the rest of the family. Someone's bound to come up with a clever idea.

Building the family Web site

In Chapter 6, I list several locations on the Web where you can build a free Web site. If you decide to create a Web site for the reunion, you can save a lot of work by converting this site into an online family newsletter.

Presenting the family newsletter on the Web is efficient and cheap — no postage necessary. Plus, when you add new information, the family newsletter is updated instantaneously.

If you want help creating a family Web site, check out `www.myfamily.com`, which provides site-building tools, genealogy tips, and a surname search feature.

If you're concerned for family members who don't have Internet access, the solution is simple. Print copies of the Web site and send them by mail to folks who may not have Internet access.

The basics

Setting up your family Web site is similar to creating a family tree. The Web starts at one central location — the main page — and branches out to other pages. The main page is called a *home page*.

This home page contains *links*, usually in the form of buttons, that you click with your mouse. These links navigate you to pages of the Web site, and the pages link back to the main page (see Figure 11-1 for an example). You can make pages that feature individual family units, or you can create pages that contain information on certain subjects, such as upcoming events or family news.

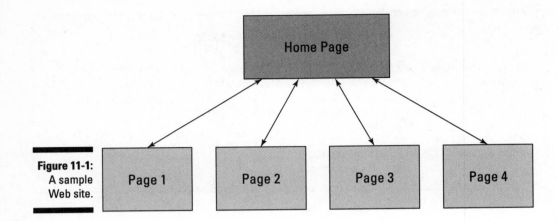

Figure 11-1:
A sample
Web site.

When creating a home page, I suggest that you include the following elements:

- ✔ **The title of the Web site:** You can invent something snazzy like "The Wheeler Family Wagon" (if your last name is Wheeler) or stick to something basic, such as "The Wilson Family Web site." Place the title at the top of the home page.

  If you create a family logo (see the sidebar "Creating a family logo," in this chapter, for more details), place it near the title.

- ✔ **A few paragraphs about the family Web site and why you created it.** Perhaps you're creating it to get ready for your next reunion or just to help family members keep in touch with each other.

- ✔ **A list of links:** Like a table of contents, this list is a directory for the linked pages, which may contain photos of the most recent reunion, a birth announcement for the newest baby, or the family's genealogy information.

- ✔ **Your e-mail address:** The visitors can contact you to update information, share stories and photos, or to suggest Web site improvements.

In the following sections, you can find a few more pointers to consider when designing your family Web site.

Artful tidbits

To make the site really sing, add family-related clip art. You can find clip-art collections on CD-ROM at software stores. Prices for these collections range from less than $15 to more than $60.

The price reflects the number of pieces of clip art available on the CD, which can range from a few hundred pieces to thousands of pieces. ***Note:*** The less you pay, the fewer clip-art images you get.

Use clip art in interesting ways. For example, you can use a baby bottle or bassinet icon to announce a new baby, a diploma to celebrate a graduation, or food or pots and pans to decorate a family-recipes page.

You can also find free clip art on the Internet. Using the search engine on your browser, type in *free clip art*. You'll find hundreds of sites featuring clip art in every subject. I suggest checking out many sites before you make selections. You may spend a good deal of time searching, but it's worth it if you don't want to pay for clip art.

Most sites provide free clip art with the intent that the end user (you) uses it only for personal sites. In most cases, free clip art should not be used on commercial sites. If you have any questions regarding the use policy, send an e-mail to the appropriate address listed on the home page.

Nifty additions

You can add lots of neat things to your Web site. Some are helpful to you, and others are simply amusing.

Include a *hit counter* if you want to keep track of how many *hits* (visitors) your site receives. You can also add a *guest book,* which registers online visitors and records their comments.

Privacy issues

Posting your family information on the Web site is all fine and dandy, but post it safely.

Never include personal information on your Web site. This includes the addresses and phone numbers of family members, their exact dates of birth, and other personal bits of information. Anyone can access this Web site — good people and bad people alike. Keep your family safe by using good sense.

For more information, check out *Building a Web Site For Dummies* by David A. and Rhonda Crowder (Hungry Minds, Inc).

Remembering family birthdays

Some people say that they hate birthdays. I like to pretend that my birthday doesn't exist and that I don't want anyone to go through any trouble just for my birthday. I don't want to realize that I'm another year older — my birthday is no different than any other day of the year.

Pshaw! The truth is, I love it when people remember my birthday. So does everybody else — no matter what they say.

If you want your family members to feel warm and fuzzy on their special days, be sure to bring a box of birthday cards (with envelopes) to the reunion and have people sign them (see Chapter 9 for more details). A couple days after the reunion — while you're still in reunion-planning mode — follow these steps so you can send the birthday cards on time:

1. **Compile all the birthdays from the family group sheets (see Chapter 13) or the directory information sheets (see Chapter 7) and add them to a master calendar.** This calendar will be your official birthday reference.

2. **Prepare the envelopes.** One the backside of each envelope, write the person's name and birthday _in pencil_ (because you need to erase it later). Prepare an envelope for everyone in the family.

Don't worry about pre-addressing the cards. Just be sure to keep contact information up-to-date because folks are mobile these days — their addresses may have changed since the reunion.

3. **Place the envelopes in the card box in order of birthdays.** Start with the January birthdays and keep adding envelopes until you get to December.

4. **Place the calendar and the box of sorted cards in a safe location.** Keep them out of harm's way, but not so out of reach that you forget where you put them (which I have done on more than one occasion).

5. **Check the calendar for birthdays at the beginning of each month.** I also suggest checking the calendar toward the end of each month so you can catch first-of-the-month birthdays as well.

6. **Pull the relevant envelopes out of the box and write the addresses on the cards.** Keeping family addresses current makes this task easy.

7. **Pop the cards in the mailbox at least one week before the birthdays.** Be sure to erase the name and birthday from the backside of each envelope before mailing.

Imagine the smile on the recipient's face when he opens his card and realizes that everyone remembered his birthday. He may even laugh when he notices that everyone at the reunion signed it — including the recipient.

TIP

Think before you type

Your family members may enjoy reading the family newsletter, but keep in mind that the amount of news that a person can absorb in one sitting is limited. Consider yearly Christmas cards — well-meaning friends and relatives sometimes write long, drawn-out letters that chronicle the events of their lives for the past year. Unfortunately, these letters can bore people to tears.

So when you're creating a family newsletter, you may want to write a short letter that reads like a shopping list rather than a bad novel. In the following list, I give you some do's and don'ts for creating a family newsletter.

Here are some do's:

✔ **Ask other family members to contribute a small story to the newsletter.** Before changing someone's wording, ask for permission to edit. If the piece is awful and needs some work, tell the person that you want to expand on the story a bit. But if the work is long-winded, tell her that space is limited and you need to shorten the material.

✔ **Include amusing stories or anecdotes in the newsletter.** If you give your family members a good laugh, they may look forward to reading the next newsletter.

✔ **Consider including a section just for kids.** Let the kids write for their section.

✔ **Have someone proof your newsletter for typos, misspelled words, or anything that sounds off-key.** Make sure that a fresh pair of eyes looks over the newsletter. Someone else may find errors that you didn't notice.

And here are some don'ts:

✔ **Don't describe everything about your family members' lives in great detail.** Instead, include the highlights.

✔ **Don't be too boastful about your own family's accomplishments.** You don't want to toot your own horn too much, either. Give everyone an equal amount of praise.

✔ **Never gossip.** Family gossip may be interesting, but you don't want to be the one to dish the dirt — leave that to the family busybody.

✔ **Don't give one side of the family more attention than another side.** Discussing one side of the family in great detail but giving little ink to the other can hurt feelings. Try to give everyone equal consideration.

✔ **Don't ignore grief.** If you find out some unpleasant information, such as a death, relate the news in a gentle way. You can include a nice memorial in your newsletter, or you can thank the family for all the wonderful cards and letters of support that the surviving family members received during the difficult time.

Chapter 12

Putting Your New Skills to Good Use

In This Chapter

▶ Realizing your reunion-planning accomplishments

▶ Branching out and helping others

▶ Bringing together old friends, roommates, or military buddies

▶ Planning other events — from weddings to food drives

*I*f you carefully follow my advice in the previous chapters of this book and then plan (and pull off) a fabulous family get-together, you may want to take on a new challenge. When it comes to planning family reunions, you can say, "Been there, done that." How about putting your skills to use in other ways?

In this chapter, I give you suggestions for taking the skills earned as a family reunion planner and applying them to other types of reunions. Now that you have these new skills, you might as well use them to their fullest!

Evaluating Your New Skills

Consider all the new things that you experienced while planning your family reunion. You organized an entire event from start to finish.

Here's a list of your accomplishments to refresh your memory.

- ✔ **You planned early and efficiently.** Giving yourself plenty of time to plan the reunion helped make it a success.

- ✔ **You organized your information.** Being organized — keeping your information in files or binders for easy reference — is one of the most important skills that any planner can have.

✔ **You thoroughly checked out potential reunion sites and determined each location's best and worst features.** Objectivity is important when choosing a reunion site.

✔ **You handled the task of working with vendors.** Managing the caterers, disc jockeys, rental companies, and/or entertainment is a major responsibility, especially with all the other factors that need to be considered when planning a reunion.

✔ **You kept the family entertained during the reunion.** The games and activities that you planned kept everyone involved and content.

✔ **You cleaned up the mess.** The rental equipment and supplies were picked up, packed up, and put back. All the trash was picked up, too.

✔ **You managed your reunion committees like a fine-tuned machine.** While designating responsibilities you were a kind and gentle "boss."

What a track record! I bet that you didn't realize that you accomplished so much while planning one event.

Planning Other Reunions or Events

Now, you can use your reunion-planning skills to organize other events. You may think that I'm crazy for even suggesting such an idea, but why not? In the next few sections, I suggest some ways that you can put your savvy skills to use again.

Putting together a military reunion

If you or your spouse served in the armed forces, consider planning a military reunion. The biggest challenge with this type of gathering is finding folks.

If you want to reacquaint yourself with your military buddies, a good place to start people searching is the Internet, where you can find many clubs set up specifically for veterans of the military. Using your favorite search engine, type in your branch of the service, along with the keyword *clubs,* and see what comes up. You may want to try searching for specific regiments, ships, or fleets, too.

Yahoo! has a special section for military clubs. Go to http://clubs.yahoo.com and click the links to browse the lists of clubs. You can also create a new club from this site. Sites exist for virtually every branch of the service for every country. You can also find local clubs and information by checking with your local veterans' center.

After finding the club of your choice, sign up for its newsletter and join in the camaraderie. After you get to know the club members, suggest having a reunion and see what types of responses you get. You may be pleasantly surprised!

Rounding up folks from your youth

Feel like reliving your glory days? Plan a high school or college reunion!

Although most alumni groups plan events for 10- and 20-year reunions, few groups plan events for anything beyond that. If your 30-, 40-, or 50-year reunion is just around the corner and no one is planning a get-together, take charge!

To find your old pals, call your school and ask whether someone is organizing a reunion for your graduating class. If you find out that no one is handling it, this is your call to action.

To find fellow alumni, ask the school for leads or try the following Web sites:

- Classmates.com
- Alumni.net

These sites feature lists of alumni organized by country, state, and city. Search for your school and your year of graduation and see who has signed up. Start sending e-mails and build a list of potential reunion attendees.

Be aware, however, that these sites require you to pay a membership fee to fully utilize the site and gain access to alumni e-mail addresses. You can, however, post your name and year of graduation to the list for free and use the Web site's message boards to communicate with fellow alumni. You can then request e-mail addresses directly from other alumni who post to the message boards.

Be sure to choose an interesting theme for your class reunion! You can use any of the ideas from Chapter 5 or create other themes based on your school's name, mascot, or the time period in which you graduated. A sock hop, disco dance or prom theme would be really neat!

Gathering your fraters and sorors

If you were a member of a fraternity or sorority in college, gather your old *fraters* (brothers) and *sorors* (sisters) for a reunion. You can make this reunion a blast from the past, complete with togas and all the other trappings that you enjoyed as a member of the Greek system. If you prefer a calm atmosphere, you can organize a breakfast near the university.

Contact your university and ask if your alumni group can take a tour of the sorority (or frat) house and meet with current members. This is a nice way to stay active in your fraternity or sorority.

Reuniting members of a club or organization

People are constantly coming and going at various clubs and organizations, such as Kiwanis, Elks and Moose, Rotary, and the Masons. But with a little planning, these folks can become like family or alumni to you.

Consider planning a reunion for past and present club members. A reunion allows the members not only to keep in touch but also to brainstorm about future community service projects.

Pondering another family reunion

Don't laugh! The earlier you begin planning the next family reunion, the smoother everything will go. Advanced planning is the key. In fact, a year is best.

Form the next group of committees and get started. Replace the do-nothing committee members from the previous reunion with folks who expressed an interest in helping out with the next reunion.

Going beyond Reunions: Other Neat Ways to Use Your Skills

You can use your new skills for other type of gatherings, too! The parties need not be huge — you can use your expertise for smaller get-togethers, such as those meant to bring together your community or your close friends.

Assembling a block party

Gather your neighbors together for a block party. You can organize the party around a holiday, such as Independence Day, Memorial Day, Mother's Day, or Labor Day. Or you can just pick any day and make it a day for a party! Pick a site in your neighborhood that can accommodate everyone, such as a park, community center, pool, schoolyard, or even the end of a cul-de-sac (be sure to get the approval of the cul-de-sac occupants before blocking off access with tables and chairs). Send out notices in the form of an invitation or flyer to every neighbor. In the notice, ask your neighbors to bring barbecues, chairs and picnic tables, and their own plates and utensils. Set up a potluck table and have a terrific time.

Be aware, however, that opening anyone else's mailbox is against the law. If you're going to hand deliver an invitation or flyer, leave it at the front door.

In lieu of a holiday event, plan a *work party* and clean up the neighborhood. Have the participants bring rakes, shovels, and work gloves for the neighborhood beautification project. Also have them bring food items and lawn chairs so everyone can share in a potluck supper afterwards. A work party is a terrific way to get to know your neighbors — old and new.

If your neighborhood has an association, let them know that you want to organize a community event. They'll be grateful!

You need to plan this type of party only a month or so in advance. Be sure to give people enough time so they can plan to attend, but not so much time that they forget about the event.

Organizing a community or charitable event

If your community has a planning committee for special events, join the crew and pitch in! If an event isn't planned for your community, jump-start the process by making suggestions. For example:

- **Plan a pancake breakfast or CPR class at the local fire station.** The proceeds can go toward purchasing emergency equipment, or they can go to needy families in your community.

- **Plan a food drive.** In my community, a *walk-and-knock* food drive is planned each fall. The participants fill paper grocery sacks with nonperishable food items and other necessities (such as soap, toothpaste, and diapers) and set them on their front porches. Then the local scouts and club members drive through each neighborhood and pick up the sacks. The gathered items are donated to the local food banks and homeless shelters. You can organize the same sort of event in your community.

Service projects are a great way to use your planning skills, no matter how large or small your community. Helping your neighbors is also a terrific way to expand your circle of friends and get to know others in your area.

Planning your niece's wedding

A wedding is sort of like a family reunion, with the addition of a bride and a groom, a white dress, a mile-high cake, and flowers.

Leave the planning for large-scale weddings to the experts, but do consider planning small intimate weddings. As with the family reunion, advanced planning is the key, but you also need to be keenly aware of the budget. For more help with wedding planning, you can consult *Wedding Kit For Dummies* by Marcy Blum and Laura Fisher Kaiser (Hungry Minds, Inc.). By combining what you've gleaned from this book and what you'll get from that one, you'll have it made!

Holding a religious event

Consider using your reunion-planning skills to help your church, temple, or synagogue. You can plan a get-together for members or help with charitable events sponsored by your faith. You can also help out with special ceremonies, such as First Communions, Confirmations, Bar and Bat Mitzvahs, and so on.

Throwing a birthday bash

We eventually reach certain milestones in our lives that are causes for celebrations. (Unfortunately, some of us have celebrated more milestones than others.) Now that you have pondered the effects of gravity on your body and adjusted your reading glasses with each passing year, here are a few options:

- **Sweet sixteen:** This is the first big milestone in a young person's life. This teen is now old enough to drive, and you're thinking of staying off the streets for good. Nonetheless, celebrate the occasion with a party.

- **Twenty-one and finally legal:** With the flick of an ID, she can now enter buildings marked "No minors allowed." Instead of partying at a bar, throw a safe party — at home.

- **The big 5-0:** Hang a disco ball and hire a disc jockey — it's going to be a wild night! You're getting better (not older), and you get to prove it. If the room spins later when you lie down in bed, keep one foot on the floor.

- **The golden years:** Hosting a party for a family member who is turning 75 or older is a great excuse to hold a family reunion! Go to the front of the book and start all over again.

Hosting a graduation party

Honor your high-school or college grad with a party. Gather family and friends to help the graduate celebrate his or her big accomplishment. You can organize any type of event, such as a breakfast or brunch, a luncheon, a dinner, or (for older graduates) a cocktail party.

Part V
From Branches to Roots: Researching the Family Tree

The 5th Wave   By Rich Tennant

"Hold your horses. It takes time to locate the ancestors for someone of your background."

In this part . . .

*L*ike peanut butter and jelly, a family reunion and genealogical research make a great pair. Because a good many branches of your family tree are at the reunion, it's a great time to start your family history research. This part contains the basic information that you need to get started. In Chapter 13, I guide you through the process of filling our family group sheets and pedigree charts (family trees). Chapter 14 helps you locate research materials, such as documents and photographs. In Chapter 15, I give you various methods of keeping track of your research and correspondence, and in Chapter 16, you can get a quick overview of how to use your computer to help in your genealogical research.

Chapter 13

Getting into Genealogy

f you're planning a family reunion, you likely have an interest in *genealogy* (the study of family history or descent). Perhaps you've wondered where Aunt Martha gets her red hair or why Tommy — your 15-year-old nephew — is tall enough to play professional basketball. Or maybe you want to know about your family's medical history, or you're simply curious about your ancestors.

To start growing your *family tree* (a genealogical chart showing the relationship of ancestors and descendants in a family), you simply record facts from your personal memories and from asking your grandparents, parents, aunts, and uncles about their memories.

In this chapter, I give you advice on gathering, recording, and organizing your information so you can begin your genealogical research. (After you lay the groundwork for your family history, you can check out Chapters 15 and 16 for tips on digging deeper into your family roots.)

Starting with Yourself

The easiest way to begin your building your family tree is to write down information about the person you know best — yourself. This material doesn't need to be lengthy or complete — even the smallest seeds can turn into grand trees. You can always fill in missing information later.

Just write about your life. Follow these steps to get started:

1. **Jot down some information about your birth, including the date and location.** Make note of the county and the country, if you were born outside the United States.

2. **List the full names of your parents.** Be sure to list your mother's maiden name, not her married name.

3. **Note information about your christening or baptism (if applicable).** Give the date and location of these events, if possible.

4. **Explain some of the seemingly mundane details of your youth.** For example:

   • The names and locations of your primary and intermediate schools

   • Your high school and college graduation dates

   • Your former addresses (It may not seem possible now, but someday your descendents will be curious about you and find all this stuff terribly interesting — really!)

5. **Write down all your wedding information, including the date and location (including county and country) of your ceremony, if you're married.** Also be sure to note the names of the witnesses and the person who officiated the ceremony.

6. **Record the births of all your children, providing the same information that you did for yourself, including place of birth and christening information.** Although it may be painful, don't forget to include the names and birth dates of deceased children — they are a part of your life, too. If your children are grown, married, and have children of their own, include this information as well.

7. **Write down your interests and hobbies, your occupation(s), and some physical characteristics, such as hair and eye color.** Although this information isn't necessarily genealogical, you may later discover that other relatives have similar traits.

If you can't remember or locate dates or other important pieces of information, write down what you do know and fill in the rest of the information later. You can always ask your mother or father or find the missing information in personal documents that you may have in your possession, such as your ancestor's birth certificate.

You likely also want to include health information. This issue is very important, because many illnesses are hereditary in nature. It's always good to know if your family is susceptible to certain problems, so be sure to pass the information along to the younger generations so they can be aware of hereditary issues that can affect them or their children.

After you get your own basic information written down, repeat the process for each of your parents. Be sure to include their full names, dates and places of birth, and when and where they got married. Also include their hobbies and interests, and anything else that you deem worthy of recording for posterity.

Next, go through the process for your *maternal grandparents* (your mom's parents) and for your *paternal grandparents* (your dad's parents). Ask your family members to help you fill in any missing information.

Diggin' in the Dust

After you write down information about your immediate family, you can start compiling material about your ancestors. This task isn't always easy. In fact, you'll likely need to dig for information in dusty old records and documents that you or another family member may have tucked away somewhere in the house.

Here's my suggested plan of attack for getting started:

1. **Pull out all the family memorabilia that's lying around the house.** This includes old Bibles, books, documents such as wills or insurance policies, correspondence such as letters and postcards, photos, journals, and anything else that may be stuffed into boxes in the attic or under piles of paperclips in desk and file drawers.

2. **Contact your immediate family members and ask them what pieces of memorabilia they have and if you can borrow it.** Your family members will probably be more than happy to assist you with your research. Be sure to tell them that you will return the original materials to them as soon as you make copies — usually within a month. Some family members may just give you the stuff to keep!

3. **Use the Research Source Log shown in Figure 13-1 (and included on the CD) to keep track of the items that you find in your house as well as the ones that you borrow from family members.** This way, if you ever need to borrow an item again, you know who has it.

4. **Pile everything on the kitchen table and then read through it and take notes.** Old Bibles may contain the dates of birth and death for members of an entire family. Documents and correspondence may contain information that can lead you to a family member's final whereabouts, which in turn can lead you to information about other relatives — look at the postmark or the date of the item for a clue.

5. **Turn over old photos to see if anything is recorded on the back.** Have copies made of the fragile originals before doing anything else with them. Be sure to record any information on the copy that was on the

back of the original. Be sure to promptly return borrowed items to their owners after making your copies. And if items have been given to you, make copies of these items and store the original in a safe, dry location, such as a safe or bank vault.

Research Source Log		
Date found	Description of item	In whose possession?

Sources to consider: Family Bibles, old postcards and letters, journals and diaries, deeds, photographs, inscriptions or dedications in old books, wills and testaments, engraved inscriptions on jewelry and watches, old phone books and city directories, school photos and yearbooks, and so forth.

Figure 13-1:
Research
Source Log.

Finding treasures in the family Bible

Family Bibles were produced abundantly during the 18th and 19th centuries and were an international success. Virtually every family has one of these huge tomes in their parlor.

These large-size volumes included pages in either the front or back to record family events such as births, christenings, marriages, and deaths. However, the material recorded in these Bibles may have been penned well after the

events took place, so I suggest backing up any family information found within them with primary documentation, such as birth, marriage, and death records (see Chapter 15 for more details).

Because these Bibles are elaborate and contain dates of family events, they're often passed down through the generations. The Bibles became family heirlooms!

One Is Not the Loneliest Number — In This Case, at Least

When you have some basic material gathered in the form of your family notes, assorted documents and photos, it's time to begin compiling your genealogy.

Because you start your genealogical research with yourself, you're number one on your family tree. (How nice to find out that after all these years, you're number one at something, right?) To complete the tree, assign the rest of your relatives and ancestors a number, based on a system known as *ahnentafel,* a German word meaning "ancestor" (ahnen) and "table" (tafel).

Using the ahnentafel system in your research helps you keep track of the entire clan from a numerical perspective. For example, you assign each male ancestor an even number, starting with 2. Likewise, you assign each female ancestor an odd number, starting with 3. All you need to remember about the numbering system is that the boys are even-numbered and the girls are odd-numbered. It's not rocket science — merely basic math.

Figure 13-2 shows you an example of the *ahnentafel* numbering system. You can find a blank version of this diagram on the CD. Feel free to print out a copy and fill in your own information.

Writing to the Relatives

Eventually, you will exhaust the supply of information flowing from your *immediate family* (the first generation surrounding you, including your parents, your siblings, and your children). When this happens, you have to widen your circle of knowledge by writing to other family members, also known as your *extended family* (people who are related to you by blood, but are not in your immediate family). This task can be difficult for beginning family historians because family members sometimes ignore requests for information. So, I give you my best advice: Gather your relatives' addresses and get ready to beg.

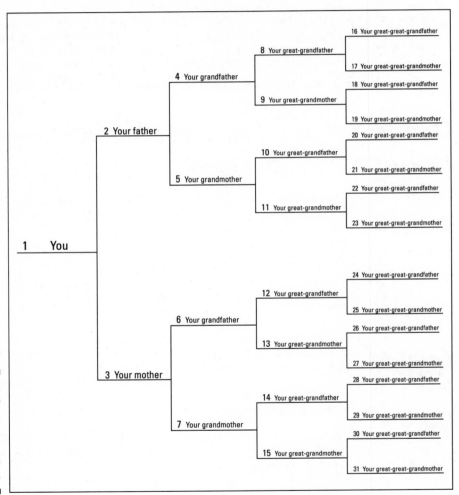

Figure 13-2:
Basic family tree showing the *ahnentafel* numbering system.

The biggest mistake a beginning genealogist can make when approaching family members for information is to ask for too much information at one time. Don't send huge packets of blank family group sheets and pedigree charts (shown later in this chapter). Also keep in mind that because the information you want is personal, some family members may not share it willingly if they barely know you — and especially if they've never met you.

Instead, draft basic short letters asking folks for specific information on common ancestors. For instance, if you need to find out your Great-grandpa Frank's place of birth, ask a relative who is a direct descendent of his. You can also safely request that your relative include any other information that she has on Great-grandpa Frank, such as the names of his siblings or parents. In fact, you may want to ask your family member to write a few words recalling a special memory that she has of a common ancestor.

Starting with a simple request often opens the floodgates to more information. Be patient and persistent. And don't forget that you may have to try a few times before you get replies from some family members.

Because you'll likely be sending out a lot of letters, you need to organize your information. To keep track of whom you write to and who replies, you can use the Correspondence Log on the CD. (See Figure 13-3 for an example.) This log allows you to note whom you send letters to, whether or not you receive a reply, and what additional material your relative shares with you.

After you open the lines of communication and begin corresponding with your kinfolk, you may want to ask them if they want to participate in the family research project by providing information about themselves and their immediate family. Don't harp on the issue if they're not interested, but asking them is certainly worth a try, especially if they're receptive to your original letters!

Managing Your Information

After you write down all the information that you can remember or track down, you need to begin transferring your material to genealogical data sheets or to a family-history computer program. I include a ready-to-use family history program on the CD that comes with this book, called Brother's Keeper. See the CD Appendix for technical information regarding this program.

If you don't use the program, you can use the following tools to help manage your genealogical information:

- **Family Group Sheets (or FGS):** Enter all the data you can in the fields indicated on the Family Group Sheet (see Figure 13-4). You use one FGS for each *family unit* (which consists of the husband, wife, and children). If an ancestor was married more than once, provide a separate FGS for each marriage.

✔ **Individual Records:** Whereas the FGS records all the *official* information about a family unit, the Individual Record (see Figure 13-5) lists the tidbits of personal information that you collect about each person in your family.

For each family member, use the Individual Record form to list details and events, such as the following:

- **Baptism, christening, confirmation, or other church ceremonies:** Include the name and address of the church as well as the names of the officiating clergy and the witnesses.

- **Bar or Bat Mitzvah:** Give the names of the officiating rabbi and the witnesses. Note the location of the synagogue as well.

- **Schools attended:** Be sure to jot down commencement dates and degrees received.

- **Military information:** Include such information as branch of service, rank, induction, and discharge dates, if applicable.

- **Special achievements or commendations:** Note such things as community service awards or job promotions.

- **Hobbies and interests:** Give a quick summary of what the person enjoyed doing in his or her free time.

- **Important medical information:** Write down details about health-related issues, such as dates of injury or diagnosis, names of diseases, surgeries, the nature of the surgery (what was wrong with the patient), and the hospital where the procedures were performed

- **Addresses of past and present residences:** Include all residences — apartments and homes and the date your ancestor lived there. Better yet, take a photo of each residence and add it to the family history. It's always fun to see photos of old residences!

- **Burial information:** List the date of burial, the address of the cemetery and include a map (ask for one from the cemetery office or caretaker) or brief explanation of where the headstone is located within the cemetery.

- **Emigration information (if applicable):** Note specifics such as the date your ancestor arrived in the country and get copies of naturalization papers or passports, if possible.

Not everything you record on the Individual Record will be accompanied by a date, such as hobbies and medical information. It's perfectly okay to leave the date area blank. However, do record the source — the person who gave you the information — so that you can check back with them if necessary.

✔ **Pedigree Chart:** Put your ancestor's basic information, such as name, date of birth, and date of death, in the Pedigree Chart (see Figure 13-6 for an example). A *pedigree chart,* which provides a visual layout of lineage, is often referred to as a *family tree* because of its branching nature. On the CD, you can find a blank family tree that you can print and use for your research.

Correspondence Log			
Date	Name and address	Replied	Material rec'd

Figure 13-3: Correspondence Log.

Family Group Sheet

Husband: _____ ahnentafel #

Born: in:
Married: in:
Died: in:
Father:
Mother:

Wife: _____

Born: in:
Died: in:
Father:
Mother:

Children:

1 Name: M or F
   Born: in:
   Married: in:
   Died: in:
   Spouses:

2 Name: M or F
   Born: in:
   Married: in:
   Died: in:
   Spouses:

3 Name: M or F
   Born: in:
   Married: in:
   Died: in:
   Spouses:

4 Name: M or F
   Born: in:
   Married: in:
   Died: in:
   Spouses:

5 Name: M or F
   Born: in:
   Married: in:
   Died: in:
   Spouses:

6 Name: M or F
   Born: in:
   Married: in:
   Died: in:
   Spouses:

Sources and notes:

Figure 13-4:
A sample of
a Family
Group Sheet
(FGS).

	Individual Record	
For: _____		Ahnentafel number: _____

Date	Description of comment	Source

Figure 13-5:
A sample
of an
Individual
Record.

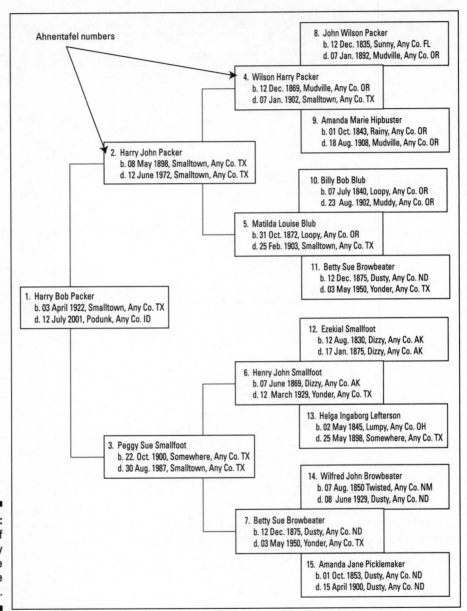

Ahnentafel numbers

8. John Wilson Packer
b. 12 Dec. 1835, Sunny, Any Co. FL
d. 07 Jan. 1892, Mudville, Any Co. OR

4. Wilson Harry Packer
b. 12 Dec. 1869, Mudville, Any Co. OR
d. 07 Jan. 1902, Smalltown, Any Co. TX

9. Amanda Marie Hipbuster
b. 01 Oct. 1843, Rainy, Any Co. OR
d. 18 Aug. 1908, Mudville, Any Co. OR

2. Harry John Packer
b. 08 May 1898, Smalltown, Any Co. TX
d. 12 June 1972, Smalltown, Any Co. TX

10. Billy Bob Blub
b. 07 July 1840, Loopy, Any Co. OR
d. 23 Aug. 1902, Muddy, Any Co. OR

5. Matilda Louise Blub
b. 31 Oct. 1872, Loopy, Any Co. OR
d. 25 Feb. 1903, Smalltown, Any Co. TX

11. Betty Sue Browbeater
b. 12 Dec. 1875, Dusty, Any Co. ND
d. 03 May 1950, Yonder, Any Co. TX

1. Harry Bob Packer
b. 03 April 1922, Smalltown, Any Co. TX
d. 12 July 2001, Podunk, Any Co. ID

12. Ezekial Smallfoot
b. 12 Aug. 1830, Dizzy, Any Co. AK
d. 17 Jan. 1875, Dizzy, Any Co. AK

6. Henry John Smallfoot
b. 07 June 1869, Dizzy, Any Co. AK
d. 12 March 1929, Yonder, Any Co. TX

13. Helga Ingaborg Lefterson
b. 02 May 1845, Lumpy, Any Co. OH
d. 25 May 1898, Somewhere, Any Co. TX

3. Peggy Sue Smallfoot
b. 22. Oct. 1900, Somewhere, Any Co. TX
d. 30 Aug. 1987, Smalltown, Any Co. TX

14. Wilfred John Browbeater
b. 07 Aug. 1850 Twisted, Any Co. NM
d. 08 June 1929, Dusty, Any Co. ND

7. Betty Sue Browbeater
b. 12 Dec. 1875, Dusty, Any Co. ND
d. 03 May 1950, Yonder, Any Co. TX

15. Amanda Jane Picklemaker
b. 01 Oct. 1853, Dusty, Any Co. ND
d. 15 April 1900, Dusty, Any Co. ND

Figure 13-6:
A sample of
a Family
Tree
(pedigree
chart).

Organizing Your Research

If you follow my advice in the previous sections in this chapter, you've been filling out forms, asking relatives for information, and tracking down memorabilia. In fact, you're probably starting to generate a lot of paperwork. So, to keep everything straight, you need to get organized.

Get yourself a big three-ring binder, a bunch of eight-tabbed notebook dividers, some clear pockets for photos and documents, and get ready to organize the whole wad. Organizing this material takes time, but it makes a great evening-in-front-of-the-tube project. Besides, if you follow these easy steps, you can get organized in a jiffy:

1. **Make a tab for yourself and for each male in your family tree and attach it to the divider.** For example, the first tab should read, *#1 (your name).* The successive tabs should read, *#2 (your father's name), #4 (your grandfather's name), #6 (your great-grandfather's name),* and so on. Keep adding and naming tabs until you have a tab for every male in your family. (For more on the numbering system in your family tree, see the section "One Is Not the Loneliest Number — In This Case, at Least," earlier in the chapter.)

Only males get to be included on the tabbed dividers because they are most often the heads of household. I realize that women are sometimes the heads of the household, but even if the woman has a child, the father of the child is still considered the head of household (even if the birth is legitimate). It's just a quirk of genealogical research.

Figure 13-7 gives an example of the tab system based on the fictional family tree shown in Figure 13-6. Except for the names, your tabs should look identical to the sample.

2. **Hole-punch your forms and place them in the binder behind the tab for each family group.** Slide copies of family photos and other documents into the protective sleeves to keep them safe.

Before slipping photos and documents into your family binder, be sure to make copies. Never store originals in your working binder — they can be easily lost while you tote your binder around to relatives' houses, the library, and the family reunion. Store the originals in a secure location, such as a safe deposit box or a fireproof home safe.

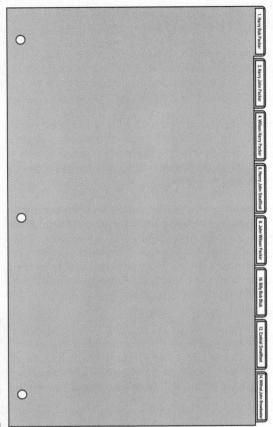

Figure 13-7:
Sample
tabbed
dividers for
the family
binder.

Makin' It Last

An old saying has been floating around the genealogical community for years. No one knows who started it, but it certainly makes sense: "Ink fades and paper deteriorates at a rate inversely proportional to the value of the data recorded." What this saying basically means is that the more important the information, the greater chance you have of losing it. This is usually due to time and deterioration. Acids and chemicals in paper and ink cause rapid destruction of paper materials.

So, you have to be sure to save your data for posterity. I suggest two ways to accomplish this task:

✔ **Print your materials on acid-free paper.** Doing so ensures that your materials don't yellow and deteriorate over time due to the naturally occurring acids and chemicals in the paper. Acid-free paper is available at most stationery stores and nearly every craft-supply store.

✔ **Save your files on a computer disk as a backup file.** You can save your computer files easily by following the instructions that accompanied your family history software. Be sure to resave all information to your backup disk every time you make a change in your records.

Keeping Track of Family Treasures

After a while, you may discover that you're accumulating a tremendous amount of family memorabilia as a result of genealogical research. To help you keep track of it, I include a Family Memorabilia Inventory Sheet on the CD. See Figure 13-8 for an example. This form differs from the Research Source Log earlier in this chapter because you use this form to record and catalog the items you get to keep, not simply those you borrow and return to their owners.

Add items to this form as soon as you get them. Items that have been borrowed need to be returned to their owners, but items that have been given to you to keep, need to be catalogued and stored. Eventually these items will be passed along to the next generation, and having them catalogued makes it easier for the recipient to know what exactly they have been given.

When storing your treasures, be sure to wrap them in acid-free tissue. Chemicals and acids from typical tissue can transfer to your precious items and cause them to deteriorate more quickly. Be sure to store all memorabilia in a clean, dry location.

Now that you have all the memorabilia inventoried and properly stored, you can share it at a moment's notice with other family members. Be sure to bring nifty family treasures, such as Bibles and photo albums to the reunion!

Family Memorabilia Inventory Sheet			
Date rec'd	Description of item	Condition	Where stored

Figure 13-8:
Family
Memorabilia
Inventory
Sheet.

Chapter 14

Exploring a World Full of Records

Y ou may be surprised to find out how much of your family history is public record. Fortunately, the information isn't typically obtainable by just anyone.

In this chapter, I tell you about the different types of family-history records and how to get your hands on them. Some of the records are easy to track down, whereas others can be a bit more elusive. Hang in there!

Getting Started: Visiting Libraries and Archives

Libraries and archives contain a wealth of genealogical information from all over the world. Both are organized by a catalog system.

You can find the library's genealogy collection in the reference section. If you can't locate it, track down a librarian — he or she will be glad to help. What you find may be an eye-opener about your family's history!

Archives may be either public or private and may contain government materials such as military records and census records. There are also church archives that are responsible for storing documents and materials of a religious nature. Not all materials are available or worthwhile to genealogical researchers. You can find archives of interest by checking with local sources, such as genealogical societies, local libraries, and church offices.

Canvassing the community libraries

If your family is a local one (in other words, having lived in the same area for multiple generations), you are indeed lucky. Your community libraries house valuable sources of information, such as old address and business directories, newspapers, maps, land records, census and county information, published family histories, photographs, and other historical data.

But even if your ancestors were not the town founders, you can still find plenty of terrific information through — if not in — your local library, as I explain in the next few sections.

Newspapers and periodicals

Libraries keep copies of old newspapers on *microfiche* (also known as fiche) and *microfilm*. Fiche are small sheets of film containing reduced photographs of printed documents that you can view one page at a time with a special viewer. Similarly, microfilms are wound on reels and viewed with a machine that resembles an old movie projector.

Newspapers on fiche or film can contain lots of helpful information for family historians. If you're willing to spend the time looking through the materials, you can find marriage and birth announcements and obituaries. You may also find interesting articles about family members. Be certain to bring these articles to your next reunion and share the stories with the clan.

You need to keep the following things in mind when working with microfiche and microfilm:

- ✔ The fiche and film are indexed by date, so you need to know an approximate date on which to begin your hunt.

- ✔ You can make a copy of a page by placing the film on a special machine and taking a picture of it. This service typically costs around 50 cents to one dollar per copy, depending on the library's fee schedule.

- ✔ You must view fiche and film at the library — you can't take these sources home with you.

When fiche cause you fits . . .

Viewing fiche and film is hard on the eyes, and moving rolls of film across a projector can cause tummy discomfort similar to motion sickness. This happens to me all the time! If you are prone to motion sickness, eat a light meal or snack before viewing the film and take frequent breaks. If you still find yourself getting queasy, take an over-the-counter motion sickness medication at least a half-hour before going through the film.

Old phone and business directories

Old city directories can be very good places to search for your kin. These directories were created long before the invention of the telephone and were printed for most cities beginning around 1850. Nowadays, they're just referred to as the White and Yellow Pages.

You can find these old directories beneficial to your research in several ways:

- ✔ **They contain addresses that can help you figure out the ward or census district where your family members resided.** Knowing this information can save you endless hours of work by preventing you from having to search every district in an area.

- ✔ **They usually list the occupation of the head of the household.** Finding a woman listed as the head of the household gives you a clue about when her husband passed away, because directories were often published annually or biannually. Knowing the occupation of the head of the household can be an interesting addition to the family story. For example, a boot clicker (the person who cuts boot leather with a knife) no longer exists in this age of technology. But, adding details of the occupation and its place in your history adds interesting information to the family saga!

- ✔ **They also include reverse directories.** Indexed by the street name or street number (rather than by the name of the head of household), the reverse directory can help you determine whether family members with different last names were living at one address. For example, you can find out if your great-grandmother Ella Jones's unmarried sister, Mary Smith, was living with her. Mary would have used her maiden name, which would be noted in the reverse directory.

If your family members aren't listed in the directories, don't despair. Often, entire neighborhoods, especially working-class or ethnic communities, were left out of the directories, as were people residing in boarding houses or those staying in temporary residences.

Published family histories

Libraries often contain published family histories indexed by name. These sources get to the library in a couple ways:

- ✔ **If your family is a founder of your community, a local historian or the historical society may have compiled and donated a family history.** These histories can save you a tremendous amount of research time — someone else has already done much of the work. Be sure to look over the material carefully.

- ✔ **Patrons who have spent years researching their family histories often donate their family files to libraries.** Patrons typically want to make their findings available to other folks who want to research the same surnames or family lines.

Beware of offers for published family histories that suddenly appear in your mailbox! These sources are usually no more than directories listing families that have your same surname and live all over the United States. They're expensive and won't do you much good.

Interlibrary loans

If your local library doesn't have the information you need for your research, you can often request it from another library through an *interlibrary loan.* This program allows libraries to borrow material from one another for a short period of time — usually a few weeks — so you can view the material and search for ancestral clues.

Making sense of Soundex

The Soundex (which keeps track of census data) is a coded surname index that is arranged *phonetically* — by the way a word sounds — rather than alphabetically. The Soundex system enables you to find a surname even though it may have been recorded under various spellings. Surnames that sound the same, like Myers and Meyers, have the same code and are filed together.

When assigning a Soundex code, the first letter of the last name stays as is. Double letters are treated as one letter, and vowels as well as W, Y, and H are disregarded completely. The consonants are given a numerical code, as follows:

- ✔ 1 is used for B, F, P, and V
- ✔ 2 is used for C, G, J, K, Q, S, X, and Z
- ✔ 3 is used for D and T
- ✔ 4 is used only for L
- ✔ 5 is used for M and N
- ✔ 6 is used only for R

Take my last name, for example: Fall is assigned the same code as the names Fall, Fahl, Foll, and Fahle, based on the letters F and L. Therefore, Fall, Fahl, Foll, and Fahle all use the letter F with the number 4. Short names, such as Fall, that

have only one or two numbers in the code need to be brought up to one consonant with three numbers by placing a zero (0) on the end. This makes the Soundex code for Fall F400.

A few more Soundex quirks to remember: Mc and Mac are not used in Soundex coding, and if your name begins with Van, Von, Le, De, D' or Dela, search the Soundex system both with and without these prefixes, just in case. It may or may not be listed using these prefixes.

This system sounds weird and even a little complicated, but the Soundex is actually an easy system to use. And given the variations in surname spellings or the misspellings that occur during census reviews, the Soundex is a blessing for researchers.

If you have trouble figuring out your surname Soundex code, here are a couple sites on the Internet that can help you: **(Note:** The first site can convert any name into a soundex code automatically.)

- ✔ **Surname to Soundex Code:** rootsweb. com/cgi-bin/soundexconverter
- ✔ **Soundex Machine:** www.nara.gov/ genealogy/soundex/soundex.html

You often have to use interlibrary loan materials at your local library — you can't check them out and take them home with you. This is especially true for reference materials, such as directories and published family histories. Check with your librarian if you're in doubt.

Analyzing the archives

Libraries generally collect books and other published items, whereas an *archives* contains the official records of an organization or the private papers of an individual or family. You can usually find a comprehensive catalog listing all the holdings of an archives at your local library.

You can also use the National Archives to search for clues to your ancestors. You can find information about these archives at `www.nara.gov` or by visiting a National Archive in person.

Archives contain tons of records, but not all of them are available to the average researcher due to innumerable laws and restrictions. Here's a rundown of the records that are available:

- ✔ **Census records:** Provides census data for the years 1880, 1900, 1910, and 1929. This data is indexed by last name using the *Soundex system,* which I discuss in greater detail in the sidebar "Making sense of Soundex," in this chapter.

- ✔ **Federal slave-trade documents:** Includes Freedmen's Bureau records and African American military records.

- ✔ **Congressional records:** Provides information about private claims and legislation. If your ancestors squared off with the government over land issues, this is where to find that information. It adds an interesting historical touch to your family history

- ✔ **Court records from various states:** These are only helpful if your ancestors sued or were sued by someone or had some other run-in with the courts. Again, this can add some interesting information to the family history.

- ✔ **Immigration and naturalization records:** Documents the granting of United States citizenship through judicial proceedings and gives you insight concerning ships' records and passenger arrivals.

- ✔ **Holocaust records:** The National Archives contain copies of prisoner lists from concentration camps and other documents that are of interest to those with a holocaust connection. This material can add a thoughtful, poignant touch to your family history data.

✔ **Maritime and war records:** Includes material from the War of 1812, the Mexican-American War, the Civil War (both Union and Confederate), the Spanish-American War, the Boxer Rebellion, World Wars I and II, and the Korean and Vietnam Wars.

✔ **Native American records:** Shows Indian bounty land records and tribe-specific information.

You can visit National Archives in the following states: Alaska, Arkansas, California, Colorado, District of Columbia, Georgia, Illinois, Iowa, Kansas, Maryland, Massachusetts, Michigan, Missouri, New York, Ohio, Pennsylvania, Texas, and Washington state.

Going Further: Finding More Sources of Records

You can find many more sources of information about genealogical research in addition to the materials that you find at the library or the archives. Because I can't possibly cover all the sources available to you, the information in the next few sections is meant only to whet your appetite.

The Family History Center

The *Church of Jesus Christ of Latter Day Saints* (LDS) is home to the *Family History Center* (FHC). This center is a genealogist's dream library because it contains books, records, fiche, and films specifically for genealogical research. The FHC is staffed by friendly and knowledgeable folks with passions for genealogy. These folks may prove to be your best allies in your research.

Family History Centers are conveniently located worldwide. You can find one by calling your local LDS church or by looking up *Family History Center* in the telephone directory.

Family History Centers contain the following databases that you can use:

✔ **International Genealogical Index (IGI):** This is a list of millions of individuals already in records submitted or collected by LDS members and nonmembers. Searchable by surname.

✔ **Ancestral File:** This database contains millions of names available in family group sheets and pedigree charts (see Chapter 13 for examples and explanations of these items).

✔ **Family History Library Catalog:** This catalog contains a list of all the books and publications available through the LDS libraries, including published genealogies.

The Family History Center also offers a staggering collection of microfilm records. By paying a small fee, which covers the cost of mailing the films to the local FHC library, you can view records from every country on the planet. You can find church records, birth and death records, baptismal records, military records, war records, and so on.

You can also access many of the LDS databases online by visiting the FamilySearch Web site at `www1.familysearch.org`.

Historical societies and local museums

Many states (and some individual towns or cities) have an historical society or museum that documents the origins and growth of the community. These places often contain local family histories, old maps, directories, land and court records, census records, and other useful research tools specific to your location. In fact, if your family is a local one, check the museum or historical society first. You may find quite a bit of useful information.

Cemeteries: Marble orchards not to be taken for granite

If you know the town or parish your family members came from, you may want to look into cemetery records. You can often find information on hard-to-find relatives, and you may discover ancestors that you never knew existed. Modern cemetery records contain only basic bits of information, such as dates of birth and death, last residences, and locations of tombstones. However, cemeteries in centuries past often contained the burials of entire families stretching back for many generations.

Large present-day cemeteries usually have offices that you can visit or write to for information. Some cemeteries prefer that you send your request in writing, so be sure to find out the cemetery's family-research policy before you visit.

When calling or writing to a cemetery, give the full names of the relevant ancestors, their approximate dates of birth and death, and the names of their spouses or children. Provide as much information as possible to the person searching the records.

Old cemeteries no longer in use — they're still standing, but burials haven't taken place for generations — can also prove helpful. These cemeteries usually don't have an official caretaker or office. If burials had to be registered with the county clerk rather than the caretaker, the only way to find out information about your ancestors is to visit the cemetery.

When visiting old cemeteries, take along a notebook and pencil and record the headstone markings for anyone with your family surname. If the cemetery is a small one, record all the names, because you may find connections to them in your family tree at a later time.

You can also find dozens of Internet sites that contain cemetery transcriptions. Just type *cemetery transcriptions* into your favorite search engine and then search the sites by state and town.

In Chapter 16, I give you Web addresses for many genealogy sites, many of which provide cemetery information or links to transcriber organizations. Be sure to look for these links!

Churches

Because civil registration is a relatively new phenomenon — only 100 years old or so — you need an alternative source for older information. This is where church records come in handy.

Churches have kept records of all the births, marriages, and deaths in their parishes for centuries. You can find these records in the church archives. (Local church officials can tell you where the archives are located.) LDS (see "The Family History Center" earlier in this section) provide microfilms of many old church records, which you can request and search through at your local Family History Center.

Be aware that deterioration, fire, tornadoes, and other natural disasters have destroyed many old records. When this happens, you may have run into the proverbial brick wall, and research on this branch of the tree comes to a screeching halt. This happens to all genealogists — just move to a different branch and keep going!

Running Down the Records and Their Uses

Throughout this chapter, I mention all kinds of records available to family history researchers, but you may be wondering what significance each of these sources has. In this section, I explain the different types of records in greater detail.

County records

County records include all official records dealing with birth, marriage, and death in the United States. Indexed by county of residence, these records date back to the late 1800s. If you want earlier records, you need to locate town or church records from your ancestor's place of birth.

The availability of county records varies from state to state depending on laws and restrictions imposed by each state. Usually, the person requesting the record must be kin, and you may not be able to access birth records on persons who are not yet deceased, unless you are the parent (or child) and can provide proof. Also, county birth, death, and marriage records can be expensive, ranging from $10 to $15 per certified copy.

When requesting documents, always provide as much information as possible to assist the person tracking down the information. Be ready to give the names of the person's parents and grandparents, the name(s) of siblings, the mother's maiden name, and approximate (or better yet, exact) dates. If you're unsure of a particular date, try to give an estimate. For instance, if Great-grandpa Joe was born in Colorado sometime in the late 1800s, provide a date estimate with a range of 5 years or so — between 1875 and 1880, for example.

Census records

Family historians never die — they just lose their census. Okay, they don't lose it — they just misplace it now and then. Seriously, folks, using census records is an excellent way to add information to your family history. Because census data is taken every 10 years, census records are helpful for tracking your family's migration from one part of the country to another.

Census data is also valuable because it lists the head of the household, his or her occupation, every living child of the family, and any other adults living in the household at the time. So, if Granny was living with the family at the time of the census, she should be listed, too! You can often find an entire family in one census record, which can add a dozen names to your family tree!

Immigration and naturalization databases

Every genealogist (except those who are Native American) must examine immigration and naturalization records. Did Great-great-great-grandpa Willie come to the United States by ship? If so, you may be able to find him in passenger lists of ships that entered America. However, searching through ship records may not be the best way to find information about him due to the sheer number of passenger lists that you would have to search. You'll be doing yourself a big favor if you can find out as much information about your ancestor as possible before consulting these records.

Because ship's records include both the port of departure and arrival, it's good to know where your ancestor originated. This information includes country and state/province or county. Try to find a ship that left from the port closest to your ancestor's place of origin, during the time period (give or take 10 years) that you think your ancestor left the old country.

Another great new source for folks researching their immigrant ancestors is the Ellis Island Web site. You can search for your ancestor by name at www. ellisislandrecords.org.

Tax and land records

If you want to find out more details about your ancestors' lives, you can access their tax and land records.

Tax records show figures for property taxes, inheritance taxes, and church taxes (although the latter is rare). Use these records to find the location and size of the family farm or property.

By accessing land records, you can get copies of old maps from county records that show the exact location of the property. If the place still exists, you can pay it a visit. Take a couple photos and add them to your family information.

Military records

Military records contain concrete data (such as a person's name and date of birth) and other interesting tidbits (like the dates of induction and discharge and notations about a person's military career). For the most part, these records enrich the family history by showing an ancestor's progress from a private to another rank.

Military records can be stepping stones to other records, such as Civil War *muster rolls* (lists of persons in military units) that were printed in area newspapers. If you're putting together a family biography, these sources can add a lot of character.

School records

If you search the community library for old yearbooks from area schools, you may discover what schools your family members attended. It's also interesting to see if your relatives participated in school activities, such as playing the tuba in the marching band or throwing a baton as a majorette.

Some schools post alumni records online. To locate them, type the name of the school and the city in your favorite browser and see what comes up.

Wills and probate records

Where there's a will, I wanna be in it! All kidding aside, wills and probate records can be useful resources for finding family history information. *Wills* and *probate records* are legal documents filed with the courts on behalf of an individual. Wills are created by individuals before their death to allocate their belongings, and probate records are those approved by the court for the purpose of an executor to carry out the terms of the will.

Wills and probate records often contain a list of all the heirs of a particular individual, such as children and grandchildren. They also contain the place and date of birth of the deceased. Through these records, you may find out that Great-grandpa Joe left all his money to a brother you never knew existed.

The Social Security Death Index

The *Social Security Death Index* (SSDI) contains the names, places and dates of death, and Social Security numbers for every person in the United States who was eligible for Social Security benefits. Whenever a claim for death benefits is filed, the deceased person's name is added to the file. This file is considered a public document.

The Social Security Administration (SSA) began to use a computer database for processing requests for benefits in the early 1960s, but it's not an index of all deceased persons who held Social Security numbers — it contains only those deaths that were reported to the SSA. Although most SSDI records date from 1962, some may go as far back as 1937.

This index can be helpful if you're having difficulty establishing a person's date of birth or place of residence when he died. It can also tell you who received the death benefit, which is usually the spouse. If the spouse did not receive the death benefit, you can safely suspect that the spouse passed away first.

Chapter 15

Separating Family Fact from Fiction

*E*very family has its share of myths, legends, and wild stories. Although these stories are fun to record and pass down to future generations, they may not contain a shred of truth. In fact, you may need to shake the family tree a bit to get the truth to drop out.

In this chapter, I explain why proper documentation is critical to your genealogical research. This process requires a lot of careful work (not to mention patience), but it's the only way good family historians can separate the facts from the fiction. Don't let errors in the family tree get you stumped!

Getting Your Hands on Documentation

When gathering details about your family history from various sources (see Chapter 14), you want to request documentation so you can verify the information. Documentation can take many forms — from *official* information, including birth, marriage, and death certificates issued by a government office to *unofficial* material, such as newspaper clippings or word-of-mouth information. I discuss the differences between the two types of sources in greater detail in the next few sections.

Get copies of all the documents that you find while researching your family's history. Doing so makes your work much easier in the long run because you can back up dates and events that took place in the lives of your ancestors.

Finding primary sources

In general, a primary source is a record created at the time of a particular event by a person with firsthand knowledge of the event. For example, a birth certificate is a primary source for the name and birth date of a baby, because the record was created at the time of birth by someone (in this case, a doctor) with firsthand knowledge of the event. Likewise, a marriage certificate is a primary source for the names of a bride and groom and the date of their wedding, and a death certificate is a primary source for the name of a deceased person as well as the date of his or her death. As for the other information found on primary sources (like the parents' names on a baby's birth certificate, for example), you can use it to aid in your research, but you shouldn't consider it primary, absolute information.

Photographs, other printed documents (such as school certificates or wills and testaments), or information provided by a person who actually lived the event and can provide a firsthand account are also considered primary sources. You can use photographs to help establish a time period for an individual — just study the clothing worn by the person in the picture. Also, old photos often have the name of the photography studio printed somewhere on the front or back. Alas, Sherlock, a clue!

Interviews with people who lived through certain events are invaluable. These folks can provide the lively details that enhance your family history. How else can you find out that Gramps used to chase skunks for fun, other than from someone who witnessed his antics when they happened? Be aware that interviews also provide secondary sources of information that still need to be verified, such as birth, death, and marriage dates for other siblings or family members.

Likewise, census records are considered primary source of information, because the census is an official count of a population and recording of its economic status, age, gender, and so forth. Census records list the names of all the residents living under one roof. These records also include the ages and occupations of the residents, as well as their relationships to the head of the household. They're a boon for genealogists sniffing along family trails. However, be aware that census records can be difficult to read or may contain misspelled names. When in doubt, obtain an *additional* source of primary information, such as the ones I talk about earlier in this section.

Through birth, marriage, and death records, you can sometimes obtain information about several generations of ancestors. For example, birth certificates before 1900 listed not only the names of the child and the parents, but often the names of the paternal and maternal grandparents as well.

However, keep in mind that a birth certificate is recommended as a primary source only for the person whose birth is recorded. Often you may notice that a birth certificate also indicates the ages or dates of birth of the child's parents. The dates of birth given for the parents of the child are considered secondary sources of information.

The reason for this is that the age of the parent(s) may have been reported incorrectly to record keepers. For example, an underage mother may have told the doctor or the record keeper that she was of age to avoid embarrassment. Or, perhaps an illegitimate birth was recorded as legitimate.

Documentation doesn't necessarily refer to a document — it can also refer to a reliable account or photograph. To keep your research true to the events in the lives of your ancestors, always strive to back up all your information with documentation.

Securing secondary sources

A secondary source is a record created well after a particular event by someone with only secondhand knowledge of the event. Examples of secondary sources include oral stories passed down through the generations, published family histories, family legends, and rumors. Some other secondary sources of information masquerade as primary sources — such as newspaper articles and ship passenger lists.

Newspaper articles (including the obituaries) are tricky because they can contain errors. These errors range from incorrect dates and places of birth and death to incorrect ages or misspelled names. Always back up information found in a newspaper, such as an obituary, with documentation, such as a death certificate.

Ship passenger lists are another form of secondary information. Although these lists can often point a family researcher down the right path, they're sometimes filled with misspelled names and erroneous information.

Moreover, ship lists contain a minute amount of information, often containing only basic details, such as the dates of travel and the names and ages of the passengers, as well as their place of origin. For example, if your ancestor, Thomas Smith, sailed from England sometime in the mid-1800s and landed in New York, you may find dozens of Thomas Smiths who match this criteria on ship passenger lists — but not a single one may turn out to be your ancestor! Thus, you want to use ship passenger lists only as research aids.

You may also encounter dilemmas with secondary information obtained from family histories. Published family histories can be terrific resources, but they can also be misleading. A friend once mentioned that her great-grandfather was a sea captain, and she found his name in a book in the library. Great — but how does she know that this person is *her* ancestor? Without proper research, she could very well be barking up the wrong family tree.

However, secondary sources can serve as springboards to finding more reliable primary sources. For example, a family rumor once surfaced in my own family about an ancestor who was a priest. For years, I wrote to the appropriate archive, but I received nothing. Finally, in desperation, I wrote to the small town hall where my ancestor supposedly lived and asked that my request be forwarded to the parish, if it still existed. The parish did indeed exist, but my ancestor was not a priest at all — he was a *notary* (lawyer) for the church, which is why the main archives never had any record of a priest bearing his name.

Other legends may not be as easy to substantiate, so I recommend shaking the family tree a bit. Interview as many family members as possible and record every variation of the story. Then go through the information and find common threads. Doing so can give you some insight about the direction your research should take.

Never accept a secondary source as gospel. When it comes to your family research, make it a rule to never knowingly pass on a rumor as a fact. Always research the issue.

Requesting documentation

Requesting documentation — especially official records — is easy, but somewhat expensive.

To request government records, follow these simple steps:

1. **Call or write to the registrar in the county where the record is located, and ask about documentation fees.**

2. **Write a letter describing exactly what you're requesting (such as a marriage or birth certificate), the exact date (or within a year give-or-take), and a check or money order for the fee(s) previously established.**

Some states will not release family information to anyone except the next of kin. Funny thing is, "next of kin" tends to mean different things to different people. At one time, this term meant you had to be the parent, child, or sibling (brother or sister) of a particular person. Today, the term is used more loosely and can refer to any direct relationship, such as being the person's grandchild, niece or nephew, or cousin. If you need to request information from a state that enforces the "next of kin" rule, be sure to include your relationship to the ancestor in your letter. For instance, you can tell them that you're researching the life of your great-grandfather, followed by the information that you want, and the date.

The same scenario applies when requesting information from other sources, such as archives, libraries, or churches. Include as much information as possible in your request, including your relationship to the person named, dates, and necessary fees.

When requesting information from *any* source, be sure to include a *self-addressed, stamped envelope* (SASE). Doing so makes it easier for the person on the other end to reply to your request. For international requests, enclose a self-addressed envelope and an *International Postage Coupon,* which is available from your local post office and can be exchanged for postage in the receiving country.

With a little luck, you'll get a reply back in a few weeks.

Digging for the Truth — No Matter What

Documenting the facts behind all the family stories is a tough job. As you get deeper into your research, you're bound to come across family facts that aren't pleasing, and you may disprove stories that your family has believed for generations. However, you shouldn't be disappointed with such results.

When fiction is stranger than truth

A Spanish friend of mine was thrilled to hear that his great-great-great-grandfather was a duke. What a proud family history! All his aunts verified the legend, so he was ready to jump in, reclaim the family coat of arms, and have a plaque made for his office wall. Then reality set in.

After spending hours in the provincial archives poring over old documents and reports, my buddy discovered something that he never expected. As it turned out, my friend's ancestor wasn't a duke at all. His great-great-great-grandfather was the guy who clanged the anvil while making horseshoes for the duke's stable. Basically, he was just an average guy.

This experience taught my friend how family stories can change and mutate over time. He also found out the importance of always questioning a legend in order to become an effective family historian.

If you come across displeasing family information, remember a well-known genealogy saying: "If there's a skeleton in your family closet, you may as well make it dance." So, I suggest writing about your experience and including your story with the family group sheets (see Chapter 13). For example, if you find that your ancestor was a sheep farmer rather than a baron, you can start the tale with something like "Farmer Gramps" and then add some humorous anecdotes about your fact-finding experience. Your family will appreciate getting the true story rather than an outlandish story that's been fabricated over time.

Keeping Track of Your Progress

Because you'll be sending out a lot of requests for documentation, you must keep track of what you send, where you send it, and when you get a reply. If you don't keep track, you can easily find yourself forgetting important tasks or repeating the ones that you've already completed.

To help you keep track of the whole shebang, you can use the Task Tracking Record shown in Figure 15-1 (and included on the CD). This list can help keep you on task and organized.

If you need logs to help keep you organized when you're digging up family memorabilia, corresponding with your kin, and inventorying your family treasures, check out Chapter 13.

You need to cite a source for every page of genealogical data that you collect, whether you obtain the information manually by networking with your relatives and writing for documents (see Chapters 13 and 14) or electronically from the Internet (see Chapter 16).

Recording your source is important because you may need to revisit your facts. For example, if what you find out about your family tree is different from what Aunt Betsy tells you, you know that she's the person to contact to work out the details.

You also need to record sources for information gleaned from the Internet. If you find a site that includes your family members' names on an old census record, you may need to revisit the record sometime in the future to research other branches of the same line. To record information found on the Internet, record the *URL* (Web site address), the date, and the name of the hosting organization. Remember that sites often change hands and that URLs can change. By recording as much information as possible, you should be able to find the source again if necessary.

Task Tracking Record		
Date	Description of task	Follow-up / Rec'd date

Figure 15-1:
Task
Tracking
Record.

The gene pool needs a bit of chlorine

My husband was given a photo of his Great-Aunt Dixie several years ago. He and I were intrigued by the glamorous photo of a striking young woman wearing a wide-brimmed, feather-trimmed hat from the early 1900s. A cousin said that Aunt Dixie was trying to become a silent-film actress and that this snapshot was likely a "publicity photo." It was publicity all right, but not the type that we expected!

After a great deal of time spent interviewing relatives and looking through old letters and postcards, we tracked her migration from Minnesota to South Dakota and finally up to Alaska. That's when we made quite an amusing discovery. Aunt Dixie was no actress at all. Instead, she was the madam of the local brothel, and she had quite a record at the county courthouse! She never did make it to Hollywood, instead retiring and marrying a rich man and moving to Oregon.

My husband has suggested that during the next reunion we blow up her photo (see the accompanying figure) to poster-sized dimensions and create a game called "Pin the feather on the madam." Don't worry — his entire family has the same warped sense of humor.

Madame Dixie

Want another example of surprises in the family gene pool? I have copies of old newspapers from Minnesota that indicate one of my husband's ancestors being cited for disrupting church services and another one being arrested for bootlegging.

Chapter 16

Partnering with Your 'Puter

. . . .

In This Chapter

▶ Reviewing popular family history software

▶ Finding Web sites and online message boards for family historians

▶ Using genealogy mailing lists

. . . .

My computer, otherwise known as 'puter, is one of my best pals. If you're like me, you feel that the computer is the greatest invention since ice cream.

If you want to make your family research simple and enjoyable, you should partner up with a computer and take your research to the Web. In this chapter, I give you lots of useful Web sites and other bits of information that can help you find your ancestors.

The material in this chapter is basic and can get you started on your family research. But if you want a source that can guide you through the hundreds of sites on the Internet in an easy-to-use format, I recommend *Genealogy Online For Dummies* by Matthew L. Helm and April Leigh Helm (Hungry Minds, Inc). The authors give you a wonderful tour of the Internet from a family history point of view. I found out about things I never knew existed by using this helpful and handy guide.

Selecting Software for Genealogy Junkies

Several excellent computer programs are available for family genealogists. The software ranges in price from about $10 to as much as $100. The software that you choose depends on your needs, your budget, and your devotion to your family-history project.

You can also use the sample program Brother's Keeper, which is included on the CD-ROM that comes with this book. This easy-to-use program guides you through the process of filling out forms and charts. (See the CD Appendix for installation instructions.)

If you want a more detailed program, you can buy software packages with multiple CDs that include such diverse tidbits as other people's family trees, ship passenger lists, and so on. You can find these programs at any computer-software store.

Because so much software is available for family genealogists, choosing a program can be challenging. In the following list, I give you my top software choices, based on ease of use, value for the dollar, research tools, and usefulness of the printable materials.

- **Family Tree Maker** (`http://www.genealogy.com/soft_ftm.html`): Top-rated for more than 10 years by various genealogical magazines and organizations, this program is easy to use, generates nice-looking printouts, and comes with some wonderful research tools, such as CD-ROMs and links to Internet sites. Check out the Web site for more information.

- **Legacy Family Tree** (`www.legacyfamilytree.com`): Another terrific program, you can download this software directly from the Web. It's also highly rated by fellow genealogists, easy to use, and generates professional-looking printouts.

- **Ancestral Quest** (`www.ancestralquest.com`): A great beginner's program that's easy to use and navigate. I haven't tried it personally, but I have spoken with many folks who have, and they're very happy with it.

No matter what program you choose, be sure that it allows you to save your data as a GEDCOM file. *GEDCOM* (an acronym for Genealogical Data Communication) is a common file format that allows users to exchange genealogical files between different programs.

The majority of genealogy software programs allow you to read and export GEDCOM files, but if you use old or second-hand software, check the instruction manual for details on compatibility with other programs.

Searching the Internet for Ancestors

As the Internet continues to grow, online genealogy research expands and improves. Currently, ancestor surfers can choose from thousands of sites, but I can think of several that really stand out. The next section takes a closer look at these sites.

On Web sites

The following list includes my favorite Web sites. These are sites that I use regularly in my own research because of the sheer amount of material available. I'm particularly fond of sites that feature searchable surname databases and message boards.

Because these sites are multipurpose (they not only give great advice, but also feature searchable databases, helpful links, and other materials), I list them here as a group, rather than in bits and pieces elsewhere.

- ✔ **Rootsweb.com** (www.rootsweb.com): This site is a bonanza for genealogists. You can read the latest and greatest genealogy news and search for ancestors by surname (see the next section, "Using surnames," for more information). This site also links to search pages and allows access to dozens of databases.

  In addition, you can subscribe to mailing lists and post queries to message boards (see the section "Mailing lists and message boards," later in the chapter for details) and get help with any genealogy topic, both domestically and internationally.

- ✔ **Ancestry.com** (www.ancestry.com): Here's another terrific site, full of data, searches, and links. First-time visitors can even get a guided tour of the site. Be sure to visit the site's surname communities. Enter your surname to see postings from others who share your surname.

  You can also search military and census records, obituaries, and many other official records. Access to some types of records requires a paid membership, which is worth the cost because of the additional records (such as census records) that you can search online. In addition, membership often gets you some nifty freebies, like CD-ROMs and newsletters not available to nonmembers. Membership fees depend on how long you want your membership to last. For example, you can pay $25 for a three-month membership or $99 for a year.

- ✔ **Cyndi's List of Genealogy Sites on the Internet** (www.cyndislist.com): Cyndi Howells is a favorite of genealogists worldwide. This site is the mother lode, folks. You can search for information by geographic location, surname, and category. You can also find links to adoption issues, *heraldry* (the study of family coats of arms and crests), immigration and naturalization, ship passenger lists, and more.

- ✔ **World GenWeb** (www.worldgenweb.com): This is your link to the world of international genealogy. To use this site, select the country you need to research and dive in. Be sure to come up for air now and then.

- ✔ **Helm's Genealogy Toolbox** (www.genealogytoolbox.com): Matthew and April Helm, the authors of *Genealogy Online For Dummies,* created this outstanding site. Here you can find lots of tips and news for genealogists, links to helpful sites, searches, and databases. This site is beginner-friendly.

✔ **GenealogyPortal.com** (`www.genealogyportal.com`): This site features eight different search engines to help you locate genealogy information. You can find information on specific families and ancestors, census and official records, local histories and collections of data, research help, and genealogical services and materials, including books and family history forms.

✔ **Internet Family Finder** (`www.genealogy.com`): Using surname and geographic location, this site searches many databases for cemetery records, ship passenger lists, family homepages, messages, census records, and more. It also searches through online indexes of many genealogy books and historical records.

✔ **Genealogy Today** (`www.genealogytoday.com`): Here's a basic, easy-to-use site where you can browse through searchable surname queries (also known as *message boards*), genealogy news, and articles about other family history links.

✔ **Social Security Death Index** (`www.ssdi.genealogy.rootsweb.com/cgi-bin/ssdi.cgi`): Updated regularly, this index lists individuals whose deaths have been reported to the Social Security Administration since 1962. Although this site doesn't tell you much about your ancestor per se, it can give you basic information, such as full name, dates of birth and death, last-known residence, Social Security number, and the state that issued the number.

Using surnames

The Web contains dozens of sites that you can search for a particular *surname* (last name) and watch the results multiply. Try the following sites for your surname search:

✔ `www.Mytrees.com`

✔ `www.gendex.com`

✔ `www.surnameweb.org`

These sites can help you connect with other genealogists who may be studying the same surname that you are.

Uncommon surnames are some of the easiest names to research on the Internet. In fact, you can often find entire sites devoted to the origin and preservation of old, unique surnames. Just type your surname (such as *Abbersnapper*), the country of origin (*Australia,* for example), and the word *surname* into your favorite search engine. ***Note:*** If your surname is fairly common, you can still find plenty of information using the same method.

Typing in the word *surname* along with your name and country helps narrow your search to published surname and genealogical information. In other words, you don't receive unnecessary material in which the name Abbersnapper appears with the term Austrailia.

If you are of Irish ancestry, you can find information on Irish surnames and origins at `www.ucc.ie/research/atlas`. The National University of Ireland sponsors this site.

Using one-name studies

A *one-name study* is just what it sounds like — a study based on one particular surname. Usually, these studies are created by individuals who bear the name, have spent years researching its origins, and want to share their information with others who have the same surname. A one-name search is similar to a surname search, except that the information contained in a one-name study is extremely detailed, much like a thesis or a research paper. Some folks find that one-name studies are just what they're looking for, whereas others think that the studies deliver too much information.

You can find sites created specifically for one-name studies. The Guild of One-Name Studies (`www.one-name.org`) is one example. Visit the site to subscribe to newsletters, find out how to become a member of the guild, or to search for your surname.

If you can't locate any one-name studies of your surname at genealogy or surname sites, you can always search for them through your favorite search engine: Type in *one-name study* followed by your surname. For example, if your surname is Rooster, type *one-name study Rooster*. See what hatches when the search engine returns your results.

Through online newsletters

If you're looking for another genealogy-research option on the Internet, check out the online newsletters available to family historians. In the following list, I give you my recommendations:

- **Update** (`www.familytreemagazine.com/newsletter.asp`): From *Family Tree Magazine,* this free e-mail newsletter, which is delivered weekly, includes genealogy news and tips, links to helpful sites, book and product reviews (such as for genealogy software), and interesting articles.

- **Missing Links** (`www.rootsweb.com/~mlnews`): This is a fun site with links to obscure genealogy-related articles — hence its missing link theme. Includes family humor and nice stories.

- **Shaking Your Family Tree** (`www.rootsweb.com/~rwguide/syft`): A syndicated weekly newspaper column that includes tips and ideas for searching by country of origin and using online resources. Back issues are filed by subject.

- **Genealogy Times** (`www.genealogytoday.com/roots/news/quarterly.html`): A quarterly newsletter featuring a variety of genealogy topics, including country directories, product reviews and research tips. Subscribe by filling out a form online.

- **Genealogy Review** (`www.genealogytoday.com/roots/news/weekly.html`): Of special interest to those researching outside the United States, this weekly newsletter focuses on a different country each month. Weekly topics include research how-to's and basic genealogy information.

- **Family Tree Digest** (`www.genealogytoday.com/roots/news/daily.html`): You can subscribe to this online newsletter to receive updates on what's new in the world of genealogy.

To find more information, use your favorite search engine and type *genealogy newsletters*. Your search should return dozens of potential sites.

More heritage help

If you're serious about researching your family history, I recommend that you supplement your online research by subscribing to a *snail-mail* (postal) magazine that focuses on genealogy. Like online genealogy newsletters, these publications provide general research news, information on new and current Web sites, software recommendations, and other handy research. Plus, you get all the latest information in one source, instead of having to keep up with many Web sites simultaneously. A subscription to any of the following magazines is money well spent:

- **Heritage Quest Magazine**, 669 West 900 North, North Salt Lake, UT 84054; phone 800-760-2455. Price: $28 for one year (bimonthly).

- **Family Tree Magazine**, 1507 Dana Avenue, Cincinnati, OH 45207; phone 888-419-0421. Price: $27 for one year (bimonthly).

- **Everton's Genealogical Helper**, Everton Publishers, Inc. P.O. Box 638, Logan, UT 84323; phone 800-443-6325. Price: $23.95 for one year (bimonthly).

These magazines also feature handy Web sites that offer online newsletters, downloadable forms and templates, research tools and tips, and links to other sites. You can access these sites at `www.familytreemagazine.com`, `www.heritagequest.com`, and `www.everton.com` for more information.

By mailing lists and bulletin boards

Many of the Internet sites that I mention in this chapter allow you to sign up for mailing lists, or they allow you to post *queries* (general search questions) to message boards in hopes of a response. Through mailing lists and message boards, you can network with hundreds of other researchers from the comfort of your computer chair.

My problem, however, is that I tend to lose track of time when reviewing queries and messages on mailing lists and message boards. The messages are so interesting that 10 minutes easily turns into 3 hours. Time flies when I'm having fun. Yours will too, so be sure that you don't have any appointments or deadlines looming.

Joining a mailing list

Mailing lists are extremely helpful, especially for the beginner. If you sign up for a mailing list, you can also receive e-mail from other researchers posting their questions. Who knows, maybe you can help them, maybe you will find some long-lost cousins, or maybe you'll do both!

To use a mailing list, you must first sign up. Because sign-up procedures can vary, follow the directions indicated on the Web site. After signing up, you get a welcome e-mail, and you can begin sending in your questions.

When you send an e-mail to the list, the message is routed to all the list members so they can read your question. Anyone who feels that they can help you will respond to your e-mail. Everyone on the list also receives the message and can benefit from the advice. *Note:* Unlike a message board (see the next section), mailing lists don't require you to visit a specifc Internet site to receive your messages. All mail comes directly to your mailbox on your computer.

You can find specific genealogy mailing lists based on country, or state of origin, or surname. For example, if you're researching your ancestors from New York, you can sign up for a New York–only mailing list, post your information, and wait for help.

For a comprehensive RootsWeb mail list, check out `http://lists.rootsweb.com`, where you can find lists for surname, country of origin, religious affiliation, software, and so on.

Navigating online message boards

A *message board* allows you to communicate with participants in ongoing discussions in a public forum — that is, you post messages that remain visible to members of a particular Web site.

Unlike a mailing list, a message board doesn't send you personal e-mails regarding your topic. Instead, you go to a particular Web site and sign in. And because messages remain on a message board for a long period of time, you can browse and search the messages for specific topics and pick up some tips in the process.

All the Internet sites that I recommend in this chapter host message boards for family historians. Look for the appropriate links on the sites.

Writing Life Stories

If you're interested in writing the life story of one of your ancestors, you can find help through several different online sources. For example:

- **Genealogy.com** (`www.genealogy.com/bio`): This site has a downloadable Biography Assistant, which contains guidelines for writing a biography as well as lists of topics and questions to consider when compiling your information.

- **Mystorywriter.com** (`www.mystorywriter.com`): This site offers an inexpensive piece of software (about $20) that can help you write your personal biography or the biographies of your ancestors.

If you prefer to let a professional handle the task, you can locate one online. Visit the Association of Personal Historians (APH) at `www.personal historians.org`. This organization, founded in 1994, is made up of hundreds of family historians from all over the world just itching to help you — for a fee, of course.

Privacy on the Web

Although the Internet is a great place to conduct family research, it's also a great place to get scammed. Unfortunately, some folks are just waiting for you to post your family information so they can take advantage of you. To combat the problem, some states (and countries) have made it illegal to share a living person's private information without his or her written consent.

Here are a few basic rules to follow to keep your kin (and yourself) safe on the Net.

- Never post any private information about a living relative. This includes date of birth, address, phone number, and Social Security number.

- When including the names of living family members on a family history Web site or when submitting them to companies that compile genealogical information, include the word *private* for birth dates and other personal information. Doing so lets other genealogists know that the person they're looking for is still living and that you want such information to remain confidential.

- When posting your family-history information to a Web site or sharing it with the company that produced your genealogy software, carefully read the instructions on the Web site or those that came with the software. If you make a mistake on your submission (such as including personal information that should be kept private), you may not be able to make corrections after it's been submitted.

- If you are unsure about the data that you're posting, you can download a free utility (a piece of software) called *GEDClean.* This utility helps you remove private information regarding living relatives before you share your files with others. You can find it at `www.raynorshyn.com/gedclean/ Compare.html`.

And, always remember my genealogist's Golden Rule: Post only as you would have others post about you. I certainly don't want my personal information shared with the rest of the world!

Part VI
The Part of Tens

The 5th Wave   By Rich Tennant

"Well, your cousin from England's here with a bunch of his loud friends. I suppose he'll want to 'help' contribute with a handful of beads again..."

In this part . . .

Readers familiar with the *For Dummies* series know that near the end of every book, you can find a bevy of top-ten chapters. To that end, Chapter 17 includes some helpful hints to get you through common reunion trials and tribulations. Chapter 18 takes a look at some terrific books (besides this one, of course) to help you plan a reunion or another type of get-together. Chapter 19 explains how to preserve your family treasures, and finally, Chapter 20 offers several more great reunion-theme ideas.

Chapter 17

Ten Lessons in Family Dynamics

· ·

In This Chapter

▶ Handling family-related problems

▶ Dealing with the busybodies and the not-so-busy bodies

· ·

*Y*our family members have unique personalities, and sometimes, these personalities can clash — big time. Clashing personalities can result in hard feelings and unexpected reactions among family members. This phenomenon is called *family dynamics.*

Your cast of family characters may include such personalities as Mr. Negativity, Nosey Parker, Miss Congeniality, the psychic, and the know-it-all. No matter what you call them, you likely have some relatives who like to climb on the soapbox and stir up family controversy.

At your family reunion, you get to see these personalities interact, and in some cases, you may need to try your hand at conflict resolution. In this chapter, I give you ten common conflicts in family dynamics and suggest ways to deal with them.

Aunt Agnes Won't Go if Uncle Hubert Will Be There

I know what you want to say to Aunt Agnes. I'm not a mind reader, but I have experienced the same situation. You're thinking, "Fine, with that attitude, don't come to the reunion!"

However, this approach isn't necessarily a good idea. Instead, chat with Aunt Agnes and explain that her attendance is important not only to you, but to everyone else — especially the guest of honor (if you have one). Be sure to mention that the reunion can't be complete without her.

Remind Aunt Agnes of an old Chinese proverb: "A journey of a thousand miles begins with a single step."

Billy and Bobby Are Fighting Again, but Their Parents Do Nothing

I bet that you're thinking, "I'm going to lock the little offenders in a dark, cramped closet."

I'm kidding, of course! But even if you think that you can better handle the situation, you can't parent other peoples' children. Instead, you need to parent the parents.

However, before you approach the parents, determine who is bothered by the situation. If you are the only one annoyed by the children, try to ignore them and move on. Visit with the folks on the other side of the room for a bit. If several other people have disgusted looks on their faces, you need to act fast.

The most painless way to handle this problem is to pull the parents aside and explain the situation. Let them know that the kids' behavior is unacceptable but somewhat expected, considering the exciting atmosphere. Kids tend to get worked into frenzies, especially in front of willing audiences.

Tell the parents that in order for the whole family to enjoy the reunion, everyone — including the children — needs to exhibit good behavior. Give the parents several opportunities to correct the situation before you take the most drastic action, which is asking them to leave. Do this only as a last resort because it's their reunion, too.

Cousin Sue Changed Junior's Dirty Diapers in front of Everyone

If you set up a diaper-changing area like I suggest in Chapter 6, this situation likely won't happen — especially if you keep a tidy little stack of diapers and baby wipes nearby.

If you set up a changing area, make sure that you point it out to parents. Most parents prefer *not* to change dirty diapers in front of the whole family.

Fifi and Fido Made Boo-Boos

Cousin Pixie brings her uninvited four-legged guests. She considers them her "babies" and won't go anywhere without them. One of the furry ones makes a mess, but Cousin Pixie seems oblivious to the malodorous pile. What do you do?

First, point out the problem to the owner of the pooch — in this case Cousin Pixie — and ask if you can assist by providing her with a plastic bag for cleanup. Hopefully, she'll take you up on your offer.

But, if she decides not to clean up after her pets, you really don't have an option — you have to put up and clean up before someone steps on the smelly landmine. Grab a plastic sack, scoop up the offending piles, and deposit them in the nearest trash bin. If you can handle this task before anyone else sees, smells, or steps in the muck, you've done beautifully.

That's Not the Way It Happened!

Memory is a strange thing. Many people can witness the same event at the same moment, but each person remembers it differently. Some people, such as myself, have memories that last only as long as the blink of an eye.

While at the reunion, you may try to gather family stories for your genealogical research. Of course, you want these stories to be accurate. Explain this fact to the people at your reunion, but if they can't agree on the details of a particular event, simply ask them to move on to the next great memory.

This Stuff Tastes Like Roadkill!

Kids can say such silly (or blatantly honest) things. For example, say you have a potluck reunion and one of the kids blurts out that someone's dish tastes bad.

If the stuff really does taste awful, discreetly get rid of it when the cook isn't watching. Scrape most of it into the trash bin, leaving only a scoop in the dish. Cover the food you throw out with other trash so the cook doesn't find it. When he sees that his dish is almost all gone, he'll assume that the hungry tribe gobbled up his secret recipe.

Sally and Lindsey Are Squealing like Greased Pigs

What to do? First, find out what they're squealing about. If they're just overly boisterous with their reminiscing, join in the fun! If they're arguing, pull them aside and explain the purpose of the reunion — to enjoy being with family, not to listen to two grown women have a catfight. Meow.

If they keep it up, I have a sure-fire cure, to be used only as a last resort and only if you have a tape recorder handy. Grab the recorder, microphone, and a blank audio cassette and record the squealing. Then play it back for them so they can hear what they sound like. They may even get a good laugh out of the situation.

If nothing works, ask them to leave if they're going to continue their argument. They can return to the reunion after they get the fighting out of their system.

Uncle Bill Won't Participate — As Usual

If Uncle Bill isn't typically a social person, leave him be. You don't want to make him uncomfortable. Some folks are happier observing the goings-on rather than participating in them.

Perhaps he will join in the reunion festivities later. Encourage his participation, but don't push.

Uncle Fred Told You It Wouldn't Work

Uncle Fred is torn between being the family psychic and the family know-it-all. Throughout the reunion, he stands over your shoulder and tells you how to manage the activities.

If whatever you try to do doesn't work out, he is usually the first person to remind you. But don't let his remarks irritate you. Instead, ask him for advice on handling the next situation. If you give him a chance to take the helm, he may back off. He probably doesn't want to turn the tables and risk being criticized.

Mr. Negativity Wants to Settle an Old Argument

This situation is a common problem at family reunions. Unfortunately, some folks try to give their opinions about things that happened long ago. In fact, an issue may be so old that only Mr. Negativity himself remembers what he's talking about. Some issues are so trivial that you wonder why folks bring them up in the first place.

Simply put, a family reunion is *not* the place to settle a family feud. You need to pull Mr. Negativity aside and explain once again the purpose of the family reunion — to enjoy and celebrate your family.

Chapter 18

Ten Terrific Reads

In This Chapter

▶ Finding books for reunion planning

▶ Collecting cookbooks to help with reunion menus

▶ Locating other useful entertainment books

In this chapter, I give you my ten best recommendations for books about reunion planning, menu planning, and general party planning. These books give you lots of tips and ideas for themes and decorations — and other great excuses to host a party.

Family Tree Maker For Dummies

Matthew L. and April Leigh Helm provide the ultimate reference book for people new to Family Tree Maker, the most popular brand of genealogy software. The authors guide you through every aspect of genealogy, including where to start and how to proceed when you run into an inevitable research problem. The humor will give you the giggles. This book is published by Hungry Minds, Inc.

Genealogy Online For Dummies

Here's the perfect introductory book for researching genealogy online. If you plan on using your computer to its fullest while researching your family history, this book can provide dozens of tips, tricks, and helpful Internet sites to make your research proceed smoothly and efficiently. This book is written by Matthew L. and April Leigh Helm and published by Hungry Minds, Inc.

The Source: A Guidebook of American Genealogy

This book by Sandra H. Luebking (and published by MyFamily.com Inc.) is a wonderful source for American genealogists. It's been completely updated and revised, making it a favorite of family historians. This book guides readers through all facets of family research and helps them locate the rich body of information available through a wide range of sources, including published histories, private collections, archives, and libraries.

Betty Crocker's Great Grilling Cookbook

Family reunions and barbecues go hand in hand. This cookbook (published by Hungry Minds, Inc.) gives you lots of yummy barbecue recipes, tips, and ideas. The book offers at-a-glance timetables for cooking meat, poultry, and vegetables, plus full-color photos that are sure to inspire you to fire up the grill. In fact, this book includes recipes for breakfast, lunch, dinner, and even dessert!

Betty Crocker's Fast & Flavorful: 100 Main Dishes You Can Make in 20 Minutes or Less

A reunion planner's dream come true — fast, easy recipes that can be doubled for a crowd. The book features a full array of no-fuss meals from appetizers to main dishes and desserts. Another bonus is that the recipes in this book use readily available ingredients and prepackaged products found in your kitchen or at your local supermarket. The book is published by Hungry Minds, Inc.

The Buffet Book

The Buffet Book by Carole Peck (and published by Viking) is an all-around buffet book with recipes, theme ideas, and general entertaining tips. In addition to a wide range of crowd-sized recipes, this cookbook and entertaining handbook features ideas for buffet table designs and hundreds of helpful entertaining tips. This book is definitely one of this author's favorite resources!

Gala!

Although not family-reunion specific, this book by Patti Coons (and published by Capital Books) offers some wonderful advice for putting together events with large numbers of attendees, including tips for selecting sites, setting up, and keeping yourself organized.

The Joys of Entertaining

One of my favorites since the day I brought it home, this "Bible" features lots of great ideas for large and small gatherings, along with gorgeous full-color photos to inspire your entertaining creativity. Published by Abbeville Press, this book is written by Beverly Reese Church and Bethany Ewald Bultman.

Entertaining For Dummies

This book (another in the *For Dummies* family published by Hungry Minds, Inc.) is an easy-to-understand reference for any party planner. This no-non-sense planning guide (written by Suzanne Williamson) features tips for every kind of social gathering from a picnic to a formal holiday dinner, plus tips to ensure that you — the party giver — enjoy your own party.

Great Parties

Martha Stewart has done it again! This wonderful book, published by Clarkson N. Potter, is full of appetizing party menus, lots of helpful tips for party themes, and interesting decorating ideas to help you plan a successful get-together.

Chapter 19

Ten Tips for Preserving Family Treasures

Your family likely has a box or two of memorabilia in need of conservation. Such memorabilia can include photos, letters, diaries, newspaper articles, books, Bibles, and other treasures. Of course, these items fade and deteriorate over time, and you don't want future generations to lose precious family history and traditions.

In this chapter, I offer you some advice about restoring damaged items and preserving them for future generations.

Preserving Family Photos

Photos tend to deteriorate faster than other family heirlooms. However, with proper preservation techniques, you can keep the nifty snapshots around for your descendents to enjoy.

Black and white photos can last a century or longer, whereas color photos rarely last more than a few decades. (The chemicals used during processing make color photos fade faster than black and white ones.) However, keep in mind that all types of photos are subject to wear and tear and become easily damaged by light, heat, and humidity.

To keep your items safe, store all photos and negatives in a cool, dry location. Don't store photos in a basement, because the air is too damp. Also, don't store photos in the attic, because the heat destroys them.

Never display photos in bright sunlight. The *UV* (ultraviolet) rays from the sun damage the paper and cause the photos to fade. If you decide to display some of your family photos, be sure to frame them using UV protective glass, and don't display them in areas where the sun can directly hit them.

Reproducing Photos

If you want to restore severely worn photos, take them to a professional restoration service for reproduction. These folks can work magic on your old family photos!

The restoration experts reproduce your photos electronically and create new negatives as well. While the photo is still in its electronic format, restoration experts touch up the photo by repairing tears, cracks, lines, and even areas missing from the original.

This process can be expensive, especially if you plan on restoring a stack of photos. But in my opinion, reproducing photos is the best way.

Copying Photos and Documents

You eventually get to the point when you need to make copies of your original treasures if you want future generations to enjoy them.

You can make copies of original photos using a photocopier, scanner, and printer or laser copier. The copies can last for 10 years or more — with the proper care.

Whatever method you choose, be sure to print your photos on acid-free paper. Doing so helps prevent the yellowing and deterioration caused by the acids in common paper. You can find acid-free paper at camera shops and craft stores.

The same idea applies to documents. The acids in everyday paper can cause your precious family documents to yellow and deteriorate in a very short period of time. To extend their life, photocopy the documents onto acid-free paper — you'll need to bring your own to the photocopying store — and store the originals in a clean, dry location, sandwiched between sheets of acid-free tissue.

Maintaining the Quality of VCR Tapes

Videography is a popular way to preserve memories. Who hasn't seen proud parents at a local ball game videotaping their child in action?

However, the truth is, a videotape is even more fragile than a photograph. The mix of chemicals used in creating the tape, coupled with the mechanical wear-and-tear of viewing, makes even the best-quality tape deteriorate quickly. Poor-quality videotapes typically last only a year or two, and good-quality videotapes last only a few years longer.

To preserve your VCR tapes, you can choose from several options, which aren't foolproof. But until tape manufacturers come up with a way to make videotapes more stable, try the following methods:

- **Use the best-quality VCR tape you can afford.** These tapes range in price from $2 to $4 for a good quality tape.

- **Make several back-up copies.** You can make copies from one VCR to another at home or use a professional video service. You can find their listings in the telephone book under "video." ***Note:*** Don't play the copies until the main tape is no longer viewable. This keeps your copies pristine.

- **Fast-forward and then rewind all your tapes at least once a year.** Doing so helps keep the tapes supple and avoids any problems that may occur from the film being tightly coiled for long periods of time.

- **Clean your VCR regularly.** Dirt and dust can damage the sensitive coatings on the tapes.

Saving Old Letters and Newspapers

Lots of families have collections of old letters or newspapers stored in trunks and boxes. However, storing paper items in this manner invites disaster, because most paper is made from wood pulp that's treated with various chemicals during manufacturing.

Newsprint is the worst type of the wood-pulp paper and decays the quickest. The combination of the poor-quality paper, its inherent acids, and the type of ink used in printing contribute to the demise of newsprint. If you take a look at a wad of week-old newspapers, you can see that the papers are already beginning to yellow and fade.

Another problem with newsprint is that it damages any paper that it comes in contact with. This process is called *acid migration*. For example, say you insert a slip of newsprint, such as a newspaper article, into a letter and store it for a while. While the newsprint deteriorates, it releases an acid that migrates to the adjoining paper, leaving brown marks on the letter paper.

Some paper items are made from cotton papers, and these items don't deteriorate as quickly as wood-pulp papers. However, you should care for them in the same way that you care for wood-pulp items. Because distinguishing between the two types of papers is difficult, treat all your items as if they were made from wood pulp.

To preserve your paper items, including documents, letters, news clippings, and photographs, store them in an acid-free box in a cool, dry location. Don't store paper items in wooden boxes, because like wood-pulp paper, wood contains chemicals and acids that can migrate to the paper. As with photos, never expose the papers to bright light.

Before storing, all papers need to be opened flat with a piece of acid-free paper inserted between the layers. Doing so keeps them safe, avoiding cracks and discoloration along the folds. If acid from any of the items migrates to the layers of paper separating the letters, replace the separating papers with fresh ones twice each year.

Laminating Your Treasures

Laminating paper does not help preserve it. In fact, it often has the opposite effect. During the lamination process, everything on the paper (including dust, mold spores, and moisture) is sealed inside a clear sheet of plastic. This becomes a breeding ground for bacteria, and as a result, the paper can quickly deteriorate. However, you can store paper items in plastic wrapping, as long as you make small holes or vents in the plastic so air can circulate.

Making Memory Books and Scrapbooks

Some families have been creating scrapbooks and memory books for generations. These books often contain old letters, ticket stubs, photos, and other items mounted on a heavy sheet of paper.

Memory books and scrapbooks come with their own set of problems because of the materials — even the new and improved materials — used to create them. The two most common materials (and problems) are the following:

✔ **Paper:** The pages of the scrapbook or memory book and usually the items that go on the pages. As I explain earlier in the chapter, wood-pulp paper yellows, and the acid in it damages any item it comes into contact with. Make copies of items that you will be adding to the pages using acid-free papers and then store the originals.

✔ **Adhesive:** The sticky substance or material used to fasten your mementos to the paper. Unfortunately, tape doesn't last long, and neither does most glue. In fact, after 10 years, glue breaks down and leaves an ugly, discolored, sticky residue. You can't undo such damage in old scrapbooks and memory books. However, when creating new books, you can purchase acid-free tapes and glues to adhere your memories to pages. You can find acid-free adhesives in craft stores.

When storing old scrapbooks and memory books, place them flat on a level surface. Don't store them upright with the spines facing outwards, because the bulky material stored in these books is hard on the bindings.

Keeping Bibles and Books

Bibles and books are subject to the same deterioration factors as paper, photos, and scrapbooks. Store them wrapped in acid-free tissue or in archival quality (acid-free) boxes lying flat on a level surface, just like I recommend for scrapbooks (see the preceding section). You can purchase these archival quality boxes at most stationery stores or photo-supply houses.

If you prefer to keep your old Bibles and books on shelves, avoid setting them (or any other books) on bare wood. When the wood comes into contact with the paper, discoloration can occur. Instead, store the books on bookshelves that have been well sealed. You can also place pieces of acid-free tissue under the books on the shelf. Tuck the tissue under the books so that it can't be seen.

Holding On to Heirloom Textiles

I love heirloom linens, and I have a large collection of them. My grandmothers and aunts made most of them, but I frequently purchase them at antique stores, flea markets, and estate sales.

Laundering and storing *textiles* (items made of fabric) requires a little TLC (Tender Loving Care) if you expect to pass them on to future generations. By using some special techniques, you can be sure that these items last for a long, long time. For example:

✔ **Wash the textiles as soon as you acquire them.** The first thing that most folks tend to do is shove the textiles in the linen cupboard. Don't do it! Instead, wash them properly to remove the dust, mold, and chemicals that can damage the textiles. However, don't wash anything that is already deteriorating, because washing only makes the damage worse.

✔ **Take the items to the dry cleaner, if necessary.** If you're unsure of the fiber content or if the tag says "dry clean only," don't wash the items in the washing machine.

✔ **Don't use bleach on your linens unless it's absolutely necessary.** If you do decide to use bleach, use it sparingly. Bleach damages textiles, and the damage can't be repaired.

✔ **Lay the linens to dry on a flat surface after laundering.** Hanging the linens causes the fibers to stretch. When the items are almost dry (just slightly damp), iron them to remove the rest of the moisture. After the items are thoroughly dry, fold them, wrap them in acid-free tissue, and store them.

For larger items, such as tablecloths or bedspreads, you can roll them around acid-free tubes or carefully hang them from hangers in the closet. Thus, when you want to use them, you don't have to iron out a bunch of creases.

✔ **Don't starch your linens before you store them.** Storing crisply starched linens causes damage along the folds. I recommend that you starch your linens when you're ready to use them.

✔ **Take your linens and textiles out of storage and inspect them for damage two times per year.** Each time you store them, fold them differently so you don't cause permanent crease damage.

With the proper care, your heirloom textiles can last for generations. Enjoy them and share them with your family by using and displaying them with care.

Saving Your Other Memorabilia

Preserving and storing other treasures depends entirely on what they are made of. For example, you can treat old dishes and crystal with soap and water and safely display or store them. And you can give metal objects a polishing now and then and display them as usual.

Use your best judgment and the tips in this chapter to store or display your family treasures so you can keep them fresh and ready to enjoy for generations to come.

Chapter 20

Ten More Great Reunion Ideas

- -

In This Chapter

▶ Sharing tips for ethnic-themed reunions

▶ Combining multicultural traditions at your reunion

- -

In Chapter 5, I give you some tips and ideas for reunion themes, but in this chapter, I give you ten more possibilities for even more variety. Having a theme really gives the reunion a sense of unity. Decorations, food, and even costumes combine to make a themed reunion a treat for all the senses.

If your family has some sort of ethnic origin, I encourage you to incorporate your ethnic background into your reunion plans. Doing so allows your family members to reconnect with their roots.

If your family has more than one ethnic affiliation, you can use this distinction to show your creativity! For example, if your family is from England and Spain, you can combine the English and Spanish aspects of your family heritage and throw a "Spang-lish" reunion. You can serve English tea and seafood paella (although probably not at the same time!). Likewise, if your family is from Italy and Japan, you can plan an "Ital-ese" festival.

In this chapter, you can find a list of ethnic-related items for reunion planning. However, this list isn't exhaustive, because I don't have enough space to cover every nationality. If your culture isn't included in this chapter, refer to one of the examples as a guide.

Chinese Gala

Bring the exciting, colorful aspects of a Chinese gala to your family reunion through the addition of festival-style foods and décor. Ask your family members to wear costumes (if they have them) to further enhance the theme. Try serving the following foods:

Fried and/or steamed rice

Assorted *dim sum* (a type of Chinese finger-food)

Chicken chow mein

Steamed pork buns (a rice-flour dough that surrounds tasty pork filling) wrapped in colorful paper

Egg-flower soup (An egg added to this vegetable soup near the end of the cooking time gives the appearance of flower petals floating in the broth.)

Rice candy (delicious candy made from rice products)

Decorate the reunion site with paper lanterns and flowers. You can also hang brightly painted umbrellas upside down from the ceiling for a tossing game (similar to the hoop toss in Chapter 7) or just for decoration. Use your imagination. Celebrate the evening with a fireworks display after dark.

Northern European Celebration

Northern European parties often include lots of pickles, sausages, breads, and good-quality beer. Polka music inspires spontaneous dancing and singing, so be sure to bring along tapes or CDs and a mode of playing them to lighten the mood. Consider these food items for your reunion:

Potato *pierogis* (potato turnovers, often made with cheese and onion added)

Grilled meats

Grilled sausages

Assorted breads, cheeses, and cold cuts

Assorted mustards, pickles, and condiments

Assorted salads

Steamed vegetables

Assorted sweets for dessert

Cover the tables with brightly embroidered tablecloths. Place a centerpiece of vivid flowers on each table. Playing some polka music after dinner can liven things up considerably.

Nordic Fest

Families of Norwegian, Swedish, and Finnish descent (among just a few Nordic cultures) may enjoy having a family reunion based on a Nordic theme. *Note:* If you're making Lutefisk, keep the air freshener handy! Consider serving the following foods:

Assorted pickled fish (herring, salmon, and so on)

Open-faced sandwiches on rye

Pancakes with toppings

Lutefisk (dried cod, rehydrated and cooked in a sauce — very smelly)

Grilled salmon

Assorted salads

Steamed vegetables

Potato Lefsa (a flat bread made from potato flour)

Breads, cheeses, and cold cuts

Fruit dumplings, cakes, or fritters for dessert

Enhance the Nordic setting by decorating in blue and white. For folklore-inspired décor, place a ceramic troll, like the kind found in a garden center, on each table as a centerpiece. Ice sculptures and snowflakes are a nice touch, even in summer.

A Little Bit of Italy

Ahhh, Italia! The food, the festivities, and the fun! Even families who aren't of Italian descent can appreciate an Italian reunion theme. The colors of red, white, and green, combined with fresh, tasty pasta dishes bring a smile to every face. Think about serving some of the following dishes:

Assorted *antipastos* (appetizers)

Minestrone or various soups

Brushetta (toasted breads with yummy toppings)

Pasta, pasta, and more pasta

Polenta (a cornmeal mush topped with sauce)

Grilled meats and vegetables

Pizza (the kids' favorite!)

Fruit and cheese

Zabaglione or *tortas* (Italian ice cream or layered cakes, respectively) for dessert

Dress the tables in red and white-checkered cloths and napkins. A simple bunch of wildflowers in a glass jar or bottle makes a lovely centerpiece, especially if surrounded by baskets of old-world-style breads. Place a few bottles of Chianti on the tables and encourage folks to pass them around. The smell of pasta is all you need to get the clan running to the food tables.

Japanese Traditions

Japanese families may want to consider a reunion based on Japanese foods, music, and decoration. Do you have a sushi chef in your family? Ask him or her to volunteer as your official sushi maker! To make cleanup easy, you can buy packages of disposable chopsticks at Asian markets. Here are some foods to consider:

Bowls of steamed *edamame pods* (soybeans still in their pods, steamed and eaten with hands) as snacks

Steamed rice

Green salad

Assorted sushi and *sashimi* (raw fish dishes)

Miso (soup made from fermented soy products) or *soba* (buckwheat) noodles in broth with accompaniments

Vegetable and shrimp *tempura* (batter-coated, deep-fried, and absolutely delicious!) with dipping sauce

Rice balls

Grilled *yakitori* (skewered meats) with condiments

Sake or sake-based cocktails

Assorted *wagashi* (sweets, such as cookies and pastries) for dessert

You can make tablecloths from lovely Japanese-inspired textiles, which you can find at any fabric store. For a *tatami* (floor-style dining) setting, place the tablecloths on low tables and spread out straw mats and cushions on the floor. If your family prefers to sit at standard tables, use the textiles as tablecloths and the straw mats as table runners. Simple, individual floral arrangements and traditional Japanese music are all you need to complete the theme.

A Taste of Spain

Olé! My family is from Spain and this, of course, is our very own reunion theme. My grandfather made the best paella on the planet! Flamenco-inspired music, dance, and costume always add the festive flair that my family members adore. Here are some possible menu ideas for planning your own Spanish festival:

Tapas

Assorted cheeses and cold cuts

Olives

Crusty bread and olive oil for dipping

Paella (a traditional rice and seafood dish) cooked outdoors

Green salad with garlic dressing

Garbanzo salad

Grilled fish

Roasted pork

Flan (custard), tortas, sweets, or *Crema Catalana* (another type of custard) for dessert

Set the tables with embroidered table linens. Huge bouquets of wildflowers or olive branches in pottery pitchers make terrific centerpieces. For a vineyard theme, you can lay grapevines across the tables. Serve plates of olives and cheese. Classical guitar music completes the theme.

Middle Eastern Fantasy

Families of Middle Eastern descent can create an enchanting cultural theme for their reunion. Low tables, cushions, ethnic foods, and music all help to create the fantastic theme. Consider some of the following foods:

Assorted grilled meats, such as lamb and chicken

Vegetables for dipping

Dipping sauces for meats and vegetables

Humus and pita or flatbread

Mixed vegetable salad

Green salad with lemon dressing

Couscous (grain-sized semolina pasta) or *goulash* (a mixed vegetable dish in tomato sauce)

Phyllo pastry stuffed with favorite fillings

Assorted cakes and sweets

Set the tables with rustic tablecloths in shades of saffron, lemon, deep green, and cinnamon. Placing a finger bowl of rosewater or orange-blossom water at each place setting for hand washing adds traditional, old-style charm. Fill lots of baskets with fruit for décor and serve the food family-style on huge brass trays. Mint tea served after dinner soothes digestion.

Proper British Fare

Celebrate your British heritage with an English-themed reunion. Your guest of honor (if you decide to have one) can be your reunion king or queen. Don't forget to provide the royal guest with a crown and throne! Here are some foods to serve:

Assorted finger sandwiches

Sausage rolls

Pears with *stilton* (a terrific but stinky cheese)

Bangers (sausage links) and mash (*mashed potatoes*)

Steamed vegetables

Assorted salads

Roast beef with Yorkshire pudding

Black tea and assorted stout ales

Profiteroles (cream puffs, British-style), cakes, or tarts for dessert

Set the tables with lace tablecloths and linen napkins — or white paper if you're going for the disposable thing. A bouquet of imitation or homegrown roses on each table makes a lovely centerpiece. Place a pretty china teacup and saucer at each place setting and have plenty of sugar and cream on the tables for tea.

German Biergarten

Here's a theme that is sure to bring a smile to the faces of Germans and non-Germans alike! I can almost hear the oom-pah-pah of the music and the festive atmosphere as I write! The following foods will no doubt add to your German atmosphere:

Grilled bratwurst

Blackforest ham (type of cured ham available at any deli counter)

Assorted hand-made breads

Assorted mustards and pickles

Sauerkraut and *schnitzel* (meat dish)

Assorted cold salads

German potato salad (made with bacon and vinegar, served hot)

Beer

Chocolate cake and *stollen* (a fruit-studded sweet bread) for dessert

Set a lively table using a mix of brightly-colored linens. Daisies in white ceramic pitchers make nice centerpieces. Playing polka music after dinner will get your family members on their feet.

Greek Festival

If your family is of Greek descent, you've probably been to several dozen family reunions already. Family has always been an important aspect of Greek life — and of course the food is terrific! Create your own Greek festival using these menu ideas:

Grilled meats, especially lamb and chicken

Skishkabob or *bifteki* (grilled beef)

Assorted grilled vegetables

Eggplant dishes

Marinated tomatoes, feta cheese, and olives

Gyro sandwiches

Pita bread with assorted dips, such as *tzatziki* (cucumber dip)

Assorted sliced sausages

Baklava and honey-based desserts

Decorate with sun-drenched colors, such as blue, white, orange, and yellow. Large wooden or ceramic bowls or baskets filled with fruit make nice centerpieces. To make this theme even more entertaining, ask family members to dress up as their favorite Greek gods and goddesses.

Part VII
Appendixes

The 5th Wave   By Rich Tennant

"I'm not sure I want to be claimed by a family whose home page has a link to the Zany Zone."

In this part . . .

Part 7 contains a few more resources to help streamline your reunion planning. In Appendix A, for example, you can find out how to use the CD-ROM that comes with this book. In Appendix B, you can check out dozens of Internet resources, such as reunion-planning and family-research sites that can provide additional tips and advice. Appendix C lists contact information for your state department of tourism. You can use it to scout out possible reunion locations. And finally, Appendix D is chock-full of crowd-sized recipes provided by the Betty Crocker kitchens to help with your menu planning. You're sure to find something to please even the finicky family members!

Appendix A

About the CD

System Requirements

Make sure that your computer meets the minimum system requirements in the following list. If your computer does not match up to most of these requirements, you may have problems using the contents of the CD:

- ✔ A PC with a Pentium or faster processor or a Mac OS computer with a 68040 or faster processor.

- ✔ Microsoft Windows 98 or later, or Mac OS system software 7.6.1 or later.

- ✔ At least 32MB of total RAM installed on your computer. For best performance, I recommend at least 64MB of RAM installed.

- ✔ A CD-ROM drive.

- ✔ A sound card for PCs. (Mac OS computers have built-in sound support.)

- ✔ A monitor capable of displaying at least 256 colors of grayscale.

- ✔ A modem with a speed of at least 33,600 bps (56K recommended).

If you need more information on the basics, check out *PCs For Dummies,* by Dan Gookin; *Macs For Dummies,* by David Pogue; *iMacs For Dummies* by David Pogue; *Windows 95 For Dummies, Windows 98 For Dummies, Windows 2000 Professional For Dummies, Microsoft Windows ME Millennium Edition For Dummies,* all by Andy Rathbone.

Using the CD with Microsoft Windows

1. **Insert the CD into your computer's CD-ROM drive.**

2. **Open your browser.**

3. **Click Start ⇨ Run.**

4. **In the dialog box that appears, type D:\START.HTM.**

   Replace *D* with the proper drive letter if your CD-ROM drive uses a different letter. (If you don't know the letter, see how your CD-ROM drive is listed under My Computer.)

5. **Read through the license agreement, nod your head and smile, and click the Accept button if you want to use the CD.**

   After you click Accept, you jump to the Main Menu. This action displays the file that walks you through the contents of the CD.

6. **To navigate within the interface, simply click on any topic of interest to go to an explanation of the files on the CD and how to use or install them.**

7. **To install the software from the CD, simply click the software name.**

   You see two options — the option to run or open the file from the current location or the option to save the file to your hard drive. After you choose to run or open the file from its current location, the installation procedure continues. When you are done with the interface, close your browser as usual.

To run some of the programs, you may need to keep the CD inside your CD-ROM drive. This is a Good Thing. Otherwise, the installed program would require you to install a very large chunk of the program to your hard drive space, which would keep you from installing other software.

Using the CD with the Mac OS

To install the items from the CD to your hard drive, follow these steps:

1. **Insert the CD into your computer's CD-ROM drive.**

   After a moment, an icon representing the CD appears on your Mac desktop. The icon may look like a CD-ROM.

2. **Double click the CD icon to show the CD's contents.**

3. **Double click the Read Me First icon.**

This text file contains information about the CD's programs and any last-minute instructions that you need to know about installing the programs on the CD that I don't cover in this Appendix.

4. **Open your browser.**

5. **Double-click** `start.htm` **to open your browser and display the license agreement.**

   If your browser doesn't open automatically, open it as you normally would by choosing File⇨Open File (in Internet Explorer) or File⇨Open⇨Location in Netscape (in Netscape Navigator) and select *Family Reunion Planning Kit For Dummies.* The license agreement appears.

6. **Read through the license agreement, nod your head and smile, and click the Accept button if you want to use the CD.**

   After you click Accept, you jump to the Main Menu. This action displays the file that walks you through the contents of the CD.

7. **To navigate within the interface, simply click on any topic of interest to go to an explanation of the files on the CD and how to use or install them.**

8. **To install the software from the CD, simply click the software name.**

   You see two options — the option to run or open the file from the current location or the option to save the file to your hard drive. After you choose to run or open the file from its current location, the installation procedure continues. When you're done with the interface, close your browser as usual.

What You'll Find on the CD

The following sections are arranged by category and provide a summary of the software and other goodies that you can find on the CD. If you need help with installing the items provided on the CD, refer back to the installation instructions in the preceding section.

Shareware programs are fully functional, trial versions of copyrighted programs. If you like particular programs, you can register with the authors and receive licenses, enhanced versions, and technical support — for a nominal fee. *Freeware programs* are free, copyrighted programs such as games, applications, and utilities. Unlike shareware, these programs do not require a fee or provide technical support. *Trial, demo, or evaluation* versions of software are usually limited either by time or functionality (such as being unable to save projects). Some trial versions are very sensitive to system date changes. If you alter your computer's date, the programs will "time out" and will no longer be functional.

Helpful software

Acrobat Reader

For Mac and Windows

Freeware version

This program lets you view and print the *Portable Document Format* (PDF) files like the files on this CD. To find out more about using Adobe Acrobat Reader, choose the Reader Online Guide from the Help menu, or view the Acrobat.pdf file installed in the same folder as the program. You can also get more information by visiting the Adobe Systems Web site at www.adobe.com.

Brother's Keeper

For Windows

Shareware version

Brother's Keeper is a genealogical shareware program that allows you to store information about your family and create detailed charts and reports based on that information. If you decide to keep it after the 30-day trial period and register your copy after trying it out, you can follow the instructions on the Brother's Keeper for Windows Web site at http://ourworld.compuserve.com/homepages/Brothers_Keeper. As of this time, there is not a Mac version of this software.

Calendar Builder

For Windows

30-day trial version

This program creates custom calendars to help you keep track of important dates in the course of your reunion planning. If you decide to keep it and register your copy after trying it out for 30 days, or to learn more about the program, you can visit the Web site or follow the instructions for registering the product at http://www.rkssoftware.com/cbinfo.htm.

Free Agent

For Windows

Freeware version

Free Agent, from Forte, Inc., lets you read and participate in ongoing group discussions on the Internet via Usenet newsgroups. Among the program's features are its capability to let you read newsgroup articles offline, which could conceivably save you Internet connection and phone charges. For more information about how to use Free Agent, visit the Web site, `www.forteinc.com`.

MusiFind Pro

For Windows

Shareware version

This database software allows you to organize your music collection, whether on CD, cassettes, or vinyl (records). It has an easy-to-use wizard to help you enter your information and query wizards for more detailed searching. Plus you can find customizable categories for different types of music media. Other features include song, album, and DJ logs and playlist reports. If you decide to keep it after the 30-day trial period, you can pay $8 for the standard version or $12 for the Internet version. Visit the Web site at `www.authord.com/MFP/` for more information.

Paint Shop Pro

For Windows

Evaluation version

Paint Shop Pro, from JASC, Inc., is a multipurpose graphics tool that lets you view images in virtually any graphics format available on the Internet. In addition, you can edit and crop images, convert images from one file to another, and even create pictures from scratch — all of which can be helpful when creating your family reunion Web pages. Visit the program's Web site at `www.jasc.com/psp.html` for more information.

Professional Bartender 2000

For Windows

30-day trial version

This nifty program contains recipes for more than 1,000 drinks, both alcoholic and nonalcoholic. You can also add your own recipes to the database or modify any of the included recipes to create your own unique concoctions. The search facility lets you search for recipes by liquor, ingredients, temperature (hot or cold drinks), season, type of drink, or intended glassware (such as a martini or old-fashioned glass). If you decide to keep it, register and pay $19.95 at the Web site `http://www.probartender.com/`.

StuffIt Expander

For Mac

Commercial version

StuffIt Expander, from Aladdin Systems, Inc., is an invaluable file decompression utility for the Macintosh. Many files on the Internet are compressed — shrunken in size through the use of special programming tricks — both to save storage space and to cut down on the amount of time that they require to be downloaded. You may also occasionally receive compressed files as e-mail attachments. After you have a compressed file on your hard drive, use StuffIt Expander to decompress the file and make it useable again. To learn more, visit the Web site at www.aladdinsys.com.

TreeDraw

For Windows

A shareware product for use with GEDCOM genealogy software

This software creates professional-looking charts with graphics and color-printing options. You can add additional text and information easily by clicking your mouse and typing — very user-friendly! You can also import descendant and ancestral charts from any software that uses the GEDCOM format.

WinZip

For Windows

Shareware version

WinZip, from Nico Mak Computing, Inc., is an invaluable file compression and decompression Windows utility. It works to compress and decompress files in the same way that StuffIt Expander does (see the StuffIt Expander program description earlier in this section). To find out more about WinZip, visit the program's Web site at www.winzip.com.

Zip Code Companion

For Windows

Shareware version

This handy software allows you to quickly find or verify zip codes, cities, states and area codes in the United States. Includes all 5-digit zip codes in the U.S., FPO (Fleet Post Office) and APO (Army Post Office) and all area codes in the United States. It also includes access to the U.S. Postal Service's ZIP+4 service through an HTML link. If you decide to keep it, pay $19.95. You can find out more about the program at the following Web site: www.pc-shareware. com/zipcode.htm.

Author-created material

The following table is a list of all the documents on the CD. Each form is available to you as a PDF file and almost every form is available as a Rich Text File (.rtf). You'll need Adobe Acrobat Reader (available on this CD) to view and print the PDF files. You can use your favorite word processor to view, print, and edit the .rtf files.

Figure number	Description
2-1	Sample letter of request
2-2	Sample letter to an old address
3-2	Master Committee List
3-3	Committee Members and Responsibilities
4-1	Reunion Survey
4-2	Location Research Log
4-3a	Budget form — page 1
4-3b	Budget form — page 2
4-4	Vendor Checklist
4-5	Stuff to Rent
4-6	Stuff to Borrow
4-7	Stuff to Buy
4-8	Decorations and Setup Checklist
5-1	Potluck Tracking Sheet
6-1	Sample invitation
6-2	Invitation and RSVP Log
6-3	Accommodations Checklist
7-1	Attendance List
7-2	Family Directory Information Sheet

(continued)

Figure number	Description (continued)
7-3	Activities Checklist
7-4	Human Scavenger Hunt checklist
8-1	Family Bingo Sheet
8-2	Scavenger Hunt List
8-3	Sample award certificate
10-1	Knockdown and Cleanup List
10-2	Post-Reunion Evaluation Form
13-1	Research Source Log
13-3	Correspondence Log
13-4	Family Group Sheet
13-5	Individual Record
13-6	Empty pedigree chart (family tree)
13-8	Family Memorabilia Inventory Sheet
15-1	Task Tracking Record

Internet Links

The Internet links section on the CD-ROM provides links to all the Web sites mentioned in this book. Having these on the CD makes it easier for you to visit the sites, because instead of sitting at your computer retyping everything you read, you can just click on the hyperlink to the URL and go directly to the site. Isn't technology wonderful?

If You Have Problems (Of the CD Kind)

I tried to include programs that work on most computers with a minimum amount of system requirements. However, every computer is different, and some programs may not work properly for some offbeat reason.

The two likeliest problems are that you don't have enough memory (RAM) for the programs you want to use, or that you have other programs running that are affecting installation or running of a program. If you get an error message like Not enough memory or Setup cannot continue, try one or more of the following methods and then try installing or using the software again.

- ✔ **Turn off any antivirus software that you have on your computer.** Installer programs sometimes mimic virus activity and cause your computer to incorrectly believe that a virus is infecting it. Also, antivirus software running in the background can use up a lot of system resources.

- ✔ **Close all running programs.** The more programs you're running, the less memory is available to other programs. Installers also typically update files and programs. So if you keep other programs running, installation may not work properly.

- ✔ **Have your local computer store add more RAM to your computer or add it yourself.** This isn't as scary or drastic as it sounds, and adding more memory can greatly increase the speed of your computer and allow more programs to run at the same time.

- ✔ **Reference the ReadMe:** Please refer to the ReadMe file located at the root of the CD-ROM for the latest product information at the time of publication.

If you still have trouble installing the items from the CD, please call the Hungry Minds, Inc., Customer Service phone number at 800-762-2974 (outside the United States: 317-572-3994) or send e-mail to techsupdum@hungryminds.com.

Appendix B

Terrific Internet Resources

* *

*I*f you use a computer and have access to the Internet, you have many reunion-planning options indeed, my friend! In this appendix, I list lots of terrific sites for anyone interested in finding out more about planning and hosting family reunions or in delving into genealogical research.

Many of the sites that I include have search engines, as well as links to other sites. For the most part, these sites are easy to navigate and full of helpful information.

This is just a small sample of what's available on the Internet. To find more sites, type one of the following keywords into your favorite search engine:

- ✔ Family reunions
- ✔ Party planning
- ✔ Event planning
- ✔ Genealogy

Locating Great Reunion-Specific Sites

Finding Web sites that are family-reunion specific can be tough, but don't despair, because I give you plenty of examples. Check out the following sites:

- ✔ **Family-Reunion.com** (www.family-reunion.com): A family-reunion organizer's dream site, where a cute little character called Mister Spiffy guides you through every aspect of reunion planning and provides lots of humor. You can also find helpful planning lists, menu ideas, and software that you can order to help you plan a smooth-running reunion.

- ✔ **Reunions Magazine** (www.reunionsmag.com): A useful site for folks planning large reunions (with 50 or more people), it provides links to reunion products, services, and locations. This site also offers a *snail-mail* (postal) subscription to its magazine. If you plan on putting your newly acquired reunion-planning skills to other uses, you can find a lot of ideas on this site.

- **ReunionPlanner.com** (www.reunionplanner.com): This site can be helpful for planning not only family reunions but class and military reunions, too! You can order support books directly from the site, or you can search the site for helpful reunion-planning tips. You can also search for locations to hold your reunion and download a trial version of reunion-planning software. If you decide to keep the trial software, you'll have to pay a fee.

- **Reunion Research** (www.reuniontips.com): Here you can find planning tips and information on products and resources for group reunions (such as family, school, and military reunions). This site also provides some terrific genealogy links, proving once again that family reunions and genealogy go hand in hand.

Be sure to check out other reunion-planning sites, including those for school reunions. Many of the same tips and strategies apply to planning family get-togethers.

Finding Genealogy Sites with Reunion Information

If you're researching your family history online, you can find many sites dedicated to genealogy. But if you're also planning a family reunion, you may as well pick up a few reunion-planning tips along the way. So in this section, I give you sites that combine genealogy with family-reunion information. For example:

- **Family Tree Magazine** (www.familytreemagazine.com): A user-friendly site with search engines, research advice, tools, and resources for people interested in genealogy and family reunions. You can also subscribe to the bimonthly snail-mail magazine.

- **Golden Gate Genealogy Forum** (www.genealogyforum.rootsweb.com): Simple and easy-to-use, this site is packed with lots of great ideas for family-reunion coordinators. Here you can find links to other helpful reunion and genealogy sites as well.

- **Ancestry.com** (www.ancestry.com): A must-visit site for anyone interested in genealogy and family reunions, it provides lots of searches, links to other sites, and all-around great advice.

- **Genealogy Today** (www.genealogytoday.com): Features tips and ideas for reunion planning, genealogy information and links, and a free database that allows you to post your family reunion information.

✔ **Cyndi's List** (`www.cyndislist.com`): Heaven on Earth for people working on genealogy. You can find so much good stuff here. Although this site is famous for its genealogy links, you can also search the site to find tips for planning and hosting family reunions. If you're visiting for genealogy research, you won't be disappointed. This site has links to every genealogy subject, from country-specific research to individual surname studies.

✔ **RootsWeb.com** (`www.rootsweb.com`): Another great site to research your genealogy on the Internet. You can search by surname or place of origin. You can also join the genealogy mailing lists and post your genealogy questions or surnames to the message boards, which are great ways to interact with fellow family finders.

✔ **US GenWeb** (`www.usgenweb.org`): An all-American genealogy site that is easy to navigate and full of interesting tidbits. This site also features links for location-specific research by state. You'll love this one!

Discovering New Fun and Games

Just for fun, I typed *party games* into my search engine and came up with the mother lode! If you don't like the games included in Chapter 8 (or if you want to try some new ones), check out one of the following sites:

✔ **Party Game Central** (`www.partygamecentral.com`): This site makes the claim of being the largest party game site on the Internet — and that may be right! The games are organized by type, such as indoor or outdoor, and the site also suggests games that are age appropriate. The site is easy to use.

✔ **Party Games** (`www.kagi.com/vit/party-games.html`): This site has games grouped by collection, which can make it tough to search. However, with more than 400 games, this site is worth a visit. And it's also available in Russian, if you happen to need it.

✔ **Party Outfitters** (`www.partyoutfitters.com`): You can rent or purchase large inflatable party games on this site, as well as arcade, sports, western, and carnival-themed games (to list a few!). You can find more than 150 games in the inflatable category alone.

Leaving the Planning to the Pros

If you want to have a large reunion but you don't want to plan the entire event, consider hiring an event planner or consultant. These friendly and efficient folks can help you with multiple tasks — from creating the guest list and locating sites to planning the menu and organizing activities.

You have several options for locating event planners in your area. For example:

- ✔ Look in your local Yellow Pages under the headings *Events* and *Party*. Both areas often feature party planners that you can contact.

- ✔ Contact your local party or rental store, where folks can provide you with a list of reputable event planners. A recommendation is often worth a thousand words!

- ✔ Search for local event planners through a professional event-planning Internet site, such as the ones listed in the following section. If a Web site doesn't list any planners in your area, send an e-mail — the site may not be updated frequently.

Some of the following sites don't contain lists of event planners, but they can help you find planners if you send them e-mail. Nonetheless, all these sites are terrific resources for party-planning materials and rentals.

- ✔ **Banquetrooms.com** (www.banquetrooms.com): This site really blows me away — what a cool and efficient means of finding a reunion location, anywhere in the United States! If your location is not listed in the database, the site features a form that you can fill out for assistance. It also provides a list of recommended event planners.

- ✔ **Event Planner** (www.event-planner.com): This is a helpful site for locating event planners, entertainers, transportation companies, sites, rentals, and everything else that a reunion planner needs.

- ✔ **Special Event Source** (www.specialeventsource.com): Use this site to help you locate event planners, decorations, rentals, sites, and so on. You can also find some great articles for party planners.

- ✔ **Event Solutions** (www.event-solutions.com): A site chock-full of party-planning information, it includes menu planning, links to professional party-planners, and many party services, such as rentals and caterers.

- ✔ **PartyPOP.com** (www.partypop.com): Another useful site full of party-planning tips, games, and themes. This easy-to-use site is organized by category. You can also find a nifty budget calculator and a drop-down search menu to make locating a party planner a breeze.

You can find many more helpful sites on the Internet that offer great advice for family-reunion planners. Just type the words *reunion planning* or *party planning* into your favorite search engine.

Appendix C

Departments of Tourism

• •

*I*f you want some reunion-site ideas, check out your state's tourism Web site for links to state parks and recreation facilities, scenic attractions, cultural event calendars, and other neat things. You can also find maps, guides, and other free stuff that you can request by e-mail or over the phone.

In this appendix, I provide a list of the Departments of Tourism for all 50 states, complete with phone numbers and Web site information.

Contacting Your State Department of Tourism

Alabama
www.touralabama.org

1-800-ALABAMA (1-800-252-2262)

Alaska
www.state.ak.us

(907) 465-2012 (No toll-free number available)

Arizona
www.arizonaguide.com

1-888-520-3433

Arkansas
www.arkansas.com

1-800-NATURAL (1-800-628-8725)

California
http://gocalif.ca.gov

1-800-862-2543

Colorado
www.colorado.com

1-800-COLORAD (1-800-265-6723)

Connecticut
www.ctbound.org

1-800-282-6863

Delaware
www.visitdelaware.net

1-866-284-7483

Florida
http://flausa.com

1-888-7-FLAUSA (1-888-735-2872)

Georgia
www.georgia.org

1-800-847-4842

Hawaii

www.state.hi.us/tourism

1-800-GO-HAWAI (1-800-464-2924)

Idaho

www.visitid.org

1-800-842-5858

Illinois

www.enjoyillinois.com

1-800-2CONNECT
(1-800-226-66328)

Indiana

www.state.in.us/tourism

1-800-759-9191 or 1-800-289-6646

Iowa

www.traveliowa.com

1-888-472-6035

Kansas

www.kansascommerce.com

1-800-2-KANSAS (1-800-252-6727)

Kentucky

www.kytourism.com

1-800-225-8747

Louisiana

http://louisianatravel.com

1-877-226-7652

Maine

www.visitmaine.com

1-877-481-5986

Maryland

www.mdisfun.org

1-800-MDisFUN (1-800-634-7386)

Massachusetts

www.massvacation.com

1-800-447-MASS (1-800-447-6277)

Michigan

http://travel.michigan.org

1-800-543-2YES (1-800-543-2937)

Minnesota

www.exploreminnesota.com

1-800-657-3700

Mississippi

www.mississippi.org

1-800-WARMEST (1-800-927-6378)

Missouri

www.missouritourism.org

1-800- 877-1234

Montana

www.visitmt.com

1-800-VISITMT (1-800-847-4868)

Nebraska

www.visitnebraska.org

1-800-228-4307

Nevada

www.travelnevada.com

1-800-NEVADA8 (1-800-638-2328)

New Hampshire

www.visitnh.gov

1-800-FUN-IN-NH (1-800-386-4664)

New Jersey

www.state.nj.us/travel

1-800-VISITNJ (1-800-847-4865)

New Mexico
www.newmexico.org
1-800-733-6396

New York
http://iloveny.state.ny.us
1-800-CALLNYS (1-800-225-5697)

North Carolina
www.visitnc.com
1-800-VISITNC (1-800-847-4862)

North Dakota
www.ndtourism.com
1-800-HELLOND (1-800-435-5663)

Ohio
www.ohiotourism.com
1-800-BUCKEYE (1-800-282-5393)

Oklahoma
www.otrd.state.ok.us
1-800-652-6552

Oregon
www.traveloregon.com
1-800-547-7842

Pennsylvania
www.experiencepa.com
1-800-VISITPA (1-800-847-4872)

Rhode Island
www.visitrhodeisland.com
1-800-556-2484

South Carolina
www.travelsc.com
1-803-734-1700

South Dakota
www.travelsd.com
1-800-S-DAKOTA (1-800-732-5682)

Tennessee
www.tourism.state.tn.us
1-800-836-6200

Texas
www.traveltex.com
1-800-8888-TEX

Utah
www.utah.com
1-800-200-1160

Vermont
www.1-800-vermont.com
1-800-VERMONT (1-800-837-6668)

Virginia
www.virginia.org
1-800-321-3244

Washington
www.tourism.wa.gov
1-800-544-1800

West Virginia
www.callwva.com
1-800-CALL WVA (1-800-225-5982)

Wisconsin
www.travelwisconsin.com
1-800-432-TRIP (1-800-432-8747)

Wyoming
www.wyomingtourism.org
1-800-225-5996

Betty Crocker Recipes

Dear Family Reunion Planners,

I love family reunions! It's great to get the family together, trade stories, meet new babies, new spouses, and almost-lost kin. I can't think of a nicer way to get reacquainted than over a meal.

It's so easy to create a terrific potluck meal that's delicious, as well as economical, when everyone works together. Mail out a sign-up sheet — or send it by e-mail — and have folks sign up for dishes. To make sure you get a tempting variety of dishes, put categories on the sheet, such as main dishes, salads, breads, beverages, and desserts. Then take a look at the sign-up and see if there are areas that need more dishes. If some categories are light (maybe everyone wants to bring dessert!) then you can ask family members to bring dishes to fill in where they're needed.

In this appendix you can find some of my favorite recipes, perfect for large groups. I put in lots of slow cooker recipes, so you can spend time visiting, not in the kitchen, the day of the reunion. Make and serve carefree Sloppy Joes, a favorite for all ages, in your slow cooker, teamed with Sweet-and-Sour Coleslaw and topped off with Chocolate Chip Cookies. Want something a bit more formal? Try Turkey Breast Stuffed with Wild Rice and Favorite Green Bean Casserole, finished with fresh fruit and Pound Cake. Are there vegetarians in the family? They'll be delighted with Chunky Vegetable Lasagna.

You can find more terrific recipes and ideas for your family reunion at `www.bettycrocker.com`. And thanks for letting me help with your family reunion.

Betty Crocker

P.S. Have a great time!

Sloppy Joes

■ *24 sandwiches* ■

SLOW COOKER:
3½ to 6-quart

PREP TIME:
15 minutes

COOK TIME:
Low 7 to 9 hours
High 3 to 4 hours

3 pounds ground beef

1 large onion, coarsely chopped (1 cup)

¾ cup chopped celery

1 cup barbecue sauce

1 can (26½ ounces) sloppy joe sauce

24 hamburger buns

1. Cook beef and onion in Dutch oven over medium heat, stirring occasionally, until beef is brown; drain.

2. Mix beef mixture and remaining ingredients except buns in 3½ to 6-quart slow cooker.

3. Cover and cook on low heat setting 7 to 9 hours (or high heat setting 3 to 4 hours) or until vegetables are tender.

4. Uncover and cook on high heat setting until desired consistency. Stir well before serving. Fill buns with beef mixture.

Betty's Success Tip

Next time you're asked to bring something to one of your kid's events, bring Sloppy Joes. Kids love them. And you can keep the sandwich filling warm in the cooker for a couple of hours. Just be sure to stir it occasionally so that it doesn't start to get too brown around the edges.

Ingredient Substitution

Stir 1 cup drained sauerkraut into the mixture before serving. It will add a nice flavor twist and no one will guess the "secret ingredient."

Serving Suggestion

You can serve this tasty beef mixture over hot cooked rice or pasta rather than using it as a sandwich filling. Or spoon it over tortilla chips and top each serving with shredded lettuce and shredded cheese.

1 sandwich: Calories 155 (Calories from Fat 80); Fat 9g (Saturated 3g); Cholesterol 30mg; Sodium 270mg; Carbohydrate 8g (Dietary Fiber 1g); Protein 11g

%Daily Value: Vitamin A 2%; Vitamin C 4%; Calcium 2%; Iron 6%

Diet Exchanges: 1 High-Fat Meal, 2 Vegetable

Barbecue Beef Sandwiches

■ *12 sandwiches* ■

SLOW COOKER:
4- to 5-quart

PREP TIME:
20 minutes

COOK TIME:
Low 7 to 8 hours

FINISHING COOK TIME:
Low 30 minutes

Ingredient Substitution

If you don't have apricot preserves, you certainly may use peach preserves or orange marmalade in its place.

Finishing Touch

For a delicious kick, spread buns with horseradish sauce. Sandwiches can be served au jus. Serve the juices left in the cooker in small bowls to dip the sandwiches in while eating to make each bite extra delicious!

3-pound beef boneless chuck roast

1 cup barbecue sauce

1/2 cup apricot preserves

1/3 cup chopped green bell pepper

1 tablespoon Dijon mustard

1 teaspoon packed brown sugar

1 small onion, sliced

12 kaiser or hamburger buns, split

1. Trim excess fat from beef. Cut beef into 4 pieces. Place beef in 4- to 5-quart slow cooker.

2. Mix remaining ingredients except buns; pour over beef. Cover and cook on low heat setting 7 to 8 hours or until beef is tender.

3. Remove beef to cutting board; cut into thin slices; return to cooker.

4. Cover and cook on low heat setting 20 to 30 minutes longer or until beef is hot. Fill buns with beef mixture.

1 sandwich: Calories 410 (Calories from Fat 145); Fat 16g (Saturated 5g); Cholesterol 70mg; Sodium 520mg; Carbohydrate 39g (Dietary Fiber 2g); Protein 29g

%Daily Value: Vitamin A 4%; Vitamin C 8%; Calcium 6%; Iron 24%

Diet Exchanges: 2 1/2 Starch, 3 Medium-fat Meat

Pork Roast with Sherry-Plum Sauce

■ *12 servings* ■

SLOW COOKER:
3½- to 6-quart

PREP TIME:
20 minutes

COOK TIME:
Low 7 to 9 hours

FINISHING COOK TIME:
High 15 minutes

4-pound pork boneless loin roast

2 tablespoons vegetable oil

1 cup dry sherry

1 tablespoon ground mustard (dry)

2 tablespoons soy sauce

1½ teaspoons dried thyme leaves

1½ teaspoons ground ginger

1 teaspoon salt

¼ teaspoon pepper

3 cloves garlic, finely chopped

½ cup plum jam

1. Trim excess fat from pork. Heat oil in 10-inch skillet over medium-high heat. Cook pork in oil about 10 minutes, turning occasionally, until brown on all sides.

2. Place pork in 3½- to 6-quart slow cooker. Mix remaining ingredients except jam; pour over pork.

3. Cover and cook on low heat setting 7 to 9 hours or until pork is tender.

4. Remove pork from cooker; cover and keep warm. Skim fat from pork juices in cooker if desired. Stir jam into juices.

5. Cover and cook on high heat setting about 15 minutes or until jam is melted; stir. Serve sauce with pork.

1 Serving: Calories 240 (Calories from Fat 90); Fat 10g (Saturated 3g); Cholesterol 70mg; Sodium 400mg; Carbohydrate 12g (Dietary Fiber 0g); Protein 25g

%Daily Value: Vitamin A 0%; Vitamin C 0%; Calcium 0%; Iron 6%

Diet Exchanges: 1 Starch, 3 Lean Meat

Skillet Fried Chicken

■ *6 Servings* ■

PREP TIME: 10 minutes
COOK TIME: 45 minutes

Lighter Skillet-Fried Chicken

For 11 grams of fat and 250 calories per serving, remove skin from chicken before cooking. Use 2 tablespoons oil in step 2.

Buttermilk Fried Chicken

Increase flour to 1 cup. Dip chicken in 1 cup buttermilk before coating with flour mixture.

½ cup all-purpose flour

1 tablespoon paprika

1½ teaspoons salt

½ teaspoon pepper

3- to 3½-pound cut-up broiler-fryer chicken

Vegetable oil

1. Mix flour, paprika, salt, and pepper. Coat chicken with flour mixture.

2. Heat oil (¼ inch) in 12-inch nonstick skillet over medium-high heat. Cook chicken in oil about 10 minutes or until light brown on all sides; reduce heat to low. Turn chicken skin side up.

3. Simmer uncovered about 20 minutes, without turning, until juice of chicken is no longer pink when centers of thickest pieces are cut.

1 Serving: Calories 350 (Calories from Fat 205); Fat 23g (Saturated 5g); Cholesterol 85mg; Sodium 670mg; Carbohydrate 9g (Dietary Fiber 1g); Protein 28g

%Daily Value: Vitamin A 10%; Vitamin C 0%; Calcium 2%; Iron 10%

Diet Exchanges: ½ Starch, 4 Medium-fat Meat

Turkey Breast Stuffed with Wild Rice and Cranberries

■ *10 servings* ■

SLOW COOKER:
3½ to 6-quart

PREP TIME:
25 minutes

COOK TIME:
Low 8 to 9 hours

4 cups cooked wild rice

¾ cup finely chopped onion

½ cup dried cranberries

⅓ cup slivered almonds

2 medium peeled or unpeeled cooking apples, coarsely chopped (2 cups)

4- to 5-pound boneless whole turkey breast, thawed if frozen

1. Mix all ingredients except turkey. Cut turkey into slices at 1-inch intervals about three-fourths of the way through, forming deep pockets.

2. Place turkey in 3½ to 6-quart slow cooker. Stuff pockets with wild rice mixture. Place remaining rice mixture around edge of cooker.

3. Cover and cook on low heat setting 8 to 9 hours or until turkey is no longer pink in center.

1 Serving: Calories 400 (Calories from Fat 125); Fat 14g (Saturated 3g); Cholesterol 115mg; Sodium 100mg; Carbohydrate 26g (Dietary Fiber 4g); Protein 47g

%Daily Value: Vitamin A 4%; Vitamin C 6%; Calcium 4%; Iron 12%

Diet Exchanges: 1 Starch, 6 Very Lean Meat, 2 Vegetable, 1 Fat

Tuna-Macaroni Salad

■ *6 servings* ■

PREP TIME: 20 minutes
CHILL TIME: 1 hour

1 package (7 ounces) elbow macaroni

1 cup mayonnaise or salad dressing

1 cup shredded Cheddar cheese (4 ounces), if desired

½ cup frozen green peas, thawed

¼ cup sweet pickle relish, if desired

2 teaspoons lemon juice

¾ teaspoon salt

¼ teaspoon pepper

1 medium stalk celery, chopped (½ cup)

1 small onion, chopped (¼ cup)

1 can (9 ounces) tuna, drained

1. Cook and drain macaroni as directed on package. Rinse with cold water; drain.

2. Mix macaroni and remaining ingredients. Cover and refrigerate at least 1 hour to blend flavor.

1 Serving: Calories 520 (Calories from Fat 325); Fat 36g (Saturated 9g); Cholesterol 55mg; Sodium 780mg; Carbohydrate 30g (Dietary Fiber 2g); Protein 21g

%Daily Value: Vitamin A 8%; Vitamin C 4%; Calcium 12%; Iron 14%

Diet Exchanges: 2 Starch, 2 Medium-Fat Meat, 5 fat

Chunky Vegetable Lasagna

■ *8 servings* ■

PREP TIME: 35 minutes
BAKE TIME: 40 minutes
STAND TIME: 10 minutes

12 uncooked lasagna noodles (about 12 ounces)

3 cups frozen broccoli flowerets, thawed

3 large carrots, coarsely shredded (2 cups)

1 can (14½ ounces) diced tomatoes, drained

1 medium red bell pepper, cut into thin strips

1 medium green bell pepper, cut into thin strips

¾ cup prepared pesto

¼ teaspoon salt

1 container (15 ounces) ricotta cheese

½ cup grated Parmesan cheese

¼ cup chopped fresh parsley

1 large egg

3 tablespoons butter or stick margarine

1 clove garlic, finely chopped

3 tablespoons all-purpose flour

2 cups milk

3 cups shredded mozzarella cheese (12 ounces)

1. Cook and drain noodles as directed on package.

2. Mix broccoli, carrots, tomatoes, bell peppers, pesto, and salt. Mix ricotta cheese, parsley, and egg.

3. Melt butter in 2-quart saucepan over medium heat. Cook garlic in butter about 2 minutes, stirring frequently, until garlic is golden. Stir in flour. Cook over medium heat, stirring constantly, until mixture is smooth and bubbly; remove from heat. Stir in milk. Heat to boiling, stirring constantly. Boil and stir 1 minute.

4. Heat oven to 350 degrees.

5. Place 3 noodles in ungreased rectangular pan, 13 x 9 x 2 inches. Spread half of the cheese mixture over noodles. Top with 3 noodles; spread with half of the vegetable mixture. Sprinkle with 1 cup of the mozzarella cheese. Top with 3 noodles; spread with remaining cheese mixture. Top with 3 noodles; spread with remaining vegetable mixture. Pour sauce evenly over top. Sprinkle with remaining 2 cups mozzarella cheese.

6. Bake uncovered 35 to 40 minutes or until hot in center. Let stand 10 minutes before cutting.

1 Serving: Calories 540 (Calories from Fat 270); Fat 30g (Saturated 13g); Cholesterol 80mg; Sodium 740mg; Carbohydrate 45g (Dietary Fiber 6g); Protein 28g

% Daily Value: Vitamin A 86%; Vitamin C 68%; Calcium 64%; Iron 18%

Diet Exchanges: 2 Starch, 2 High-Fat Meat, 3 Vegetable, 2 Fat

Marinara Sauce with Spaghetti

■ 12 Servings ■

SLOW COOKER:
3½ to 6-quart

PREP TIME:
15 minutes

COOK TIME:
Low 8 to 10 hours
High 4 to 5 hours

Betty's Success Tip

This multipurpose sauce is so easy to make that you'll want to make it often and keep a few extra containers in the freezer. Ladle the cooked sauce into airtight freezer containers, and keep in your freezer up to a month. Just thaw in the refrigerator or microwave, and use in your favorite recipe.

Ingredient Substitution

The crushed tomatoes with Italian herbs add extra flavor, but you can use plain crushed tomatoes and increase the basil to 1 tablespoon and the oregano to 2 teaspoons.

2 cans (28 ounces each) crushed tomatoes with Italian herbs, undrained

1 can (6 ounces) tomato paste

1 large onion, chopped (1 cup)

8 cloves garlic, finely chopped

1 tablespoon olive or vegetable oil

2 teaspoons dried basil leaves

1 teaspoon dried oregano leaves

1 teaspoon salt

1 teaspoon pepper

12 cups hot cooked spaghetti, for serving

Shredded Parmesan cheese, if desired

1. Mix all ingredients except spaghetti and cheese in 3½ to 6-quart slow cooker.

2. Cover and cook on low heat setting 8 to 10 hours (or high heat setting 4 to 5 hours).

3. Serve sauce over spaghetti. Sprinkle with cheese.

1 Serving: Calories 255 (Calories from Fat 20); Fat 2g (Saturated 0g); Cholesterol 0mg; Sodium 670mg; Carbohydrate 54g (Dietary Fiber 4g); Protein 9g

% Daily Value: Vitamin A 8%; Vitamin C 18%; Calcium 6%; Iron 16%

Diet Exchanges: 3 Starch, 2 Vegetable

Easy Baked Beans

■ *10 servings* ■

SLOW COOKER:
3½- to 6-quart

PREP TIME:
10 minutes

COOK TIME:
Low 4 to 5 hours
High 2 to 2½ hours

2 cans (28 ounces each) vegetarian baked beans, drained

1 medium onion, chopped (½ cup)

⅔ cup barbecue sauce

½ cup packed brown sugar

2 tablespoons ground mustard (dry)

1. Mix all ingredients in 3½- to 6-quart slow cooker.

2. Cover and cook on low heat setting 4 to 5 hours (or high heat setting 2 to 2½ hours) or until desired consistency.

1 Serving: Calories 190 (Calories from Fat 10); Fat 1g (Saturated 0g); Cholesterol 0mg; Sodium 940mg; Carbohydrate 43g (Dietary Fiber 8g); Protein 10g

% Daily Value: Vitamin A 0%; Vitamin C 2%; Calcium 10%; Iron 18%

Diet Exchanges: 1 Starch, 2 Vegetable, 1 Fruit

Betty's Success Tip

This recipe is so quick and easy that you will want to make it for just the family, too. Cut the ingredients in half, and cook in a 2- to 3½-quart slow cooker.

Serving Suggestion

Spoon the beans over squares of hot corn bread or split corn bread muffins. Sprinkle with shredded Cheddar cheese and sliced green onion.

Finishing Touch

To keep this a meatless treat, sprinkle each serving with bacon flavor bits. You'll love that great smoky flavor that goes so well with baked beans.

Creamy Potato Salad

■ *10 servings* ■

PREP TIME: 45 minutes
CHILL TIME: 4 hours

Lighter Creamy Potato Salad

For 13 grams of fat and 210 calories per serving, use reduced-fat mayonnaise and 2 eggs.

6 medium round red or white potatoes (2 pounds), peeled

1½ cups mayonnaise or salad dressing

1 tablespoon white or cider vinegar

1 tablespoon yellow mustard

1 teaspoon salt

¼ teaspoon pepper

2 medium stalks celery, chopped (1 cup)

1 medium onion, chopped (½ cup)

4 hard-cooked eggs, chopped

Paprika, if desired

1. Place potatoes in 3-quart saucepan; add enough water just to cover potatoes. Cover and heat to boiling; reduce heat to low. Cook covered 30 to 35 minutes or until potatoes are tender; drain. Let stand until cool enough to handle. Cut potatoes into cubes.

2. Mix mayonnaise, vinegar, mustard, salt, and pepper in large glass or plastic bowl. Add potatoes, celery, and onion; toss. Stir in eggs. Sprinkle with paprika. Cover and refrigerate at least 4 hours to blend flavors and chill. Store covered in refrigerator.

1 Serving (about ¾ cup): Calories 345 (Calories from Fat 250); Fat 28g (Saturated 5g); Cholesterol 105mg; Sodium 480mg; Carbohydrate 21g (Dietary Fiber 2g); Protein 5g

% Daily Value: Vitamin A 4%; Vitamin C 18%; Calcium 2% Iron 8% Diet

Exchanges: 1 Starch, 1 Vegetable, 5 Fat

Sweet-and-Sour Coleslaw

■ *8 servings* ■

PREP TIME: 15 minutes
CHILL TIME: 1 hour

Ingredient Substitution

In a hurry? Use the 6½ cups packaged coleslaw mix, and omit the cabbage, carrot and bell pepper.

½ medium head cabbage, finely shredded (4 cups)

1 large carrot, finely shredded (1 cup)

1 medium green bell pepper, chopped (1 cup)

4 medium green onions, thinly sliced (¼ cup)

½ cup sugar

½ cup white wine, white vinegar or cider vinegar

¼ cup vegetable oil

1 teaspoon ground mustard

½ teaspoon celery seed

½ teaspoon salt

1. Place cabbage, carrot, bell pepper, and onions in large glass or plastic bowl.

2. Shake remaining ingredients in tightly covered container. Pour over vegetables; stir. Cover and refrigerate at least 3 hours, stirring several times, until chilled. Serve with slotted spoon. Store covered in refrigerator.

1 Serving (about ¾ cup): Calories 130 (Calories from Fat 65); Fat 7g (Saturated 1g); Cholesterol 0mg; Sodium 160mg; Carbohydrate 18g (Dietary Fiber 2g); Protein 1g

% Daily Value: Vitamin A 16%; Vitamin C 58%; Calcium 2%; Iron 2%

Diet Exchanges: 3 Vegetable, 1 Fat

Favorite Green Bean Casserole

■ *6 servings* ■

PREP TIME: 20 minutes
BAKE TIME: 40 minutes

1 can (10¾ ounces) condensed cream of mushroom, cream of celery, or cream of chicken soup

½ cup milk

⅛ teaspoon pepper

2 cans (15 ounces each) French-style green beans, drained

1 can (2.8 ounces) French-fried onions

1. Heat oven to 350 degrees.

2. Mix soup, milk, and pepper in 2-quart casserole or square baking dish, 8 x 8 x 2 inches. Stir in beans. Sprinkle with onions.

3. Bake uncovered 30 to 40 minutes or until hot in the center.

* 2 bags (16 ounces each) frozen cut green beans can be substituted for the canned beans. Cook as directed on package for minimum time; drain.

1 Serving (about ¾ cup): Calories 160 (Calories from Fat 90); Fat 10g (Saturated 2g); Cholesterol 5mg; Sodium 850mg; Carbohydrate 17g (Dietary fiber 3g); Protein 4g

% Daily Value: Vitamin A 6%; Vitamin C 6%; Calcium 8%; Iron 10%

Diet Exchanges: ½ Starch, 2 Vegetable, 1½ Fat

Scalloped Corn

■ *8 servings* ■

PREP TIME: 10 minutes
COOK TIME: 8 minutes
BAKE TIME: 35 minutes

2 tablespoons butter or stick margarine

1 medium onion, finely chopped (¼ cup)

¼ cup finely chopped green bell pepper

2 tablespoons all-purpose flour

½ teaspoon salt

½ teaspoon paprika

¼ teaspoon ground mustard

Dash of pepper

¾ cup milk

1 can (15¼ ounces) whole kernel corn, drained

1 egg, slightly beaten

1 cup cornflakes cereal

1 tablespoon butter or stick margarine

1. Heat oven to 350 degrees.

2. Melt 2 tablespoons butter in 10-inch skillet over medium heat. Cook onion and bell pepper in butter, stirring occasionally, until crisp-tender. Stir in flour, salt paprika, mustard, and pepper. Cook, stirring constantly, until smooth and bubbly; remove from heat.

3. Stir in milk. Heat to boiling, stirring constantly. Boil and stir 1 minute; remove from heat. Stir in corn and egg. Pour into ungreased 1-quart casserole.

4. Mix cornflakes and 1 tablespoon butter; sprinkle over corn mixture. Bake uncovered 30 to 35 minutes or until center is set.

1 serving: Calories 135 (Calories from Fat 55); Fat 6g (Saturated 3g); Cholesterol 40mg; Sodium 350mg; Carbohydrate 17g (Dietary Fiber 1g); Protein 4g

% Daily Value: Vitamin A 10%; Vitamin C 8%; Calcium 4%; Iron 10%

Diet Exchanges: 1 Starch, 1 Fat

Potato Casserole Supreme

■ *8 servings* ■

PREP TIME: 15 minutes
BAKE TIME: 50 minutes

1 can (10¾ ounces) condensed cream of mushroom soup

1 can (10¾ ounces) condensed cream of chicken soup

1 container (8 ounces) sour cream

½ cup milk

¼ teaspoon pepper

1 package (30 ounces) frozen shredded hash brown potatoes

8 medium green onions, sliced (½ cup)

1 cup shredded Cheddar cheese (4 ounces)

1. Heat oven to 350 degrees. Grease rectangular baking dish, 13 x 9 x 2 inches.

2. Mix soups, sour cream, milk, and pepper in very large bowl. Stir in potatoes and onions. Spoon into baking dish.

3. Bake uncovered 30 minutes. Sprinkle with cheese. Bake uncovered 15 to 20 minutes or until golden brown on top and bubbly around edges.

1 Serving: Calories 325 (Calories from Fat 135); Fat 15g (Saturated 8g); Cholesterol 40mg; Sodium 1,060mg; Carbohydrate 39g (Dietary Fiber 3g); Protein 9g

% Daily Value: Vitamin A 10%; Vitamin C 10%; Calcium 16%; Iron 6%

Diet Exchanges: 2 Starch, 2 Vegetable, 3 Fat

Garlic Bread

■ *18 slices* ■

PREP TIME: 10 minutes
BAKE TIME: 20 minutes

Herb-Cheese Bread

Omit garlic. Mix 2 tea-spoons chopped fresh parsley, ½ teaspoon dried oregano leaves, 2 tablespoons grated Parmesan cheese and ⅛ tea-spoon garlic salt with the butter.

Onion Bread

Omit garlic if desired. Mix 2 tablespoons finely chopped onion or chives with the butter.

Seeded Bread

Omit garlic if desired. Mix 1 teaspoon celery seed, poppy seed, dill seed, or sesame seed with the butter.

1 clove garlic, finely chopped, or ¼ teaspoon garlic powder

⅓ cup butter or stick margarine, softened

1 loaf (1 pound) French bread, cut into 1-inch slices

1. Heat oven to 400 degrees.

2. Mix garlic and butter.

3. Spread butter mixture over 1 side of each bread slice. Reassemble loaf; wrap securely in heavy-duty aluminum foil.

4. Bake 15 to 20 minutes or until hot.

1 Slice: Calories 90 (Calories from Fat 35); Fat 4g (Saturated 2g); cholesterol 10mg; Sodium 170mg; Carbohydrate 13g (Dietary Fiber 1g); Protein 2g

% Daily Value: Vitamin A 2%; Vitamin C 0%; Calcium 2%; Iron 4%

Diet Exchanges: 1 Starch

Zucchini Bread

■ *2 loaves, 24 slices each* ■

PREP TIME: 15 minutes
BAKE TIME: 1 hour
COOL: 2 hr 10 minutes

Cranberry Bread

Omit zucchini, cinnamon, cloves, and raisins. Stir in ½ cup milk and 2 teaspoons grated orange peel with the oil. Stir 3 cups fresh frozen (thawed and drained) cranberries into batter. Bake 1 hour to 1 hour 10 minutes.

Pumpkin Bread

Substitute 1 can (15 ounces) pumpkin (not pumpkin pie mix) for the zucchini.

3 cups shredded zucchini (2 to 3 medium)
1⅔ cups sugar
⅔ cup vegetable oil
2 teaspoons vanilla
4 large eggs
3 cups all purpose* or whole wheat flour
2 teaspoons baking soda
1 teaspoon salt
1 teaspoon ground cinnamon
½ teaspoon ground cloves
½ teaspoon baking powder
½ cup coarsely chopped nuts
½ cup raisins, if desired

1. Move oven rack to low position so that tops of pans will be in center of oven. Heat oven to 350 degrees. Grease bottoms only of 2 loaf pans, 8½ x 4½ x 2½ inches, or 1 loaf pan, 9 x 5 x 3 inches, with shortening.

2. Mix zucchini, sugar, oil, vanilla, and eggs in large bowl. Stir in remaining ingredients except nuts and raisins. Stir in nuts and raisins. Divide batter evenly between pans.

3. Bake 8-inch loaves 50 to 60 minutes, 9-inch loaf 1 hour 10 minutes to 1 hour 20 minutes, or until toothpick inserted in center comes out clean. Cool 10 minutes on wire rack.

4. Loosen sides of loaves from pans; remove from pans and place topside up on wire rack. Cool completely, about 2 hours, before slicing. Wrap tightly and store at room temperature up to 4 days, or refrigerate up to 10 days.

* If using self-rising flour, omit baking soda, salt, and baking powder.

1 Slice: Calories 95 (Calories from Fat 35); Fat 4g (Saturated 1g); Cholesterol 15mg; Sodium 110mg; Carbohydrate 13g (Dietary Fiber 0g); Protein 2g

% Daily Value: Vitamin A 0%; Vitamin C 0%; Calcium 0%; Iron 2%

Diet Exchanges: ½ Starch, 1 Vegetable, ½ Fat

Chocolate Brownies

■ *16 brownies* ■

PREP TIME: 25 minutes
BAKE TIME: 45 minutes
COOL TIME: 2 hours

Chocolate-Peanut Butter Brownies

Substitute ⅓ cup crunchy peanut butter for ⅓ cup of the butter. Omit walnuts. Before baking, arrange 16 1-inch chocolate-covered peanut butter cup candies, unwrapped over top. Press into batter so tops of cups are even with top of batter.

⅔ cup butter or stick margarine

5 ounces unsweetened baking chocolate, cut into pieces

1¾ cups sugar

2 teaspoons vanilla

3 large eggs

1 cup all-purpose flour*

1 cup chopped walnuts

1. Heat oven to 350 degrees. Grease bottom and sides of square pan, 9 x 9 x 2 inches, with shortening.

2. Melt butter and chocolate in 1-quart saucepan over low heat, stirring constantly. Cool 5 minutes.

3. Beat sugar, vanilla, and eggs in medium bowl with electric mixer on high speed 5 minutes. Beat in chocolate mixture on low speed, scraping bowl occasionally. Beat in flour just until blended, scraping bowl occasionally. Stir in walnuts. Spread in pan.

4. Bake 40 to 45 minutes or just until brownies begin to pull away from sides of pan. Cool completely in pan on wire rack, about 2 hours. For brownies, cut into 4 rows by 4 rows.

   * If using self-rising flour, omit baking powder and salt.

1 Brownie: Calories 300 (Calories from 160); Fat 18g (Saturated 5g); Cholesterol 40mg; Sodium 115mg; Carbohydrate 32g (Dietary Fiber 2g); Protein 4g

% Daily Value: Vitamin A 12%; Vitamin C 0%; Calcium 2%; Iron 6%

Diet Exchanges: Not Recommended

Chocolate Chip Cookies

■ *About 4 dozen* ■

PREP TIME: 10 minutes
BAKE TIME: 8 to 10 minutes
per sheet
COOL TIME: 2 minutes

Lighter Chocolate Chip Cookies

For 4 grams of fat and 90 calories per serving, decrease butter to ¾ cup and omit nuts. Substitute 1 cup miniature chocolate chips for the 12-ounce bag of chocolate chips.

¾ cup granulated sugar

¾ cup packed brown sugar

1 cup butter or stick margarine, softened

1 teaspoon vanilla

1 large egg

2¼ cups all-purpose flour*

1 teaspoon baking soda

½ teaspoon salt

1 cup coarsely chopped nuts

1 bag (12 ounces) semisweet chocolate chips (2 cups)

1. Heat oven to 375 degrees.

2. Beat sugars, butter, vanilla, and egg in large bowl with electric mixer on medium speed, or mix with a spoon. Stir in flour, baking soda, and salt (dough will be stiff). Stir in nuts and chocolate chips.

3. Drop dough by rounded tablespoonfuls about 2 inches apart onto ungreased cookie sheet.

4. Bake 8 to 10 minutes or until light brown (centers will be soft). Cool 1 to 2 minutes, remove from cookie sheet to wire rack.

* If using self-rising flour, omit baking soda and salt.

1 Cookie: Calories 135 (Calories from Fat 70); Fat 8g (Saturated 2g); Cholesterol 5mg; Sodium 105mg; Carbohydrate 16g (Dietary Fiber 1g); Protein 1g

% Daily Value: Vitamin A 4%; Vitamin C 0%; Calcium 2%; Iron 0%

Diet Exchanges: 1 Starch, 1 Fat

Snickerdoodles

■ *About 4 dozen* ■

PREP TIME: 10 minutes
BAKE TIME: 8 to 10 minutes
per sheet

Finishing Touch

This favorite cookie is traditionally rolled in or sprinkled with cinnamon-sugar before baking. This nonsensically named cookie originated in New England in the 1800s.

1½ cups sugar

½ cup butter or stick margarine, softened

½ cup shortening

2 large eggs

2¾ cups all-purpose flour*

2 teaspoons cream of tartar

1 teaspoon baking soda

¼ teaspoon salt

¼ cup sugar

2 teaspoons ground cinnamon

1. Heat oven to 400 degrees.

2. Beat 1½ cups sugar, the butter, shortening, and eggs in large bowl with electric mixer on medium speed, or mix with a spoon. Stir in flour, cream of tartar, baking soda, and salt.

3. Shape dough into 1¼-inch balls. Mix ¼ cup sugar and the cinnamon. Roll balls in cinnamon-sugar mixture. Place 2 inches apart on ungreased cookie sheet.

4. Bake 8 to 10 minutes or until set. Immediately remove from cookie sheet to wire rack.

* If using self-rising flour, omit cream of tartar, baking soda, and salt.

1 Cookie: Calories 90 (Calories from Fat 35); Fat 4g (Saturated 1g); Cholesterol 10mg; Sodium 65mg; Carbohydrate 13g (Dietary Fiber 0g); Protein 1g

% Daily Value: Vitamin A 2%; Vitamin C 0%; Calcium 0%; Iron 2%

Diet Exchanges: 1 Starch, ½ Fat

Pound Cake

■ *24 servings* ■

PREP TIME: 20 minutes
BAKE TIME: 1 hour 20 minutes
COOL TIME: 2 hours 20 minutes

Lemon-Poppy Seed Pound Cake

Substitute 1 teaspoon lemon extract for the vanilla. Fold 1 tablespoon grated lemon peel and ¼ cup poppy seed into batter.

2½ cups sugar

1 cup butter or stick margarine, softened

1 teaspoon vanilla or almond extract

5 large eggs

3 cups all-purpose flour*

1 teaspoon baking powder

¼ teaspoon salt

1 cup milk or evaporated milk

Powdered sugar, if desired

1. Heat oven to 350 degrees. Grease bottom and side of angel food cake pan (tube pan), 10 x 4 inches, 12-cup bundt cake pan or 2 loaf pans, 9 x 5 x 3 inches, with shortening; lightly flour.

2. Beat sugar, butter, vanilla, and eggs in large bowl with electric mixer on low speed 30 seconds, scraping constantly. Beat on high speed 5 minutes, scraping bowl occasionally. Mix flour, baking powder, and salt. Beat flour mixture into sugar mixture alternately with milk on low speed, beating just until smooth after each addition. Pour into pan(s).

3. Bake angel food or bundt cake pan 1 hour 10 minutes to 1 hour 20 minutes, loaf pans 55 to 60 minutes, or until toothpick inserted in center comes out clean. Cool 20 minutes; remove from pan(s) to wire rack. Cool completely, about 2 hours. Sprinkle with powdered sugar.

* If using self-rising flour, omit cream of tartar, baking soda, and salt.

1 Serving: Calories 225 (Calories from Fat 80); Fat 9g (Saturated 5g); Cholestrerol 65 mg; Sodium 115 mg; Carbohydrate 33g (Dietary Fiber 0g); Protein 3g

% Daily Value: Vitamin A 8%; Vitamin C 0%; Calcium 2%; Iron 4%

Diet Exchanges: 1 Starch, 1 Fruit, 2 Fat

Index

• G •

Guest List

Guest List (continued)

Shopping List

Shopping List (continued)

Notes

Notes

Notes

Notes

Hungry Minds, Inc.
End-User License Agreement

5. **Limited Warranty.**

   (a) HMI warrants that the Software and Software Media are free from defects in materials and workmanship under normal use for a period of sixty (60) days from the date of purchase of this Book. If HMI receives notification within the warranty period of defects in materials or workmanship, HMI will replace the defective Software Media.

   (b) HMI AND THE AUTHOR OF THE BOOK DISCLAIM ALL OTHER WARRANTIES, EXPRESS OR IMPLIED, INCLUDING WITHOUT LIMITATION IMPLIED WARRANTIES OF MERCHANTABILITY AND FITNESS FOR A PARTICULAR PURPOSE, WITH RESPECT TO THE SOFTWARE, THE PROGRAMS, THE SOURCE CODE CONTAINED THEREIN, AND/OR THE TECHNIQUES DESCRIBED IN THIS BOOK. HMI DOES NOT WARRANT THAT THE FUNCTIONS CONTAINED IN THE SOFTWARE WILL MEET YOUR REQUIRE-MENTS OR THAT THE OPERATION OF THE SOFTWARE WILL BE ERROR FREE.

   (c) This limited warranty gives you specific legal rights, and you may have other rights that vary from jurisdiction to jurisdiction.

6. **Remedies.**

   (a) HMI's entire liability and your exclusive remedy for defects in materials and workmanship shall be limited to replacement of the Software Media, which may be returned to HMI with a copy of your receipt at the following address: Software Media Fulfillment Department, Attn.: *Family Reunion Planning Kit For Dummies,* Hungry Minds, Inc., 10475 Crosspoint Blvd., Indianapolis, IN 46256, or call 1-800-762-2974. Please allow four to six weeks for delivery. This Limited Warranty is void if failure of the Software Media has resulted from accident, abuse, or misapplication. Any replacement Software Media will be warranted for the remainder of the original warranty period or thirty (30) days, whichever is longer.

   (b) In no event shall HMI or the author be liable for any damages whatsoever (including without limitation damages for loss of business profits, business interruption, loss of business information, or any other pecuniary loss) arising from the use of or inability to use the Book or the Software, even if HMI has been advised of the possibility of such damages.

   (c) Because some jurisdictions do not allow the exclusion or limitation of liability for consequential or incidental damages, the above limitation or exclusion may not apply to you.

7. **U.S. Government Restricted Rights.** Use, duplication, or disclosure of the Software for or on behalf of the United States of America, its agencies and/or instrumentalities (the "U.S. Government") is subject to restrictions as stated in paragraph (c)(1)(ii) of the Rights in Technical Data and Computer Software clause of DFARS 252.227-7013, or subparagraphs (c) (1) and (2) of the Commercial Computer Software - Restricted Rights clause at FAR 52.227-19, and in similar clauses in the NASA FAR supplement, as applicable.

8. **General.** This Agreement constitutes the entire understanding of the parties and revokes and supersedes all prior agreements, oral or written, between them and may not be modified or amended except in a writing signed by both parties hereto that specifically refers to this Agreement. This Agreement shall take precedence over any other documents that may be in conflict herewith. If any one or more provisions contained in this Agreement are held by any court or tribunal to be invalid, illegal, or otherwise unenforceable, each and every other provision shall remain in full force and effect.

Installation Instructions

The *Family Reunion Planning Kit For Dummies* CD offers valuable information that you won't want to miss. To install the items from the CD to your hard drive, follow these steps.

For Microsoft Windows

1. Insert the CD into your computer's CD-ROM drive.
2. Open your browser.
3. Click Start⇨Run.
4. In the dialog box that appears, type D:\START.HTM.
5. Read through the license agreement, click the Accept button if you want to use the CD — after you click Accept, you'll jump to the Main Menu.
6. To navigate within the interface, simply click on any topic of interest to go to an explanation of the files and how to use them.
7. To install the software from the CD, simply click the software name.

With the Mac OS

1. Insert the CD into your computer's CD-ROM drive.
2. Double-click the CD icon to show the CD's contents.
3. Double-click the Read Me First icon.
4. Open your browser.
5. Double-click `start.htm` to open your browser and display the license agreement. If your browser doesn't open automatically, click on File⇨ Open and select the Family Reunion Planning Kit CD.
6. Read through the license agreement and click the Accept button if you want to use the CD — after you click Accept, you'll jump to the Main Menu.
7. To navigate within the interface, simply click on any topic of interest to go to an explanation of the files and how to use them.
8. To install the software from the CD, simply click the software name.